Arthur Mee

Arthur Mee

A Biography

Keith Crawford

The Lutterworth Press

The Lutterworth Press
P.O. Box 60
Cambridge
CB1 2NT
United Kingdom

www.lutterworth.com
publishing@lutterworth.com

ISBN: 978 0 7188 9435 1

British Library Cataloguing in Publication Data
A record is available from the British Library

First Published, 2016

Cover illustration: *Arthur Mee (1875–1943), Editor of
'The Children's Newspaper'* © estate of Frank O. Salisbury.
All rights reserved, DACS 2016.
Photo credit: Nottinghamshire County Library Service.

"Biography" meant a book about someone's life. Only, for me, it was to become a kind of pursuit, a tracking of the physical trail of someone's path through the past, a following of footsteps. You would never catch them, no you would never quite catch them. But maybe, if you were lucky, you might write about the pursuit of that fleeting figure in such a way as to bring it alive in the present.

Robert Holmes,
Footsteps: Adventures of a Romantic Biographer

Contents

List of Illustrations

Note: Every effort has been made to trace copyright holders and to obtain their permission for the use of any copyright material. The publisher apologises for any errors or omissions and would be grateful for notification of any corrections that should be incorporated in any future reprints or editions of the book.

Acknowledgements

Writing is often a solitary endeavour but impossible without the support of others. My thanks go to Verity Andrews, Archive Assistant at the University of Reading Library's Special Collections Service, UK. Verity was enormously helpful in the manner in which she located Arthur Mee's letters to John Derry before ensuring that copies reached a destination on the other side of the world. I also thank the staff of the British Library's manuscripts department for their help in locating letters written by Arthur Mee to Alfred Harmsworth and ensuring that they were made available for my use.

Look and Learn Limited, who own the copyright of *The Children's Newspaper*, kindly gave permission to include in the book material from the newspaper, and I am grateful for their help. Dr Susan Pittman, Archivist at the Farningham and Eynsford Local History Society, was very helpful in providing photographs, letters written by Arthur Mee and information on Mee's home at Eynsford Hill House. Ilya, Alessandra and Saskia Kazi, the current residents of Eynsford Hill House, were very generous in locating additional material, which they provided for my use, and they have my gratitude.

Professor John Simons, Deputy Vice-Chancellor at Macquarie University, Sydney, and Katie Simons took time to examine a draft of the book. As always with John and Katie, their insightful and forensic minds were a great help, and for that and their friendship they have my thanks. Mark and Barbara d'Arbon also read the manuscript, offering their usual mixture of helpful encouragement and perceptive criticism. Professor Hugh Cunningham at the University of Kent; Dr Julia Stapleton from Durham University; Associate Professor Josephine May at the University of Newcastle, Australia; and Dr Grant Rodwell from the University of Adelaide, Australia, read and commented on drafts of chapters. Each have my gratitude for the valuable and insightful observations they made. The book is better for the efforts of these educational warriors and excellent people; any shortcomings are, of course, entirely my own.

Finally, my wife Jenny has, throughout the writing of the book, put up with my all too frequent absences in another part of the house with far more understanding than I might have been able to muster had our roles been reversed. Now the book is finished, in response to family and friends asking where I am she no longer has to reply, "He's in another room playing with Arthur." As always Jenny is the most honest of critics and for that and much more she has my love and gratitude.

Preface

This book arose out of a range of interests that combined to move me in a direction I had not anticipated, but found intriguing. For nearly a decade I had spent time researching and writing about how curriculum materials in the form of school textbooks found their way into classrooms, as well as exploring their political and ideological construction. I was interested in how school history, social studies and citizenship textbooks help shape, and are, in turn, shaped by, ideological and socio-political norms, traditions and values. I combined this work with a lifelong interest in the history of education and its cultural and sociological origins. In 2013 I committed myself to moving beyond the analysis of school textbooks to exploring an alternative form of curriculum materials in the guise of early-twentieth-century children's magazines.

While I had no interest in being sucked into the often vacuous quagmire of postmodernist theoretical gymnastics, with its dreary and tiresome massacring of language, I was interested in how children's magazines were powerful weapons in the ideological and political construction of what of the past was remembered and how it was remembered. My interest lay in exploring how the narratives that constitute a nation's past present a powerful moral authority. I wanted to focus upon how they did not simply tell stories, but stories that contained discourses from which cultural and ideological meanings were manufactured.

Originally I concentrated upon a series of articles I wanted to write on the manner in which *The Children's Newspaper*, which Arthur Mee edited between 1919 and 1943, imagined English national identity, Australia and Aboriginal Australians. Reading through the weekly editions of the newspaper, it became clear that the stamp of Arthur Mee was writ large across its pages through his editorials, articles attributed to "A.M." and the general tone and character of the paper. I came to construct a picture of Arthur Mee and his values that prompted me to want to know more, but I found little outside his writings that helped answer my questions. A major exception was a single volume on Mee written in 1946 by his lifelong friend John Hammerton. More hagiography than anything else, it is, as

Hammerton intended, not a conventional biography but a romanticised and entirely affirmative set of often sentimentalised recollections provided by Hammerton and some of Mee's close contemporaries.[1] A second helpful source was Maisie Robson's briefer account of Mee's life and career, *Arthur Mee's Dream of England*, published in 2003.[2]

Apart from these sources and in spite of the enormous appeal of his writing, which saw Mee become a household name and a major publishing brand, the man remained an almost ghostly figure. This seemed odd given that the publication most associated with Mee, *The Children's Encyclopaedia*, sold 1.5 million sets across the British Empire. The American edition known as *The Book of Knowledge* sold 3.5 million sets. Unique at the time of its publication, *The Children's Encyclopaedia* was the early-twentieth-century equivalent of the internet and was translated into numerous languages.

What interested me was why, given Mee's widespread popularity, we knew so little of him, and why he could have told John Hammerton, "I know nothing about children."[3] Arthur Mee is now most often found on the shelves in second-hand book shops, at the back of a cupboard, in an attic or deep within adult memories of childhood. Often by accident or in the name of nostalgic remembering, his name occasionally steps out of the past into a present that would have horrified and delighted him. Mee did receive what some might consider the ultimate accolade when in an episode of *Monty Python's Flying Circus* he was the host of the "All-England Summarize Proust Competition". But apart from occasional reminiscences from those recreating afternoons of yesteryear spent mulling over copies of *The Children's Encyclopaedia*, the interests, crusades and accomplishments of Arthur Mee have faded.

Known and yet wholly unknown by the huge national and international audience that bought his titles simply because they carried his name, Mee revolutionised the home-school learning relationship. Among those he influenced was Enid Blyton, whose set of *The Children's Encyclopaedia* she read again and again. In 1911, aged fourteen, Blyton entered a poetry competition in *My Magazine*, one of Mee's publications. To her delight she received a letter from him saying he would publish the poem; the result was that Mee was included in her prayers each night.[4] As well as Blyton, others known to have read *The Children's Encyclopaedia* include C.P. Snow, William Golding, the molecular scientist Francis Crick, the wife of socialist politician G.D.H. Cole, Margaret Cole, the writer and polemicist Peter Hitchens, the author Alexander McCall Smith and the historian David Starkey.

*

When John Hammerton discussed with Mee's wife Amy the possibility of writing a biography of her husband, he suggested calling the book *Child of Wonder: An Intimate Biography*. Amy's sister Lena Fratson is said by Hammerton to have liked the title because it described Mee perfectly. On his death Mee was described as a "Christian romantic", a description Hammerton acknowledges as accurate.[5] Mee was certainly a romantic and his writing bears all the hallmarks of a romanticism which appealed to his love of childhood as a time of innocence and hope and his view of the world as a magical place of wonder and imagination. The audience who bought Mee's publications believed they knew him personally and he encouraged the perception that he was a welcome and much anticipated friend who arrived fortnightly in hundreds of thousands of homes.

Mee was more than a strikingly popular editor and writer; for a generation of young readers and their parents, the name Arthur Mee meant something. For many in his audience, the narratives embedded within his writing legitimised a trinity of beliefs that for his generation lay at the heart of the national character: God, England and Empire. Aimed at appealing to the widest and most profitable readership, Mee's writing for children had education, information and entertainment at its core. Bolstered by a strong nonconformist religious faith, he saw himself as being on a mission to shape the attitudes and values of his readers with respect to what was good and bad, right and wrong, moral and immoral, true and false. His writings were what in a different context Foucault has called practical texts, "written for the purpose of offering rules, opinions, and advice on how to behave as one should".[6]

Mee lived through decades of unparalleled change. He witnessed the invention of the motor car and powered flight, the arrival of universal suffrage, the cinema, the "wireless" and BBC television, the jet engine and the radio telescope, Einstein's theory of relativity, the splitting of the atom and the discovery of insulin. He was fascinated by it all, enthralled by the excitement of scientific and technological change, appalled by aspects of twentieth-century modernity and sickened by the tragedies of poverty and war. He was an eyewitness to the First World War, the 1926 General Strike, mass unemployment, deprivation, hardship and ignorance, the rise of Hitler and National Socialism, and the Second World War. Yet in spite of all this, it is difficult to turn the pages of an Arthur Mee publication without being constantly reminded of an unfaltering optimism that remained throughout his life a defining feature of his personality and temperament. Mee always managed to sustain the belief that no matter how bad the world might be, life was always gradually and continually improving.

Mee was an ardent and patriotic Englishman with a passionate and emotional devotion to the protection of the history, traditions and values of all things English. As his world changed around him, like many of his generation, he struggled to come to terms with how best to understand a new England that both energised and dismayed him while also protecting his England of tradition and Victorian values.

Much of Mee's writing reveals an ideological and personal paradox experienced by many who lived through the decades when everything was exposed to the prospect of change. Mee always wrote and spoke of himself as a liberal and a radical one at that, and he was politically and economically libertarian in his distrust of government intervention in the lives of the people. He could be moderate and conservative, progressive and traditional. In his rhetorical attacks on poverty, ignorance and destitution, his writing reveals elements of Christian socialism. In other contexts he exhibited a strong thread of cultural conservatism borne of anxiety that his world of Victorian certainties faced crisis and extinction.

*

During the writing of his biography of Mee, Hammerton claims to have had placed at his disposal his correspondence, papers and personal records. But there is little evidence of them within the book's pages, and Mee's personal voice is absent. However, Mee was never one to be silent, and in trying to reconstruct the story of his life this book draws upon three principle sources of evidence. First, approximately 700 letters written by Arthur Mee and members of his editorial staff to his lifelong friend, mentor and collaborator John Derry, held within the Reading University Library's Special Collections. The hand- and type-written letters cover the period 1905 to 1936 and focus upon a myriad of issues and themes. These include the contributions that Derry made to Mee's publications, exploring his thoughts and opinions on this work, political, cultural and social issues and more personal issues. Also included are letters written to Derry by members of Mee's staff, notably Stella Hancock, Margaret Lillie and Hugo Tyerman.

Second, letters between Mee and Alfred Harmsworth, later Lord Northcliffe, held in the British Library manuscripts department. Mee went to work for Harmsworth in 1903 and the two enjoyed a long professional association. Covering the period 1904 to 1910, the letters reveal something of the relationship that Mee had with Harmsworth at a time when he was fast becoming the most powerful press baron in the country, as well as providing details on the early days of *The Children's Encyclopaedia*.

Third, extensive use has been made of Mee's publications. Across a career that spanned fifty years, Mee's output and range as an editor and author was prolific. Before the First World War he edited *Harmsworth's Self-Educator* (1905-1907); *Harmsworth's History of the World* (1907); *The Children's Encyclopaedia* (1909-1910); *The World's Great Books* (1909-1910); *Harmsworth's Natural History* (1910-1911); *Harmsworth's Popular Science* (1911-1913) and *The New Harmsworth's Self-Educator* (1913-1915). We can add to this list a re-issued part-publication of *The Children's Encyclopaedia* called *My Magazine* (1914-1933), and, after the First World War, *The Children's Newspaper* (1919-1964).

In addition, Mee wrote and edited books on a variety of topics, read by children and adults. These include for children *Arthur Mee's Hero Book* (1921); *Arthur Mee's Children's Bible* (1924); *Arthur Mee's 1000 Heroes* (1933); *The Children's Shakespeare* (1933) and *Heroes of the Bible* (1936). Other of Mee's books for children set out a moral framework by which he thought they should live, including *Arthur Mee's Letters to Boys* (1913) and *Arthur Mee's Letters to Girls* (1915), re-published in 1920 and again in 1924 as *Arthur Mee's Talks to Girls* and *Arthur Mee's Talks to Boys*. A further topic for his pen was his fierce loyalty to England, expressed in books including *Arthur Mee's Gift Book for Boys and Girls Who Love the Flag* (1917), *Little Treasure Island: Her Story and Her Glory* (1920), *Arthur Mee's Wonderful Day* (1923) and *Arthur Mee's Book of Everlasting Things* (1927).

Mee's writing for an adult audience included his works for the temperance movement *Defeat or Victory?: The Strength of Britain Book* (1917), *The Fiddlers* (1917) and *The Parasite* (1918). Enormously popular was the Mee-edited *The King's England*, a series of books tracing the history and romance of individual English counties, the first of which, *Enchanted Island*, was published in 1936. During the early years of the Second World War he wrote a number of polemics lauding the nation's fight against what he described as un-Christian savagery and barbarism. These include *Why We Had to Go to War* (1939); *Arthur Mee's Blackout Book* (1939), full of stories, games and puzzles for children; the enormously popular *Arthur Mee's Book of the Flag* (1941); *Call the Witnesses* (1941); *1940: Our Finest Hour* (1941); *Immortal Dawn* (1942) and *Wonderful Year* (1943).

*

In 1938 while attempting to write a biography of her friend Christopher Fry, Virginia Woolf is said to have exclaimed, "My God, how does one write a biography?" That question disturbs every biographer and few can claim to have got it completely right. I had to make decisions about how to shape the book and decided not to format it entirely in a chronological fashion; this would not have enabled me to investigate a number of themes that are important in understanding Mee and his work. I wanted to explore Mee within different contexts and to understand particular aspects of his life, values and views on the social and cultural politics of the time.

I have sought to adopt a quasi-chronological approach, employing a structure that Mee would have found familiar. When editing *The Children's Encyclopaedia* he decided that the traditional alphabetical approach to organising content was unlikely to provide his audience with a framework for learning that would generate interest or enthusiasm. The magazine's subject matter was divided into topics as a way of trying to express what Mee called "unity" by enabling readers to explore linked themes. This book has a similar structure, and while Chapter One and Chapter Two are broadly chronological, the remainder of the chapters are thematic and could be read as individual essays.

Chapter One follows Mee's life from his beginnings in Stapleford, Nottinghamshire, and contextualises his nonconformist background and school education before turning to the early days of his journalistic career in Nottingham and his move to London in 1897. Chapter Two chronicles his career as a London journalist working for Alfred Harmsworth. The chapter provides a sense of Mee as an individual through exploring the fundamentals of his personality and temperament. The intention of these chapters is to provide a narrative framework illustrating the formative years of Mee's life as he moved from being a fledging provincial writer of potential to occupy a place as one of the capital's most sought after and respected journalists.

The chapters that follow delve into aspects of Mee's life and work and are intended to examine in detail his character and the values and beliefs that drove him. Chapter Three focusses upon how Mee's journalistic career turned towards writing for children. Although forever interested in learning and self-improvement and in possession of what many regarded as a childlike imagination, Mee had not consciously thought of writing for children. But he found himself in the right place at the right time to take advantage of newly popularised theories concerning child development and how children learnt, which, with Harmsworth's backing, he exploited in *The Children's Encyclopaedia* and later within *The Children's Newspaper*. How these publications came into being, how Mee developed an approach to writing for children and who worked for Mee in their production lie at the core of this chapter.

Mee was born into a devoutly religious family, and an undiluted nonconformist faith and support for temperance remained central to his personality throughout his life. Chapter Four explores what Mee meant by religious faith, how important it was in his every thought and deed and how he made sense of it within the context of a belief in Darwinian evolutionary science. Like many of his generation, Mee was seduced by the arguments of eugenic theorising and was an avid supporter of eugenicist thinking on the "evils of drink" and arguments concerning the physical and moral degeneration of the English race, and the chapter explores his thinking on these issues.

Mee had a deep emotional attachment to England; he thought it the most culturally and economically superior nation on Earth that had for centuries been the focal point for global progress and civilisation. Chapter Five unpacks Mee's spiritual and at times mystical devotion to England, in particular his use of heroic narrative and how he symbolically romanticised the English landscape and his gardens as representative of all that was not only good about England and the English but all that was universally right.

Mee lived to see two world wars, both of which provided him with contexts through which he could laud the English nation, and the chapter also explores his attitudes towards defending an England under threat during the First World War.

Central in Mee's life was his commitment to the British Empire as a force for universal good, and he was an unabashed, although not xenophobic, imperialist. He shared many of the views of the time on Social Darwinism, cultural racism and the status of indigenous populations within the Empire. Was Mee racist? Chapter Six explores how he viewed colonial nations as versions of a white England in other parts of the world and how through the pages of *The Children's Newspaper* Aboriginal Australians were constructed and portrayed.

Mee was a lifelong liberal with an unyielding commitment to individualism and freedom. Chapter Seven examines his campaigns against poverty and ignorance and his powerful reaction to the 1926 General Strike, within which elements of conservatism and socialism emerge. Although Mee was enthusiastic about embracing modernity in its technological and scientific guises, particular features of a rapidly changing nation left him frustrated and sometimes utterly bewildered. Chapter Eight explores his culturally conservative responses to the transformation of his "Old England" during the inter-war period. This includes his abhorrence of jazz, and his reactions to the cinema, what he considered the corruption of the English language and the impact of modernisation upon the English landscape.

Chapter Nine brings Mee's story to a conclusion by focussing upon the final years of his life. The 1930s and 1940s saw Mee experience what in his words was "A Heartbreaking World". It was a time when his dreams of an egalitarian world united against violence, ignorance and poverty were crushed by the onset of the Second World War. Yet it was a time when he remained typically at his most productive and optimistic. These final years saw him begin *The King's England* series, which he called "My England Book", and the writing of war diaries within the pages of *The Children's Newspaper*. The chapter explores how Mee fought the war at his desk with pen and ink as he looked forward to what he remained convinced was a positive and confident future.

*

A word on nomenclature might help. Mee always saw himself as English rather than British and so throughout the book I refer, as Mee nearly always did, to England rather than to Great Britain or the United Kingdom. This is simply a matter of consistency and continuity and reflects the fact that during the period that Mee's influence was at its height, he and many of his generation wrote "England" when they also meant Great Britain. By the end of the nineteenth century a sense of British identity had begun to lessen and was supplanted in public consciousness by a racialist-inspired form of English national identity that left little room for Celtic national identities.[7] Certainly by the time that Mee was begin to develop his career, a sense of English nationalism was more fully emerging and can be seen in several aspects of his work and in his views of the world.

Finally, a word about the notes at the back of the book. I have tried to write a book that might appeal to a general audience as well as an academic one; hopefully there is something here for both sets of readers. Those interested in following an academic pathway are invited to examine the notes and those not interested are cordially invited to completely ignore them!

1.

Beginnings

Stapleford

Arthur Henry Mee was born in Stapleford, Nottinghamshire, on 21 July 1875. Ten kilometres south-west of Nottingham, Stapleford was in the year of his birth an unremarkable community of 2,000 inhabitants. The village economy once reliant upon agriculture had by 1851 turned towards hosiery and lace manufacture following the growth of a factory-based industry. While agriculture and coal mining remained sources of work, from the 1870s Stapleford owed a substantial growth in population to its emergence as a satellite for the lace industry in Nottingham.

In 1881 the population of Stapleford had shown a significant increase, a trend that continued following the opening of a lace factory and a new colliery on the edge of the village.[1] The population of over 3,000 in 1881 had by 1891 risen to 4,000. This prompted local historian Cornelius Brown to write, "A visitor to Stapleford after an absence of twenty years would scarcely recognise in the mass of buildings and places of business the small hosiery village that he once knew."[2]

Arthur Mee's roots lay firmly within the respectable working class. His father Henry Mee was born in the industrial town of Heanor, twelve kilometres south of Stapleford. Henry's father James Mee had spent his working life as an unskilled agricultural labourer before dying of a heart condition aged fifty. Henry Mee's mother Sarah earned a living making hosiery items on a pedal-operated machine, which, until the introduction of steam power, was a cottage industry.

In 1871, the year of his mother's death, twenty-year-old Henry Mee, his twenty-six-year-old brother James and James's wife Emma left Heanor to live in Stapleford. James Mee, who had been a coalminer, found work as a signalman on the railways but later took his family back to Heanor, where he worked as a framework knitter and then a postman. Henry Mee remained in Stapleford, lodging on Nottingham Road with a railway signalman, Alfred Charlton, and his family. He found work as an engine cleaner and was then employed on the Midland Railway as an engine driver. But most of his working life was spent as an engineer operating stationary steam engines inside hosiery and lace factories where they drove the machinery, shafts, pulleys and belts.

On 10 June 1872 Henry Mee married nineteen-year-old Mary Fletcher, whose well respected nonconformist family worked in lace manufacturing in Stapleford. Mary's father John Fletcher was a lace-maker and before marrying Henry, Mary and her eight brothers and sisters worked in the industry. Mary worked as a cotton lace winder, transferring yarn from bobbins into balls ready for weaving. The Mees set up home in Church Street around the corner from James Mee in Church Lane, before moving to 7 Pinfold Lane. Near the heart of the village's industrial development, they lived in a two-bedroom terraced house like many others built for a growing industrial population.

In 1881 Henry Mee's neighbours in Pinfold Lane were lace-makers, railway workers and unskilled labourers. Mary Mee's family lived close by; her widowed father John Fletcher lived at 5 Pinfold Lane with four of her brothers and sisters and at 6 Pinfold Lane was her elder brother Charles, his wife Janette and their three children. Once settled into married life, Henry and Mary Mee quickly became caught up in the responsibilities of raising a family. Between 1873 and 1881, Mary gave birth to six children. The first to arrive was a daughter, Annie (b. 1873); she was followed by Arthur, boys Ernest (b. 1878) and Herbert Fletcher (b. 1881) and two more girls in Mabel Laura (b. 1885) and Sarah Lois (b. 1887), who was always called Lois.

A Nonconformist Upbringing

Arthur Mee grew up in a family whose values and lifestyle were conditioned by the liberal politics and nonconformist commitments of Henry Mee. Campaigning for the separation of church and state and freedom of religious and civil conscience, nonconformists developed a natural affinity with liberal politics, and Henry Mee was a staunch Baptist and a steadfast liberal.

Drawn from the middle and upper working classes, artisans, shopkeepers and wage earners living and working within commercial and industrial centres formed the basis of nonconformist congregations. They prided themselves upon their individualism and reluctance to submit to the power of government agencies. They saw themselves as outsiders and, divorced from the religious and political establishment, a sense of independence shaped their identity. Nonconformists combined within their own communities; not only did they worship together, they lived and worked side by side, did business with each other and married into each other's families.[3] Life was shaped by family responsibility, hard work and a powerful sense of community.[4]

Piety lay at the core of nonconformity; a sober and disciplined lifestyle was essential and signs of pretension, ostentation or self-indulgence were considered improper and unacceptable. Nonconformity was more than a commitment to a set of religious beliefs and it went far beyond the chapel door in providing a programme for living an ethical and moral life. Although not exclusively the province of nonconformists, the "nonconformist conscience" matured into a set of principles designed to guide personal and public behaviour.

At the heart of nonconformity was a willingness to oppose injustice and behaviour considered morally wrong. Conditioned by a reformist zeal, nonconformist social identity included a sense of historical mission and a commitment to self-improvement, individual freedom and social amelioration. Being a nonconformist meant adopting a robust commitment to public as well as private duty and nonconformists played important roles in civic life. Political action was equated with religiously inspired reform and the pursuit of social welfare and integrity in public life. With the exercise of conscience a pre-requisite, nonconformists campaigned against poverty, unemployment, prostitution, gambling and crime and had a central role in the temperance movement.[5]

Henry Mee was an earnest, uncompromising and dedicated member of the community at Stapleford Baptist Chapel. A patriarchal and serious figure, he lived his life guided by a fixed framework of religious, political and social beliefs. As well as being a member of the congregation, Henry Mee was a deacon, helping to manage the business of the chapel. Deacons were chosen because of their spiritual piety, their grasp of doctrine and their honesty, reliability and integrity. These were qualities that Henry Mee possessed in abundance and he is said to have carried out his role with "unsmiling gravity and inflexibility of purpose".[6] Along with Mary Mee's father John and her uncle William Fletcher, Henry was involved in laying a memorial stone at the new Baptist Sunday school before giving an address to a public meeting.[7]

Henry Mee was politically active and as an act of conscience objected to the 1902 Education Act and refused to pay that portion of the local rates given to education. The Act abolished local school boards and made local authorities responsible for funding schools, including denominational schools. Nationally thousands of nonconformists rejected the idea that they should pay rates towards sectarian religious teaching in denominational schools, leading to a campaign of passive resistance.[8]

John Clifford was the recognised leader of the passive resistance movement; he was a devout Baptist and an uncompromising believer in the nonconformist conscience. At age ten his poverty stricken upbringing had seen him earning a living in a Nottingham lace factory working fifteen hours a day, six days a week. It was an experience that shaped his faith and his crusades against poverty, inequality and injustice.[9] Clifford studied at the Baptist Academy in Leicester before in 1858 becoming pastor at Praed Street Baptist Church, London, and then in 1877 at the newly built Westbourne Park Church, where he stayed until his retirement in 1915. As a member of the Nottingham Local Preachers Association, on a Sunday afternoon in the summer of 1875, a nervous Clifford preached to Henry Mee's congregation at Stapleford Baptist Church on the subject of "faith".[10]

What Clifford described as the soul of passive resistance was opposition to an abuse of individual rights that saw religion in schools dominated by Anglican and Roman Catholic rites and dogmas.[11] Failure to pay the rates usually meant a court appearance, at which point, after registering their protest, some debtors paid up. When payment was withheld, personal goods were confiscated for auction with the money raised paying the debt.[12] On such occasions resisters would often arrive in force at auctions and sometimes, with the agreement of the auctioneer, sing hymns and make speeches before the sale began.

Henry Mee was secretary of the Nottingham passive resistance committee. On 21 April 1910, along with twenty others, he found himself at an auction of goods; he bid £9 4s 2d, the amount required for the rates plus court costs, and bought all the lots, including his own.[13] It was common practice that committee funds be used for purchase and the goods returned to their owners. While other passive resisters fell by the wayside, Henry Mee did not, and on 23 April 1923 he appeared in the Nottingham Summons Court for what he described as the twenty-first or twenty-second time for failing to pay that portion of the rates provided for education.[14] This was the context within which a young Arthur Mee grew up. It was a family and community environment in which religious faith, political and social activism sat side by side.

An Ordinary Schooling

Arthur Mee and his siblings attended the Baptist Sunday school which enjoyed the facilities of a new building opened by John Clifford in April 1884. Sunday schools were hugely popular, even among those parents who were ambiguous about religion or had no religious faith. It was not uncommon to see low levels of Sunday worship and very high levels of Sunday school attendance. Prior to the 1870 Education Act, they were places parents sent their children to receive an education in basic literacy and numeracy that may have been poorly provided in day schools.

The Sunday school was an environment in which the widely held perception that religious faith and self-improvement were inseparable formed the basis of instruction. Biblical teaching was used to forge a set of ideals, focussing upon social reform, character formation and an optimistic confidence in the ultimate triumph of morality and justice. Through chapel and Sunday school attendance, Arthur Mee developed an absolute belief in the Bible's teachings, as well as being instructed in the value of self-sacrifice, hard work, honesty and thrift. He was also taught a militant rejection of gambling, tobacco and alcohol, the consumption of which was claimed to be a direct route into poverty, social humiliation and destitution.

Sunday schools were not entirely about lessons for life and conscience; they were also focal points for social gatherings, discussions and lectures. August bank holiday was a traditional day of celebration in Stapleford, the highlight of which was a march through the streets by the town's nonconformist congregations. Arthur Mee and his family would almost certainly have taken part in the celebrations, which saw the streets decked with streamers, Union Jacks, banners and placards containing texts from the scriptures. In August 1880, over 1,000 children marched in a parade with the Stapleford Temperance Drum and Fife Band leading the way. The smaller children were transported in wagons decked with ribbons, evergreens and banners. There were periodic stops at designated places for the singing of hymns, following which there was a picnic in the park attended by thousands.[15] Is it too much to speculate that a nine-year-old Arthur Mee had a small part in a performance of a drama called *Joseph and his Brethren* given by children from the Baptist Sunday school on Christmas Day and Boxing Day 1884?[16]

The learning that took place in chapel and Sunday school was augmented when in 1880 five-year-old Arthur began his formal schooling. He attended Church Street Board School the year the school opened and the year in which education was made compulsory for children up to the age of ten. With the population of Stapleford increasing and school places at a premium, locally elected school boards were authorised to build and maintain elementary schools out of the public rates. The only other school in the village was St John's Church of England National School, opened in 1837, the year of Queen Victoria's coronation. National schools were under the authority of the National Society for Promoting Religious Education and the schooling offered was in accordance with the principles of the Church of England, making it an unacceptable option for Henry Mee's family.

Throughout the 1880s, William Fletcher, Arthur Mee's uncle on his mother's side, was vice-chair and chairperson of a school board that had a significant nonconformist presence. Church Street School began life hesitatingly; attendance was low, particularly among girls, children could be found wandering the village instead of in school, and discipline was poor. Following an inspection in 1882 the teaching staff was completely changed.[17] During the years Arthur Mee spent in the infant department, teachers arrived and left with alarming alacrity.

There is no evidence of whether Mee liked or disliked his school days; what is known comes from Hammerton's biography, in which it is suggested that, while a competent student, he did not excel at anything in particular. The Victorian elementary school curriculum Mee studied was based upon the principles of working-class character formation and preparation for a life of duty, loyalty and sacrifice. Teachers came from the working class and taught a powerful dialogue of puritanical discipline and a strict and unyielding moral code. This was an education of ordinary people by ordinary people who taught the routines and habits of reliability, self-discipline, compliance and hard work required by the labour market.

During his years at Church Street School Mee was provided an education in reading, writing, comprehension, arithmetic and religious instruction, although the 1870 Education Act banned the teaching of denominational religion. In addition, singing, "drill" and object lessons involving the study of an artefact may have been added. Board Schools could, if they wished, offer classes in grammar, geography and history, for which they were awarded extra funding if, when examined, the children reached a required standard.

Mee's time at school saw him taught by George Byford, who travelled to Stapleford each day from his lodgings in Bruce Grove, Nottingham, where he lived with his eighteen-year-old brother Arthur, who worked in a furniture store. Born in Essex in 1857, Byford was a teacher from the working class; his father Eli was a coachman and servant. Byford was a committed Conservative whose political views differed markedly from those of the radical Henry Mee. Being taught by him gave Mee the chance to compare some of the uncompromising liberal principles instilled in him by his father with Byford's brand of conventional and patriotic conservatism.

Byford can be credited with ensuring that Mee left school in possession of a view of the world that added to that taught him by his father. Mee's faith in biblical narratives and his nonconformist principles remained untouched throughout his life, as did his view that conscience and character were the keys to personal success and achievement. Byford's influence saw added to this a passionate devotion to all things English and an unshakeable conviction that the British Empire was without question a universal force for good.[18]

Mee's life outside the classroom is not surprisingly shrouded in obscurity; he was, after all, an ordinary child living an unexceptional life in an unremarkable industrial village. Maisie Robson suggests that he enjoyed family life, played with his young brothers and sisters and volunteered his services as a babysitter.[19] At this point there was nothing to mark him out as in any way different or exceptional and his nonconformist surroundings ensured an orderly and regulated life of unpretentious simplicity. There was no reason to chronicle his journey towards adulthood and little is known of his youth other than that he was a small and frail child who grew into a slight and at times frail adult with poor eyesight, which, from a young age, saw him wear glasses.

Living in a house filled with brothers and sisters, and with cousins nearby, it is hardly likely that Mee would have become a reclusive or withdrawn child. Although sometimes shy and reserved, he was sociable, inquisitive and intensely curious about the world. Despite a strain of seriousness bred into him by his father, like his mother he came to possess a healthy sense of humour that in adult life emerged in a subtle and satirical brand of schoolboy wit and a tendency to giggle if he found something funny. Hammerton suggests that a young Mee had an unhappy experience learning to play the violin but had no interest in sport or any enthusiasm for a hobby apart from reading, where, influenced by his father, his tastes were confined to the scriptures and non-fiction.

There is nothing from Mee's letters to John Derry or from Hammerton's biography that throws light upon what this earnest boy did with any free time, apart from one exception: Hammerton writes of how Mee made profitable use of his reading and comprehension skills working for Henry Mellows, a grocer and nonconformist community leader in Stapleford. Mellows knew Mary Mee's family through her uncle William Fletcher, also a grocer and preacher with, like Mellows, a shop on Nottingham Road. Mellows had an interest in current affairs and each evening while he worked in his bakery, he employed the young Arthur Mee to read aloud the parliamentary reports published in newspapers. Hammerton suggests that it was this experience that prompted Mee's interest in politics, together with a fondness for sweets and pastries.[20]

The Making of a Journalist

Arthur Mee's unassuming childhood in Stapleford came to an end when in 1889 Henry Mee moved his family to Nottingham. From the mid-1880s the lace industry in Stapleford had struggled against increased competition, industrial unrest, fluctuating demands and rising costs. The manufacture of lace in Stapleford was a fraction of that in Nottingham and with a strike on the Nottingham coalfield, the town experienced a depression, and a soup kitchen was opened for the unemployed and destitute. Wages were higher in Nottingham, but if Henry Mee was seeking greater security and better paid work then he may have been disappointed; to begin with, at least, he took his family into an environment similar to the one they had just left.

In 1889 Nottingham lace manufacturers were looking to reduce wages to make them more competitive; the outcome was a three-month strike by thousands of workers and factory owners threatening to move their businesses to surrounding villages.[21] In this environment Henry Mee managed to find work as an engineer operating a stationary steam engine in a lace factory. The family relocated to the north of the city and in 1891 were living in Manning Street, Mapperley Park. From there they moved literally around the corner into 213 Woodborough Road, and then along the road to number 237. This remained Anne Mee's home until her death in 1919 and Henry Mee's until he died in 1930.

The Mees' home was close to the Woodborough Road Baptist Chapel and it was there that the family worshipped. The chapel housed 900 and was under the direction of the Liberal Rev. G. Howard James, President of the Nottingham Sunday School Movement. Henry Mee became a deacon and later a member of the chapel directorate, and Arthur Mee and his siblings attended both chapel and Sunday school.[22] Once settled, the Mees continued to add to their family and after a nine-year gap since the birth of Herbert Mee, Wilfred (b. 1890), Harry George William (b. 1892), John Neville (b. 1895) and Arnold (b. 1897) were born; Mary Mee was forty-four when Arnold arrived.

The move to Nottingham coincided with the end of Arthur's school career. Sixteen-year-old Annie Mee was already working as a cashier and thirteen-year-old Ernest as an office boy prior to making a successful career in lace manufacturing. Arthur could have left school when he was ten but at the age of fourteen it was time to begin earning a living to help the family. The job he found was as a copyholder at the conservative *Nottingham Daily Guardian* newspaper, where he was required to read aloud newspaper copy while it was checked by the proof-reader prior to being set for printing. There is nothing to suggest that Mee was looking for a job on a newspaper, but becoming a journalist required nothing in the way of formal qualifications and was a quick route into the respectability of employment. He had a good understanding of language, punctuation and grammar and having read out the parliamentary reports for Henry Mellows, it was a job for which he could provide some evidence of aptitude and experience.

Mee proved himself conscientious, hard-working and determined to grasp any opportunity he could. He perfected two skills essential to his profession by teaching himself how to take Pitman shorthand and how to type by copying down sermons and lectures he heard in chapel.[23] Having quickly proved himself diligent, enthusiastic and eager to learn, in 1891, with the support of Howard James's connections, the sixteen-year-old Mee became an apprentice journalist on *The Nottingham Daily Express* at sixteen shillings a week.

The *Express* was a radical liberal newspaper with a focus strongly influenced by nonconformist principles. Each day, as Mee walked through the front door of its building in Upper Parliament Street, he passed under the images of liberal icons Richard Cobden, William Gladstone and John

Bright. Mee took enthusiastically to his new career and his ambitious determination to succeed was quickly recognised by the editor John Derry, who later described their first meeting:

> When I first met him he was a copy-boy in the Readers' Department of the *Nottingham Daily Guardian*; that is, he read manuscripts to the print corrector, and when I saw him he had already absorbed much knowledge of writing, printing, punctuation, and newspaper affairs. The world was a wonderful place to him. Everything was wonderful, surprising, charming. That is the keynote to his life. A newspaper office was wonderful. How could one help learning all about it? Most of all, writing anything to be printed was wonderful. Most of it was done by reporters who took down speeches which were cut down to fit space. It was splendid to do every wonderful thing you could find anybody doing. That was Arthur Mee's feeling. So he went out and did some reporting on his own account, and he brought a most admirable condensed report of things worth reporting to me for publication in the *Nottingham Daily Express*, of which I was the editor. I accepted it. It was a thoroughly sound piece of work, fit to go straight into the printer's hand and full of good points. "Who are you?" I asked. "My name is Arthur Mee" he said, "and I am in the Readers' Department of the Guardian Office." "Then why don't you take this to the Guardian?" I asked. "Well, Sir," he explained, "the Guardian is a Tory paper and I am a Liberal, and while I am in the Guardian Office I am like Naaman bowing the knee in the House of Rimmon." Hullo, thought I, there's character and personality in this lad, and I said "Your report will appear tomorrow morning, and on Saturday you shall have seven-and-sixpence; and whenever you are at a meeting and can write a report like that, bring it in." That was Arthur Mee's first article, and in a few weeks he was apprenticed for five years to the *Nottingham Express* and was earning his own living.[24]

Mee's long working days as a young journalist were filled with reporting on the endless variety of political, religious and social life in a large provincial city. In comfort and discomfort, in rain, snow, wind and sunshine, he learned to work at all hours of the day and night, taking notes in courtrooms and political meetings and at the scenes of accidents and crimes and interviewing anybody who had a story to tell. His initiative and a willingness to become skilled in all aspects of reporting, writing and sub-editing found him subjecting an impressed Keir Hardie MP to a demanding interview which appeared in *The Nottingham Express*.[25] While learning his craft, Mee continued his education and, through a membership paid for by the paper, was a member of the Nottingham Mechanics Institute. Mechanics institutes were established as venues for working-class men to enjoy cultural, educational and social activities, and Mee was able to feed his mind in its classes, lectures and library and his appetite in its refreshment room.

As Mee matured as a journalist, he met three individuals who became significant in his personal and professional life. The first was John Derry, who was born in May 1854 in Donnington-le-Heath, Leicestershire, into a family of working-class artisans. In 1870, at the age of sixteen, he was a pupil teacher and, having completed his training, began a career as a schoolmaster in Camberwell, south London. In 1877 he married Sarah Jane Wilkins, also a schoolteacher, from Hugglescote, near Ashby-de-la-Zouch in Leicestershire.

In April 1877 they moved to Bourne, where Derry had been appointed headteacher of the Board School. His appointment aged twenty-three was not without controversy. There was some suggestion that a claimed relative, the Rev. William Orton, a Baptist minister in Bourne and chair of the school board, was instrumental in getting him the job.[26] Tragedy struck in April 1880 when, after three years of marriage, twenty-five-year-old Sarah Jane Derry died. Derry remained in Bourne, where, teaching in the same school, he met Rose Southwick, who, in May 1880, left to become headmistress of the Princess Road Board School in South Norwood, London. But by 1884 she was back in the north and in April married John Derry at St Andrew and St Simon Church in Leeds.

Derry was a respected and active member of the Liberal Party, engaging in charities and campaigns to relieve poverty among the working poor. Upon his election as a county councillor in January 1889, a brass band playing *See the Conquering Hero Comes* met him at Bourne Station and he was carried through the town on a wagon as part of a torch-light procession of over 1,000.[27] He was vice-president of the schoolteachers union in Lincolnshire and a committee member at the local cricket club; he took to the stage in a drama called *Poisoned* to raise funds for the Sunday school.[28] A description in *The Grantham Journal* portrayed him as a cheerful, "buoyant, breezy, and hard-working" man who took politics seriously; he was also "Big of body, broad chested, and ruddy of countenance".[29]

Derry's commitment to liberal politics saw him abandon teaching and in March 1887 he resigned as headteacher of the Board School. He was a friend of another cricket lover, Sir Arthur Priestley, the Liberal MP for Grantham who began *The Grantham Times*, and Derry went to edit it.[30] Four years later in June 1891, Derry left Lincolnshire to become editor of *The Nottingham Express* and in May 1895 left Nottingham to edit the liberal *Sheffield Daily Independent.*[31]

The Derrys were nonconformists who worshipped at Queen Street Congregational Chapel, the hub of liberal nonconformist politics in Sheffield. He was a moderate rather than radical liberal who, it has been suggested, was guided by "ardour, tolerance and principle . . . agreeably mixed".[32] In 1897 Derry became a Liberal councillor for the Burngreave

Figure 1.
John Derry, c. 1895
Figure 2.
John "Sandy" Hammerton, c. 1920

ward until he resigned in 1903. He was intimately involved in the politics of the Sheffield Education Committee, to which he was elected in 1900, and had a leading role in developing its structure post-1902.

Derry and Mee enjoyed a close relationship; he and Rose Derry were regular and greatly anticipated visitors to Mee's home and were figures of affection within his family. Twenty-one years his elder, Derry was more than a friend, and Mee latched on to him as a mentor and a sounding board. He listened to Derry, shared many of his views, valued his opinions and for over forty years relied upon him constantly as a contributor and sub-editor and as a calm, shrewd and trusted confidante.

Derry was replaced as editor of *The Nottingham Express* by twenty-four-year-old John Alexander Hammerton, already an experienced journalist and editor. Hammerton was born in Alexandria, Scotland, on 27 February 1871; his father manufactured clogs and sold them through shops he owned in Lancashire, Glasgow and Alexandria. When his father died of pleurisy at forty-one, three-year-old John Hammerton and his family left England to live in Glasgow in a three-room flat they shared with his grandmother.[33] At age fourteen, a reluctant Hammerton left school and began earning a living in the office of J. & G. Mossman, a Glasgow firm of stonemasons; it was a job he hated. Set on a career in journalism, Hammerton, like Mee, educated himself at evening classes, read widely, taught himself shorthand and by 1889, although not teetotal, was assistant editor on the temperance newspaper *The Reformer*. In 1893 he moved to the trade-union-sponsored

Glasgow Daily Echo as assistant editor, followed by a short stint at the ill-fated *Bolton Evening Echo.* 1894 found him working briefly as editor of *The Blackpool Herald* before in June 1895 he became editor of *The Nottingham Daily Express*, two weeks before Mee finished his apprenticeship. Their meeting in Nottingham began a friendship that lasted nearly fifty years.

Hammerton and Mee were very different, with Hammerton claiming that "no two friends could differ more sharply in their views of life than A.M. and J.A.H.".[34] While Mee was driven by a nonconformist sense of mission, the more pragmatic Hammerton had no inner sense of calling, religious or otherwise. While Mee demonstrated an extraordinary work ethic and became consumed by forging a successful career, Hammerton was less driven. Mee found aspects of popular literature, theatre and music sometimes offensive but more often trivial, tedious and uninspiring, while Hammerton enjoyed them enormously. While Mee was fiercely teetotal, drinking water, lemonade, coffee and tea, Hammerton liked his whiskey.

Derry and Hammerton appear frequently throughout Mee's life story, as does one other more obscurely sketched figure, Ernest Arthur Bryant, known as "Ern", one of Mee's most intimate friends.[35] Born in Brixton, south London, in 1873, Bryant met Mee while working on *The Nottingham Express*. He was known as a versatile and productive journalist with a sense of humour.[36] Later in life he suffered from insomnia, neuritis and shingles, and his health was often a worry to Mee.[37] Bryant remains something of an enigma and little is known of this more or less constant presence in Mee's life.

Bryant supported himself through journalism, including writing for *The Daily Mail* and magazines such as *The Quiver*, an illustrated middle-class evangelical and temperance magazine; *Cassell's Magazine*; and the illustrated monthly *Windsor Magazine*. Exploiting the popularity of Edwardian ideas of self-improvement, in 1908 he wrote a book called *A New Self-Help*.[38] For fifty years Mee was loyal, supportive and protective of him, providing the unmarried Bryant with an income, on occasion a roof over his head, and a place within his family. On Mee's death, Bryant, who had little money of his own, was a beneficiary in his friend's will and was left the substantial sum of £1,500.

London, Marriage and Family

In 1895, nearing the completion of his apprenticeship, Mee was appointed editor of the *Nottingham Evening News*, the evening edition of the *Express*, at thirty shillings a week. Although it was a promotion, the job had little prestige attached to it; all it required was selecting from the morning's *Express* enough interesting local news to fill the evening paper's four pages. While the job offered Mee a further opportunity to develop his skills and although he completed the work with what was now his customary ability, efficiency and enthusiasm, he had no intention of making a career on a provincial newspaper.

Encouragement came from the worldly John Hammerton who supplemented his income by writing articles for London-based periodicals and magazines, including *Tit-Bits*. Hammerton encouraged Mee to build his reputation by writing for the penny weekly. Established in 1881, *Tit-Bits* was written for a working-class and lower-middle-class audience; it was unashamedly populist and in 1890 had a readership of 500,000 a week.[39] *Tit-Bits* owner George Newnes was amongst the first to recognise that the development of mass literacy in the closing decades of the nineteenth century had created a new audience who, ambitious for information, entertainment and self-improvement, found the contents of newspapers tedious and boring.

Tit-Bits specialised in human interest stories, romantic fiction, serials, interviews with celebrities, readers' letters, competitions and entertainment news. It appealed to a readership that had little time to spare and articles were limited to a length likely to sustain the interest of a reader travelling by train or tram. The success of *Tit-Bits* led to it being widely imitated and Newnes can be credited with making the magazine a marketing and commercial template for dozens of magazines and newspapers that followed.

Writing for *Tit-Bits* saw Mee widen and enhance his reputation, and, with him being paid sometimes as much as £20 per week, added very significantly to his bank balance. But while anxious to move to London, Mee, ever cautious where his career was concerned, later warned young journalists not to leave a job on a provincial newspaper to move to London unless a firm offer had been made.[40] In November 1896 such an offer came his way when his growing visibility within the pages of popular magazines led to Galloway Fraser, the editor of *Tit-Bits*, inviting him to London to discuss joining the staff. Mee had been offered a job working for Alfred Harmsworth at his magazine *Answers*, but accepted the offer from Fraser and at the age of twenty-one began his career as a London-based writer and journalist.

As an aspiring journalist with a burning ambition to succeed, Mee's arrival in London saw him living in the largest and wealthiest city in the world, characterised by a tireless energy, vitality and dynamism. Cosmopolitan and multi-cultural, brash and self-confident, London was at once exotic, brilliant and glamorous, shocking, contradictory and dangerous. It was a place of striking contrasts where immense wealth and abject poverty existed side by side. It was a city in which an intoxicating and diverse mixture of literary, political and social representations of what it was to be modern and innovative were fashioned and refined. As it continually re-invented itself, Ford Maddox Hueffer saw London as the "apotheosis of modern life".[41]

In this dynamic world of pessimism and optimism, anxiety and hope, Mee turned briefly from building a career to getting married. On 6 March 1897, a few months after moving to London and the year of Queen Victoria's Diamond Jubilee, he married nineteen-year-old Amelia Fratson. Nothing is known of a courtship other than the claim that the two met in 1895 while they were on holiday in Skegness, a Lincolnshire seaside resort which, after the coming of the railway in 1873, became a popular destination for holidaymakers in their thousands.

Amelia, known as Amy, was born in the village of Skelton in north Yorkshire. By the time she was two, the family had moved to Melbourne in east Yorkshire where her father Charles Fratson earned a living as a joiner. A further move saw the family in East Cottingwith in Yorkshire and in July 1890, Charles Fratson, still a joiner, was adding to the family income as the landlord of the Blue Bell Inn. He was an active member of his local community, using his skills to help restore the local church and build a classroom for the Board School and joining in with the social side of village life at agricultural shows. By 1901 he had abandoned the drink trade but continued to work as a joiner and wheelwright.

Following the wedding in Wandsworth, south London, the Mees set up home at 27 Lanercost Road, Tulse Hill, in a semi-detached Victorian villa. Prior to the expansion of owner-occupied homes during the 1920s and 1930s, a majority of people from all social classes rented homes. Even if Mee had been extremely frugal it is unlikely that he would have been able to find the money it would have taken to buy a house. This is even more likely to be the case considering that the Mees began married life with a lodger, with Ernest Bryant living with them at Lanercost Road. It was in this, their first home, that Arthur and Amy Mee began their own family when on 18 August 1901 their only child Marjorie Ernestine was born.

Tulse Hill was an area of south London that experienced substantial residential development once the opening of the railway in 1868 saw it grow as a commuter suburb. Mee was able to walk each day to the station before making the short journey into the city. At a time when the occupation of the male wage earner defined a family, identifying himself as an editor in the 1901 census placed Mee firmly within the ranks of the socially reputable middle class. He was what Charles Masterman called a "suburbanite", who lived in homes each boasting "its pleasant drawing-room, its bow-window, its little front garden, its high sounding title – 'Acacia Villa,' or 'Camperdown Lodge' – attesting to unconquered human aspiration".[42]

Lanercost Road was solidly middle-class and those that rented and bought their semi-detached and detached villas there gave them names to mark out their independence, individuality and territory. In 1901 residents in Lanercost Road lived in homes called "Hillview", "Windermere", "Ashford House", "Hazelbrae", "Winbrook" and "Silverdean"; Mee's home at number 27 was "Redcot". Among his neighbours were those with respectable middle-class occupations, including civil servants and clerks working in local government, accountants, a mortgage broker, businessmen and a civil engineer. Several had that mark of middle-class respect-ability, a live-in domestic servant, although the Mees were not yet in that category.

Now with the responsibility of a home and family, after two years working at *Tit-Bits*, twenty-six-year-old Mee decided to make himself more financially secure by taking advantage of the many offers of work that were coming his way. He opted to become a freelance journalist; although the rewards could be significant, it

Figure 3.
Amelia Mee, c. 1916

was not without its pressures, something that Mee noted years later when writing that being self-employed required courage, method, hard work and the ability to write about anything at any time. He suggested a salary of £500 a year was possible, made up of work for a newspaper or magazine two days each week plus writing a daily or weekly column for other publications.[43]

This was exactly how Mee organised his working life and he was in the right place at the right time. The last decade of the nineteenth century was, as H.G. Wells noted, particularly beneficial for writers, who found themselves working in an environment of opportunity and high demand.[44] Not wishing to refuse any opportunity that came his way, in April 1898 Mee became assistant editor of the weekly *Home Magazine*, a penny illustrated religious magazine published by George Newnes. Under the editorship of George Clarke, Mee was described as having been "one of 'Tit Bits' brightest writers".[45] He also continued to write for other periodicals, including *Temple Bar* magazine, *The Young Man* and *The Young Woman*, the Newnes monthly *Strand Magazine*[46] and Alfred Harmsworth's *Answers*.

His range was impressive; he wrote about the "heroic splendour" of Robert Baden-Powell for the comic paper *Chums*[47] and a piece on the peril of cigarettes for the *Sunday School Chronicle*.[48] He wrote "The Making of Sherlock Holmes" for *The Young Man*;[49] in September 1899 he produced an article on the Baptist minister C.H. Spurgeon for the nonconformist

Figure 4.

Amelia Mee with her sister Lena Fratson behind, c. 1899. Lena lived with the Mees until her death and was Mee's private secretary.

magazine *The Puritan* and an article on Donizetti for the penny weekly *Great Thoughts*. In 1900 he also found time to act as the magazine editor on the forgotten daily newspaper *The Morning Herald*. In 1902 he was writing daily columns for the conservative evening newspaper *The St James Gazette*[50] and taking on the role of editing the illustrated weekly magazine *Black and White* at a salary of £500 per annum, a job he did until 1903.[51]

In addition to writing for magazines and periodicals, Mee added to a remarkable output by producing biographies of the Liberal politician Joseph Chamberlain (1900), the Conservative Prime Minister Lord Salisbury (1901) and also in 1901 a book on Edward VII.[52] A fourth book, *England's Mission by English Statesmen*, an edited collection of speeches from leading politicians, appeared in 1903 and was described by *The Spectator* magazine as "a very instructive volume".[53]

This output meant that Mee could afford a larger home and by June 1902 the family had moved to an imposing detached villa at 18 Court Road (now Elmcourt Road), a mile from Lanercost Road. It was here that the Mees were joined by Amy Mee's twenty-year-old sister Selina Fratson, known as "Lena". Lena lived as part of the Mee family for over fifty years and worked as Mee's private secretary, organising his home office, taking dictation and typing letters.

*

In 1891 Mee had been a sixteen-year-old apprentice journalist on *The Nottingham Daily Express*. Not much more than a decade later, he was married with a family, living comfortably and enjoying a reputation as an in-demand journalist of industry, ability and initiative. This was by any standards an impressive career trajectory, but in spite of his growing success and standing there was nothing to suggest that he would rise beyond the status of a man who, within the confines of his profession, was a respected and successful journalist and editor. Although always anxious to improve his knowledge and skills, Mee had shown little interest in education and schooling and none in developing a career writing for children.

The only discernible sign of a wider sense of purpose was Mee's determination to grasp any opportunity that offered the potential for advancement. His ambition to establish himself professionally and to attain material security for his family could not be satisfied within the life of a jobbing journalist turning out well-paid but often anonymously crafted articles. Mee wanted much more; he wanted long-term professional protection working within an environment where he could give full reign to his appetites and aspirations. The campaigning voice that would become so characteristic of his writing had not yet been heard and was unlikely to be so as long as he continued to write commissioned articles for a diverse range of magazines and newspapers. Mee needed a larger stage, one that would provide him with opportunities to be influential by carrying his values, ideas and opinions to a national audience, and for that he needed Alfred Harmsworth.

2.

Caught in the Harmsworth Web

Working for "the Chief"

Born in Dublin in 1865 into a family of lawyers and clergymen, Alfred Harmsworth began to develop an interest in journalism editing his school magazine. Having left school, he worked freelance for several magazines and newspapers, before, aged twenty, being asked to edit *Youth*, an illustrated magazine for boys, and, in 1886, *Bicycling News*.[1] But Harmsworth's ambitions went beyond writing for magazines and newspapers to owning them. His ability, some said genius, was to spot a public trend and exploit it and from the outset he was set on taking advantage of rising levels of literacy by publishing magazines and newspapers for a mass audience. The Forster Education Act (1870) had established a system of local school boards providing education for 5- to 13-year-olds and by 1880 one million new school places were available, producing increases in already rising levels of literacy. In 1871 80 per cent of men and 73 per cent of women were able to read and write; by 1897 only 3 per cent of the population were illiterate. In a letter to his friend Max Pemberton, Harmsworth wrote of the potential of a magazine like *Tit-Bits*:

> The man who has produced this Tit-Bits has got hold of a bigger thing than he imagines. He is only at the very beginning of a development which is going to change the whole face of journalism. I shall try to get in with him. We could start one of these papers for a couple of thousand pounds, and we ought to be able to find the money. At any rate, I am going to make the attempt.[2]

Harmsworth's first effort at publishing was *Answers to Correspondents* (1888), a carbon copy of *Tit-Bits*.[3] *Answers* was aggressively marketed and in November 1889 offered £1 a week for life to the reader who could guess how much money there was in the Bank of England on a certain day. The competition generated enormous excitement and increased sales to 200,000 a week, making Harmsworth significant profits from advertising revenue.[4] He put those profits into establishing The Amalgamated Press, from which he launched other titles. In 1890 he published *The Illustrated Chips* and *Comic Cuts*, a black-and-white pictorial magazine for adults that by 1892 had a weekly readership of 500,000.[5] He also entered the market for mass-produced magazines for women. *Forget-Me-Not* (1891) and *Home Sweet Home* (1893) were followed in 1895 by *Home Chat*, which reached a circulation of 250,000.[6]

Harmsworth directed his attention to daily newspapers and in 1894 bought the conservative *Evening News* for £25,000, modernised it and turned it into a profitable publication.[7] In 1896 he launched *The Daily Mail*, followed

Figure 5.
Alfred Harmsworth, c. 1920

in 1903 by *The Daily Mirror*, which became the largest selling daily newspaper, with a circulation of one million. In 1905 he added *The Sunday Observer* and in 1908 *The Times*, viewed by many as a semi-official voice of government opinion.

The Daily Mail, populist and patriotic to its core, was aimed at aspirational readers who Peter Bailey suggests wore white collars and led grey lives.[8] It was designed to exploit popular social trends by providing readers with what Harmsworth thought they wanted rather than what some thought they ought to want. He knew well the power of newspapers, claiming, "God made people read so that I could fill their heads with facts, facts, facts – and tell them whom to love, whom to hate and what to think."[9] Journalists and sub-editors were instructed to ensure that narratives "explained, simplified and clarified"[10] because they were "writing for the meanest intelligence".[11]

Although he was mocked by the social and political elite as a nouveau riche interloper lacking social or family connections, politicians knew that Harmsworth's publications had the potential to influence the views of millions. In 1904, in an effort to secure support for the Conservative Party, Prime Minister Arthur Balfour conferred a baronetcy and Alfred Harmsworth became Lord Northcliffe.

In 1903, having left the editorship of *Black and White*, Mee and John Hammerton began to explore new ideas for magazines. Hammerton had left *The Nottingham Daily Express* in 1897 to become editor of *The*

Birmingham Weekly Post. He was there for three years, before, in October 1900, moving to London to edit a group of religious and temperance magazines published by S.W. Partridge & Co. Hammerton developed an idea for a weekly newspaper to be called "Who's Who This Week". A dummy issue constructed by Mee was sent to Harmsworth, who showed absolutely no interest in publishing it. But he had a reputation for identifying and employing journalistic talent and then wondering what to do with it, and he was interested in Mee. At one time Mee had said he would never work for Harmsworth, but when the offer of a job came along he immediately accepted. While Harmsworth saw in Mee an able journalist, Mee saw in Harmsworth an employer who could provide him with a career and opportunities to develop new ideas in an innovative environment.

Mee was also attracted by the yearly salary of £1,000. It was an extraordinary sum for one still relatively young, but was consistent with Harmsworth's policy of paying his journalists well as a way of motivating them. At the Annual General Meeting of The Amalgamated Press in 1905 he told his audience that it was his policy to get the best journalistic talent available by paying them unheard-of sums. But he also told them that as nearly everybody was paid by results, the speed of promotion was matched only by the speed at which those thought inadequate were sacked.[12] With the annual wage of an unskilled and semi-skilled worker being approximately £100-£150 p.a., and that of a clerk £200 p.a., £1,000 a year furnished the Mee family with an extremely comfortable lifestyle.

Mee once told John Derry that ever since an expenses claim at *The Nottingham Express* had been cut by twopence he had thought money a "nuisance".[13] He had also been told by Harmsworth that finance was not one of his strong points.[14] But Mee always knew the value of money and was very willing to spending it on acquiring the comforts of life that pleased him artistically and marked out the successes of his career. Wasting little time in enjoying the fruits of his growing wealth, the Mees left Elmcourt Road and suburban London for the Kent countryside. By the summer of 1905 they had moved into "Uplands", a large detached house in the village of Hextable on the edge of Swanley.

The move saw the Mees join a growing exodus from London by middle-class professionals attracted to the idea of living a semi-rural life. This meant not only a physical distancing from the old to the new but a social distancing. Life in villages and hamlets within striking distance of London was considered aesthetically more appealing, far less crowded, much healthier and to offer the opportunity of living within a more secure and stable world. Hammerton claims the move into Kent was prompted by the fact that the Mees wanted Marjorie to grow up in the countryside, "amongst the little fairies".[15]

Figure 6.

*Uplands, Hextable, Kent. The Mees moved into Uplands in 1903 and
remained there until 1913 when they moved to Eynsford Hill. The house
is still there and has been divided into two semi-detached homes.*

There was nothing of note to distinguish Hextable until the coming of
the railway to nearby Swanley Junction in 1862. Subsequently the village
gained a reputation as a middle-class retreat sixteen miles from the centre
of London. At the time that Mee moved there, Hextable was growing;
one acre plots were being sold for the building of what were described
as "county cottage residences". On Rowhill Road, where Uplands was
situated, a number of large detached villas with acres of garden were up
for lease.[16]

Built in approximately 1885, Uplands was an impressive home for the
twenty-eight-year-old Mee and his family. It had eighteen rooms set in five
acres, complete with a croquet lawn, tennis court, palm house and extensively
landscaped gardens. It also had a stable for Jack, the Shetland pony that
Marjorie Mee's doting father bought for her.[17] The Mees also acquired
that quintessential mark of middle-class respectability and status, a live-in
domestic servant in the form of eighteen-year-old Elizabeth Claydon from
Stetchworth in Cambridgeshire.

To get to work Mee took the train from nearby Swanley Junction
through the countryside and urban south London into Blackfriars Station.
From there it was a short walk, taxi or bus ride through the congested
streets of central London to his office in Carmelite Street and later Temple
Chambers in Temple Avenue. Mee did not always make the reverse
journey in the evening. The frenetic pace at which he worked meant it
was usual for him to remain in London overnight. Then he would stay
at the luxurious and expensive Goring Hotel in central London with its

en-suite bedrooms, air conditioning and central heating. Mee was a regular guest at the Goring, staying there for days at a time and on one occasion spending a week there recovering from influenza.

The Harmsworth Self-Educator

Mee and Harmsworth were driven by their determination to be successful. Both had a resolute commitment to the British Empire, an enthusiasm for new technologies and a passion for the English countryside. Mee had a healthy respect for the man known by his employees as "the Chief" and had a photograph of him hanging from a wall in his office next to one of Marjorie Mee. Not all Mee's friends shared his regard for Harmsworth. In a brutally honest vignette, Mee's friend, the author Harold Begbie, portrayed Harmsworth as an opportunist who, lacking moral judgement and scruples, manipulated public opinion for personal profit.[18]

Mee knew of Harmsworth's reputation and at one time it had put him off, but now it mattered little when set against the prospect of a very well-paid career. Nor did it matter to John Hammerton, who also accepted an offer from Harmsworth to join The Amalgamated Press on £1,000 a year.[19] Hammerton quickly developed his own opinions of working for "the Chief". It was, he wrote, like being part of a volatile adventure where a strong character was required in order to withstand treatment that could be brutal.[20] Yet in spite of the demands, Hammerton writes that Mee became "caught up in the Harmsworth web in which he has ever since remained a more or less willing prisoner".[21]

Harmsworth had been involved in the publication of weekly and fortnightly magazines since 1898, including the enormously successful *Harmsworth Magazine*, and later *The London Magazine*, before in 1905 re-publishing *Nelson's Encyclopaedia: Everybody's Book of Reference*. His contribution was limited to allowing his name to be used as a marketing ploy in the title of a new edition. The encyclopaedia, originally compiled under the editorship of George Sandeman and published by Nelson's, was re-published as *The Harmsworth Encyclopaedia*. Marketed as one of the most significant publishing feats ever embarked upon and an educational work of great value, it was hugely popular.[22] In a glowing endorsement, *The Practical Teacher* claimed that it had provoked enormous demand and represented a significant contribution to public education.[23]

Mee began life on *The Daily Mail* as editor of the features page and sometimes wrote articles on issues that reflected his political and social values.[24] But Harmsworth had other plans for him and early in 1905, impressed with the sales of *The Harmsworth Encyclopaedia*, he put Mee to work developing a populist magazine to be called *The Harmsworth Self-Educator: A Golden Key to Success in Life*. The aim was to capture an audience among the aspirational working and lower middle class who had faith in self-education and were anxious to purchase a publication that told them how they could progress in life.

Mee, like many of his generation, believed unequivocally in the idea of self-improvement and progress, and with good reason; he saw it around him, lived with it and enjoyed its benefits, and there was no reason to think that it would end. The economist John Maynard Keynes looked back at those years before the First World War with a mixture of wit, mockery and melancholy. With regard to the nation's global dominance, influence and power, Keynes claims that people "regarded this state of affairs as normal, certain, and permanent, except in the direction of further improvement, and any deviation from it as aberrant, scandalous, and avoidable".[25] From his youngest days this was how Mee had been taught to interpret his world: there would always be change and, in spite of its challenges, it would always be progressive; things would always incrementally get better for everybody who worked hard and improved themselves.

Published between 1905 and 1907 in forty-eight fortnightly issues, the *Self-Educator* was a magazine designed to help readers become more qualified, get a better job and receive a better wage. It was published at a time when, as George Orwell observed, "the worship of money was entirely unreflecting and untroubled by any pang of conscience".[26] The *Self-Educator* represented, as Mee put it, "Education in Action".[27] It was "a book of modern life, of modern thought, and of modern work".[28] It contained sections on the arts and humanities, science, technology, geography, history, music and natural history and articles on trades, industries and the development of practical skills. Advertisements extolled the virtues of modern technologies such as "The New Model Remington typewriter", a self-filling fountain pen and the latest in accurate timepieces, all for the busy and aspirational worker.

Mee brought his commitment to self-education to the editing task and in the introduction announced the *Self-Educator* as a "working school of life" designed to

> lay the foundations of an adaptable and successful career for the thousands of young men and women who are bewildered by the increasing difficulty of choosing a definite aim in life, or, having a definite aim, of adapting themselves to its conditions.[29]

These aims were reflected in how Mee marketed the *Self-Educator*. Full-page advertisements in *The Daily Mirror* were intended to convince readers that it was indispensable for their futures. Many were written by Mee and reflected his view that if a worker suggested ways of increasing the profits of his employer, they could expect promotion and success.[30] A half-page advertisement included in *The Daily Mail* the day before the first issue appeared and likely written by Mee called the encyclopaedia "The fountain of Brain power" and urged readers to "Buy It. Read it. Succeed".[31] A panel advertisement in *The Manchester Courier* appealed directly to readers' sense of ambition; "Be dissatisfied with your lot," they were urged, before being asked, "Do you wish to rise in the world?" The message was that success came with ambition and with the knowledge the *Self-Educator* provided.[32]

Two weeks after the first issue *The Daily Mail* told readers that they were part of a fierce struggle for survival and that those who bought the *Self-Educator* had a head start. Those who failed to buy the magazine would forever remain locked into a life of monotony being paid all they might ever expect as well as being at the mercy of economic downturns.[33] The *Self-Educator* was a phenomenal success and by June 1906 had sold copies to the value of £500,000.[34] Harmsworth was delighted and Mee found his salary doubled.[35]

The Harmsworth Self-Educator was followed in 1907 by *Harmsworth's History of the World* (1907-1909); this was Mee's idea, although John Hammerton did much of the editing. To ease the load they negotiated a contract with William Heinemann who owned the rights to the eight-volume *History of the World: A Survey of Man's Record* (1901). Edited by the German historian Hans Helmolt, this series was what they intended to use as the basis for the publication.

The deal they struck saw Mee become the owner of his first car. In a tongue-in-cheek moment he asked Heinemann that should he receive more than £10,000 in royalties from the arrangement, he buy him a car. The £10,000 was quickly reached and Heinemann had the car delivered to Mee's office. Never having had any interest in learning how to drive, Mee had to employ a chauffeur, something he continued to do throughout his life. Such was Mee's excitement that he wrote to Harmsworth urging him to put aside this work to come for a drive.[36] Harmsworth was more hard-edged about the success of *History of the World* and, while happy with its sales, warned Mee to keep expenses down lest the circulation drop.[37] On the back of the magazine's success, Harmsworth put his "payments by results" policy into practice and Mee's salary was raised by a further £1,000 a year.[38]

"I Have to Think of My Career"

The nostalgic sentiment attached to Mee's work ignores the fact that not only was he expected to produce magazines that were popular, they had to be extremely so and also exceptionally profitable. He worked within a highly competitive business environment in which the ability to market products that would sell to a mass audience was essential. Although Harmsworth encouraged him to use his imagination, Mee knew that his professional interests and personal security were tied to his employer's demands and the consequences of failing to meet them were never far from his thoughts.

Like many who worked for Harmsworth, Mee thought he was sometimes unfairly treated, but their relationship was positive and on occasion affectionate.[39] Mee's letters are written to the "Dear Chief" and sometimes signed "Your devoted A.M.",[40] while Harmsworth's letters are often addressed to "My Dear Arthur".[41] But while his association with Harmsworth was one of admiration and respect, Mee knew that it was never remotely one of equals. Hammerton claims that while he never consciously thought of planning a career, he was incredibly surprised when Mee, faced with making a decision that might have upset Harmsworth, said, "I can't do that: I have to think of my Career."[42]

Building a career and planning for the future were integral elements of how the Edwardian middle classes shaped their identity. Enterprise and initiative were valued for the material wealth they might bring, but also attached was an ethical and moral imperative. Within a hierarchical society in which status was a defining social characteristic, the advantages of financial security in terms of respectability and prestige were enormous. Anything that threatened propriety or damaged a reputation and the status that went with it, such as unemployment or scandal, was viewed with horror and assiduously avoided.

Mee became consumed by these issues and a widespread middle-class perception that respectability was the product of financial security. Ruin and the social ignominy that might follow were genuine concerns at a time when state-sponsored safety nets remained scarce and life insurance policies and pension funds were limited.[43] For the desperate, suicide offered a way out, and the Edwardian decade saw considerable numbers of suicides by men employed in business and the professions.[44] The spectre of unemployment and the insecurity and poverty it brought saw Mee develop a strain of cautious conservatism as far as his work was concerned. He was one of those middle-class suburbanites described by H.G. Wells in *The War of the Worlds* (1898) as having "Lives insured and a bit invested for accidents".[45]

Ensuring the financial security of his family was always a priority for Mee and in May 1908 he wrote to Harmsworth asking to be paid a royalty on sales of the publications he edited. Arguing that his finances consisted of small savings and insurance policies, Mee wrote of a duty to protect his family from financial ruin if anything went wrong.[46] Claiming that it was because of him that Harmsworth's publications had become extraordinarily profitable, he argued that a royalty on the profits of future editions would provide him with long-term financial security.[47] Harmsworth's answer is unknown, although he did offer editors a percentage of a publication's profits above a particular circulation figure, ensuring that it was in their interests to make sure it sold well.

The autumn and winter of 1909 saw Mee restless. In an undated letter to Derry that fits with a chronology of November 1909, he wrote of his worry that he faced an uncertain future. He knew his efforts were reaping impressive profits for The Amalgamated Press but the nature of the work was inherently risky. What troubled him most was that nothing he was responsible for had a permanent life. After a magazine had finished its run he had to come up with a new idea and start again, and there was no guarantee that a new publication would achieve the success demanded.[48]

Mee's disquiet had been heightened by the reception of *The World's Great Books* which, jointly edited with Hammerton, appeared in October 1909.[49] Mee had convinced Harmsworth of the merits of publishing a fortnightly magazine containing comprehensive summaries of the world's great fiction and non-fiction, aimed at those who lacked the time or inclination to read a whole book.[50] The model had worked before and on the back of a nationwide advertising campaign he saw no reason why this should not be another success.

But in spite of public endorsements from the likes of Mee's friend the radical nonconformist journalist W.T. Stead, the general public greeted *The World's Great Books* with a large dose of indifference. On a tour of newsagents and bookstalls to check sales, Mee and Hammerton were left in no doubt. As one shopkeeper said, "Believe me, this is a dud. A complete dud."[51] In spite of claims that thousands were passing through London's railway stations with a copy under their arm, what Mee wrote of as his "latest Frankenstein"[52] was not selling well. Numbers were short of what was expected and a month after the first edition appeared Mee was having to cut its costs.[53] Mystified as to why the series had failed to capture the public imagination, he concluded that it offered nothing practical or tangible to readers other than aesthetic and cultural satisfaction, in which he concluded that most people had no interest. Previous publications had targeted buyers seeking to improve their careers but *The World's Great Books* had nothing of the aspirational utilitarian focus that had characterised the *Self-Educator*; there was nothing in it that might help a reader earn more money.

1910 was made more difficult for Mee by the fact that Harmsworth was becoming anxious about profit margins. Pressure arrived in the form of a letter suggesting that Mee pay greater attention to his work. Mee was a member of the Dartford Liberal Association and took an interest in politics in and around Hextable, including campaigning for the local candidate in the January 1910 general election.[54] His community involvements saw him persuade the local council to spend £20,000 on mains drainage and street lighting for the village.[55] The *Nottingham Evening Post* described Hextable as "a pleasant village which Mr. Mee, who resides there, has done much to improve and modernise without spoiling".[56] Harmsworth had a different view, believing that Mee's activities were taking him away from his work at a time when the necessity of improving the profitability of the publications for which he was responsible was acute.[57]

In October 1910 Mee sent Harmsworth a long handwritten reply expressing great concern that "the Chief" thought he was neglecting his work when all he had been doing was learning about local government and trying to make a contribution to his community.[58] The letter reveals his determination to protect his career by giving up any activity that might make Harmsworth doubt his commitment. To lose Harmsworth's confidence would, Mee wrote, be the final blow in what had been a difficult year for him.[59] Harmsworth's reply written from Paris on 1 November 1910 coaxed, cajoled and praised in reminding Mee how lucky he was and of the risks of failure. He was shrewd enough to let Mee know how much he valued his ability, energy and work while also encouraging him to concentrate and to not let anything get in the way of maximising profits.[60]

Part of what Mee described as an anxious and painful 1910 included the illness of his younger brother Harry. Harry Mee, like his brothers Arthur, Herbert and Wilfred, was making a career as a journalist on *The Nottingham Daily Express* when in May 1910 he was taken dangerously ill and brought to London for treatment. He had been suffering from headaches resulting from a brain tumour pressing on the optic nerve, causing him to lose his sight and then slip into a coma. He was operated on twice by Sir Victor Horsley.[61] On Sunday 12 June, Mee wrote to Derry telling him that Harry had come through the operations well, but then

> about last Wednesday, something changed and since then he has been delirious, remembering nothing, and the visits are painful. Even if he should recover, he will almost surely be sightless, and subject to this terrible thing again. . . . Someday when all the world goes well, we will have a happy little party.[62]

After what appeared to be a chance of recovery, Mee remained hopeful, but on 9 July in the National Hospital, Bloomsbury, eighteen-year-old Harry died. The funeral was on 13 July in Nottingham. A service took place at Woodborough Road Baptist Chapel and Harry was buried in the general cemetery with his father, brothers and uncles standing beside the grave.[63] In *Arthur Mee's Wonderful Day* (1923), Mee reflected upon his brother's death:

> Yet too sad for a word is life sometimes. In the heart of this beautiful London our brave boy lay, day after day til the days were weeks, week after week till the weeks were months, and I knew as I walked in the sun, that he would never see the sun again. All that science could do, all that money could buy, all that love could devise, had failed at last.[64]

Alfred Harmsworth sent a letter of sympathy.[65]

Mee found solace in work and his career continued to flourish. Harmsworth's suggestion that he focus upon his part-publications did not prevent him from developing his work as a writer. A contract with Hodder

& Stoughton saw the appearance of *Arthur Mee's Gift Book: For Boys and Girls Who Love the Flag* (1917), a collection of stories, articles, poetry and illustrations written during the First World War, the proceeds of which were donated to the Red Cross. He also wrote *Little Treasure Island: Her Story and Her Glory* (1920), containing patriotic articles on history, geography and literature, and *Every Child's Creed* (1921), a religiously inspired Christmas manifesto for children calling for an end to war, greed, ignorance and disease. Other titles included *Arthur Mee's Hero Book* (1921), which was for one reviewer "throbbing with the spirit of heroism that has made our world what it is and our country what she is".[66] In 1922 appeared a book for the Christmas market; *Arthur Mee's Golden Year* contained accounts of his travels in Italy, Switzerland, France, Norway and Egypt.

Mee's relationship with Harmsworth ended when on 14 August 1922, aged fifty-seven, "the Chief" died from heart disease. Harmsworth's death was not entirely a surprise. Over the years his health had deteriorated and his behaviour had become erratic, and there had been fears among some family members and friends that he was suffering from paranoia and megalomania.[67] In a considered obituary, Mee eulogised Harmsworth as a man of imagination, courage and faith, claiming, "There are millions of people who never agreed with him; there are very few who always agreed with him; but there never was a man who sowed ideas on the world's highway as he did. . . . He made journalism bright and fine."[68]

"A Most Attractive Individual"

Mee was dedicated to his career but he was far from dull or dreary company and managed to somehow combine the excessive demands of work with a rich and full life. By nature serious yet cheerfully optimistic and trusting, Mee is revealed in his letters to be a man with a self-deprecating sense of humour and somebody who playfully mocked his family and friends in ways he hoped would amuse them. Hammerton suggests Mee was known to sing hymns in his bath.[69] Possessed of an intense curiosity that helped overcome a natural shyness, Mee was always pleased to enjoy people's company and to share in conversation about everything and anything. While nothing could detract from his faith-based values, he was at ease surrounded by friends and work colleagues who had interests and views very different from his own, seeing them as a source of ideas and opinions.

Small in stature, Mee made up for a lack of physical presence with a powerful personality, and those who knew him recognised a focussed, driven and dynamic individual. He was never afraid to voice his views, and his enthusiasms and prejudices were articulated with equal passion. He might have agreed with G.K. Chesterton that "There is no such thing on Earth as an uninteresting subject; the only thing that can exist is an uninterested person."[70] Consumed with a restless energy, he had an uninhibited desire to constantly learn more about the world. Hammerton writes, "He was always anxious to know 'Who said that? Who wrote that? Who did that?'"[71] At times his enthusiasm got the better of him when what appeared to him to be an exciting new project to which he wanted immediately to devote his energies seemed to friends to be entirely unrealistic.[72] Hammerton credits himself with restraining Mee's animated eagerness:

> It will not, I trust, be regarded as in any way self-flattery if I say that I had a much more practical mind than my colleague, Arthur. . . . I was constantly translating schemes of his from the plane of the imagination to that of realism: turning, at times, quite attractive but barely workable ideas into practical possibilities.[73]

Mee had a magpie mind and was an emotive and intuitive thinker; hungry for information, he had to know a little about everything without ever knowing too much about anything. Thriving upon structure and organisation, he was an extraordinary collector of snippets of information in the form of press clippings on every conceivable subject, all meticulously filed in envelopes and indexed. These, together with his extensive reference library, he used as sources of ideas for his writing.

Loyalty and trust were important to Mee and he was impulsively generous in donating to causes he thought important, to the families of friends who had died and to work colleagues. In a 2007 letter to *The Guardian*, Donovan Pedelty, who had worked as an office boy on *The Children's Newspaper*, wrote of how at Christmas 1942 he was presented by Mee with a copy of his book *Talks for Boys*. While the book was of no interest, he found the £1 note placed inside much more appealing.[74] In his will, Mee left £10 each to his office boy and "Ross", the newspaper seller who stood outside Lever House in Blackfriars.

Apart from an enthusiasm for designing and re-designing his gardens and purchasing items to make his home more comfortable, Mee had no time or patience for anything that could be called a hobby. He did not share the enthusiasm of Marjorie Mee for botany and bird-watching or John Hammerton's keen interest in the theatre, nor did he play cards as his family sometimes did. As well as being a fan of the theatre, John Derry enjoyed fell walking, cricket and bowls and he was a good amateur golfer. None of this appealed to Mee, apart from a good walk, but he was content to follow Derry around the golf course, play bowls with him on the lawn at Uplands and get theatre tickets for him to see plays on his trips into London.[75]

As Mee got older, his dismissal of popular theatre as trivial mellowed and outings to see plays became more common. In September 1911 he went with family members to the Haymarket Theatre to see Graham Moffat's Scottish comedy *Bunty Pulls the Strings*.[76] The play was a moral, witty and sentimental exploration of human character and an enormous success.[77] Romanticism was what Mee sought from plays and James Barrie's *Dear Brutus*, a midsummer fantasy about personal redemption set within the mythical and magical fairyland of an enchanted wood, was a favourite. He also enjoyed Rutland Broughton's *The Immortal Hour*, an operatic fairy tale replete with magic, natural spirits and fairy peoples. But it was Shakespeare that Mee revered above all and he eagerly looked forward to being driven up to Stratford-Upon-Avon with family and friends to see a play.[78]

Until forced to stop by family, exhaustion or illness, work dominated Mee's waking hours. He was inordinately busy, not just co-ordinating and editing his publications and writing articles and books but also giving talks to schools and other organisations. When asked by the Hastings and St Leonards branch of the Junior League of Nations Union to plant a tree of peace at a ceremony, Mee is said to have replied in a letter, "Alas and alack, I am killing myself much too fast, and have hardly time to eat or sleep in the two or three lives I am trying to live, so must say 'No' with much regret."[79] In a 1981 interview Marjorie Mee said of her father,

> He could write in a room full of people, all talking, and then turn and join in as though he had been listening to every word. Even on journeys, he would correct proofs. He never really stopped working.[80]

Happy to see others enjoying themselves, he looked on as an amused spectator when his family became caught up in the craze of roller-skating, or "rinking", that swept the nation. The roller-skating boom of 1908-1912 saw over 500 skating rinks opened across the country; some were purpose-built while others took over existing buildings. Most were open from 10am until 11pm; patrons skated on wooden floors while an orchestra played.

Urged on by an excited nine-year-old Marjorie Mee, who had first "rinked" on a family visit to Nottingham, in April 1910 Amy Mee, Lena Fratson, Ernest Bryant and Margaret Lillie, Mee's office secretary who lived in Hextable, visited rinks in Orpington, Dartford and Gravesend. Mee was entertained by the whole idea and wrote to Derry parodying the pastime with his teetotalism, calling it "drinking" with a line through the "d". He described with feigned outrage how Uplands had been taken over by rinking as his family whirled round and round arm-in-arm "under the unbalancing influence of this sinister thing. And every one of them at Christmas was a teetotaller, not touching sherry even in plum puddings!"[81]

Alfred Harmsworth insisted that his senior staff took regular breaks from work, preferably out of the country. At a time when only the affluent could hope to afford them, holidays became an important part of Mee's life. His first trip out of England was in January 1906 when, together with his sister Lois and Cyril Duncan Cross from Cassell and Company, he visited Egypt, before, on the journey home, stopping in Paris where they were joined by Lena Fratson and Margaret Lillie.[82] He travelled throughout France, Germany, Italy and North Africa. Motoring holidays through England became a favourite, sometimes being driven by Marjorie; they invariably became opportunities to develop new ideas and were frequently interrupted by telegrams, phone calls and letters regarding work.

Mee freely admitted that pressure at work caused him to become over-tired, irritable and bad-tempered. In a letter dated February 1910 he wrote to Derry that unless he got away for a holiday he would end up dead or in a madhouse. It had been a difficult year and he needed a break but

> the back kitchen having to be papered for the spring, there are obstacles in the way says Amy, she can't go til much too late. Now I don't mind dying when my time comes, but I don't like dying to oblige a spring cleaner; therefore what should I do to be saved?[83]

The answer was for Derry to accompany Mee on a tour of Italy. He took a childlike delight in organising the rail holiday, setting out the places he wanted to see, including Pompeii, Florence, Pisa, Rome and Venice, and booking the trip, travelling first class, with Thomas Cook Travel. With a generosity that was typical, he paid all the bills.[84] For years after the holiday, Mee's letters to Derry were written to "Dear Giovanni" and signed "Artur".

In August 1911, Mee urged Derry to take the thirty-seven-year-old Ernest Bryant away on an inexpensive holiday. Bryant had little in the way of money, but he was reluctant to accept financial help and Mee was anxious not to embarrass him. He was worried about Bryant and was convinced that he owed it to himself, his family and his friends to rest if he was to regain his health.[85] Bryant's health worried Mee for the next decade and he took it upon himself to ensure that "Ern" was looked after, including taking a reluctant Bryant on an expenses paid trip to Cannes for a medically advised convalescence.[86]

While he does not seem to have experienced any major illnesses requiring hospital treatment, Mee suffered from periodic asthma attacks that at times threatened to become debilitating.[87] The asthma appears to have been checked by holidays in the sun and warmth of Italy and the south of France, but on several occasions he can be found writing from his sick bed, to which he was confined with colds, flu and chest infections, and the return of the asthma was always a concern.[88]

Eynsford Hill

Having spent ten years at Uplands, the Mees were on the move again in 1913. Seeking to escape further from the ever encroaching suburbs of London, they moved four miles south to the village of Eynsford. Considered one of the most historic and picturesque villages in Kent, Eynsford had grown up around a ford crossing the River Darent. Its attractions included a Roman

Figure 7.
*Eynsford Hill House in 1913, shortly after building was finished. This view is
the back of the house overlooking part of the extensively lawned gardens.*

villa of national significance at Lullingstone, the mediaeval Anglican
Church of St Martin and an eleventh-century Norman castle. The village
had a strong nonconformist tradition; the first Baptist church was built in
1806 and a sizeable new church constructed in 1906.

Nearing middle age, Mee wanted something about his new home
that symbolised his romanticised and emotional attachment to England,
something that would be a unique expression of his personality. On the
northern edge of the village, on a hill adjacent to a wood with views over
the Darent Valley and the Kent countryside, Mee bought a plot of land,
and, while continuing to live at Uplands, had his new home built. Named
Eynsford Hill, the house was designed by the enormously popular architect
Percy Morley Horder, who made a name for himself designing country
houses employing local traditions and materials. He had designed homes in
Surrey and Sussex, including one for David Lloyd George and another for
Harold Begbie.

By this time Mee was a wealthy man, writing mischievously to Derry,
"Am I to have golden gates or silver ones?"[89] He could afford to ensure
that the home that he, Amy, Marjorie and Lena Fratson would share until
his death was the epitome of comfort and aesthetic elegance. No expense
was spared on the construction of the seven-bedroom home or on the
lavish landscaping of its expansive gardens and woodland. Mee took a close
personal interest in every aspect of the design and construction of his home;
during the building he wrote to Derry of it being "my second wife".[90]

Figure 8.
*The front of Eynsford Hill House, which remained Arthur
Mee's home until his death in 1943*

The house was built in a vernacular revival style and included gables,
stone dressing, mullioned leaded casement bay windows, mouldings and
inglenooks, parquet flooring, mosaic tiles and oak panelling. Mee ensured
that the house had all the modern conveniences, including electric light
and central heating radiators. Inside he surrounded himself with objets
d'art and historical artifacts including ancient bronze and terracotta
statuettes, porcelain and Roman glassware. Buying objects to decorate his
home was for Mee far preferable to spending it on something as transitory
as theatre tickets.

The library contained oak bookshelves and cabinets to house the
thousands of books in his collection. There was an oak fireplace with
marble surround, a carved wooden settle and stained glass panels in the
windows. One window had Marjorie Mee's initials, M.E.M., carved into it.
The formal gardens contained terraced lawns, a flagged rose terrace, a rose-
covered pergola, a summer house, a lily pond and an avenue of yew trees
bordered in spring by foxgloves. Roman, Egyptian and mediaeval artefacts
were built into walls, seats and paths and a weather vane was erected, on top
of which was a copper reconstruction of Sir Francis Drake's Golden Hind.
Mee and Marjorie laid the foundation stone of the house and hid within it
an illustrated message, "to the Future", near the front door.[91]

Mee enjoyed an extensive circle of friends and acquaintances, which,
in addition to journalists and editors, included politicians, artists, poets,

religious figures and authors. Amongst his acquaintances was said to be George Bernard Shaw. Like Mee, Shaw was a teetotaller, but he was also a Fabian and socialist; Mee was neither, but both were committed to working-class social reform, although employing quite different strategies.

The Eynsford Hill characters in Shaw's *Pygmalion* are said to have been named after Mee's house. The connection remains a tantalising enigma too possible to dismiss, but with nothing in the way of attributable evidence to support the idea. Shaw completed work on *Pygmalion* in June 1912, a year before the Mees moved into Eynsford Hill in August 1913. Mee had bought the land in 1912. *Pygmalion*'s themes of social class, feminism and socialism were hardly Mee's concerns and he appears not to have had much time for Shaw, declining an invitation to attend a lunch with him.[92] His preference was to work and he wrote to Derry, "not all the Bernard Shaw piffle ever spoken or written is worth an hour from my Villaging".[93] Perhaps Mee met Shaw socially, perhaps in conversation he mentioned having a house built at Eynsford Hill and perhaps Shaw somewhat comically decided to use the name for the family in *Pygmalion* – it would have been typical of him.

*

Deciding to work for Alfred Harmsworth provided Mee with an environment within which his energies and commitments found a ready home. It was not without its stresses and strains; nobody working for Harmsworth could think of themselves as being completely secure. Mee knew this, and he acknowledged that he needed Harmsworth more than Harmsworth needed him. He worked within a results-driven industry in which great rewards followed great successes and failure was best avoided. His early successes with Harmsworth helped to furnish him with a measure of security and the prospect of an open road to success, provided he continued to perform well.

At this point in his career he was developing for himself a reputation as a hard-working, talented writer and editor, taking full advantage of Harmsworth's ambitions to dominate the marketplace. He was at the heart of publishing enterprises that were proving enormously popular and profitable, and he was reaping the profits of that work. Well-liked and well-respected, Mee was shrewd and worked hard at positioning himself in ways that enabled him to benefit from his efforts. As his standing grew he began to see himself constructed as a brand, further cementing his reputation and his professional and personal security. But it was to be a brand that was to take him in an unexpected direction.

3.

Manufacturing a Brand

The Idea of Childhood

Living in England during the first decade of the twentieth century was an exhilarating and unsettling experience for many, whose lives wavered between pessimism and doubt, hope and excitement. Edwardian England was stimulated by a myriad of fresh opinions, ideas, novelties, aspirations and innovations.[1] The economist and anti-imperialist John Hobson described a world in which people were "possessed by the duty and the desire to put the very questions which their parents felt shocking, and to insist upon plain intelligible answers. What is more, they want all those questions answered at once."[2]

The quickening pace and scope of change thrilled some while others looked on with despair at what was perceived as the abandonment of the unshakeable faiths of Victorian England. The Liberal politician and journalist Charles Masterman, writing of a confused and unsure society, claimed, "Expectancy and surprise are the notes of the age."[3] There seemed to be no answer to the question of whether the nation was set to enter a period of conflict and turmoil or of progress and prosperity, or to simply stagnate. It was as if, in the words of Lucy in E.M. Forster's *A Room with a View* (1908), society was in a "muddle" between the Victorian, the Edwardian and beyond.

The idea of childhood was not immune to Edwardian conversations about the changing nature of society. Embracing the new saw the emergence of childhood as a focus of debate and speculation. It came to be seen as a social construction rather than as a settled or undisputed feature of human society. Children were increasingly thought of as active rather than passive learners and educators promoted the idea that learning should be based upon how children grew intellectually, socially and emotionally. No longer were children without a childhood; instead they were individuals with particular needs, interests and ways of thinking. Although the education system remained inherently conservative, as Edwardians became infatuated with childhood, supporters of more progressive forms of teaching and learning shaped a new vocabulary through which to discuss children and the purposes of schooling.

The Board of Education's advice to teachers in 1905 was to encourage active education as a way of helping children to take greater responsibility for their learning.[4] The National Union of Teachers rejected rote learning, recommending that teachers provide opportunities for children to adopt independent approaches to their studies.[5] In their training, student teachers became familiar with books promoting child-centred approaches to teaching and learning, such as John Dewey's *The Child and the Curriculum* (1902), Edwin Kirkpatrick's *Fundamentals of Child Study* (1903) and Margaret McMillan's *Education through the Imagination* (1904).[6] Infant teachers were examined in child development and the principles of practical learning sponsored by Friedrich Froebel.

Children's literature, read as much by adults as by children, emphasised a liberated world where there was freedom to play, to dream and to explore the imagination. Edwardian children could read Rudyard Kipling's *Just So Stories* (1902) and *Puck of Pook's Hill* (1906); E. Nesbit's *Five Children and It* (1902) and *The Railway Children* (1906); Beatrix Potter's *The Tale of Peter Rabbit* (1902); Kenneth Grahame's *Wind in the Willows* (1908) and Frances Hodgson Burnett's *The Secret Garden* (1910). J.M. Barrie's *Peter Pan* exemplified Edwardian views of childhood.[7] Peter Pan, the perpetual child who refuses to grow up, tells Wendy, "I don't want ever to be a man. . . . I want always to be a little boy and to have fun. So I ran away to Kensington Gardens and lived a long, long time among the fairies."[8]

The arrival of childhood within the public consciousness presented opportunities well understood by Mee. With *The Harmsworth Self-Educator* having found a profitable audience, he turned to the idea of producing a children's magazine that would feed similar aspirations among parents. The logic was simple; if between 1905 and 1907, adults in their hundreds of thousands had purchased a fortnightly magazine aimed at education and self-improvement, would not those same adults, as parents, buy a similar magazine with equivalent aims for their children?

Context and Competition

When Mee turned his attention to writing for children he entered a ferocious market crowded with magazines and story papers, all seeking to meet the demands of a voracious and vacillating readership.[9] Early examples were based largely upon the teaching of biblical morality. *The Children's Friend* (1824-1882) appeared monthly and included poems, prayers and religious stories. In later decades secular material was added in the form of adventure fiction and articles on science, natural history, sport and hobbies and crafts, as well as competitions and puzzles. More secular titles included *The Boy's Journal* (1863-1870), Samuel Beeton's *Boy's Own Magazine* (1855-1874) and W.H.G. Kingston's short-lived monthly *Kingston's Magazine for Boys* (1860-1863). In 1866 the Reverend J. Erskine Clarke launched *Chatterbox*, a magazine designed to counter what he considered to be the immorality of juvenile literature. Alexander Strahan's monthly *Good Words for the Young* (1868-1877) was popular but its 6d price tag put it beyond the reach of many working-class families.

The most successful publisher of religious books and magazines was The Religious Tract Society (RTS), established in 1799. The evangelical mission of the RTS was to convert the industrial working classes to Christianity through the publication of low cost, high volume books. The RTS distributed tracts, religious books, penny histories and Sunday magazines and supported missionary and educational projects nationally and internationally. By the 1850s the RTS was publishing *The Leisure Hour* (1852-1908) and *The Sunday at Home: a family magazine for Sabbath reading* (1853-1940); both were weekly periodicals providing patriotic, morally inspiring and entertaining reading. The magazine's "page for the young" included short stories and moral homilies with titles such as "The Duty of a Child's Obedience", "Child's Love of the Sabbath and its Services", "Lessons From Flowers" and "The Spider and Its Prey".[10]

In 1824 George Stokes made the RTS's first serious attempt to produce books for children with a series of 51 *Short Stories for Children under Ten Years of Age*. It sold more than 5 million copies by Stokes' death in 1847. This was followed by the monthly *The Child's Companion* with its mixture of religious homilies and poetry, morally inspiring stories and warnings to children about avoiding "wickedness and sin".[11] Included were essays on natural history, geography and, on one occasion, an invitation to engage in "Spiritual Arithmetic".[12] By 1850 the society had published over 4 million copies of over 300 picture books and serials for children.[13]

But many young readers were far more interested in an entirely different genre of fiction as an alternative to the narratives of religiously grounded magazines; "penny dreadfuls" provided juvenile readers with a heady mixture of melodramatic and sensationalised fiction. Described as "the most alluring and low-priced form of escapist reading available to ordinary youth",[14] they were, according to G.K. Chesterton, at "the centre of a million flaming imaginations".[15] Sold by newsagents, stationers, tobacconists, toy shops, and street vendors or lent out by circulating libraries, they offered readers an escape from the often dull monotony and uniformity of everyday life. The content of the most sensational dreadfuls featured pirates, highwaymen, thieves and criminal gangs, macabre, supernatural tales and gothic horrors in which characters smoke, drank and kissed girls.

Many penny dreadfuls were published by the Newsagents' Publishing Company (NPC), managed by Edwin J. Brett. Brett made a substantial fortune from them and in 1866 turned his attention to publishing a new paper, *Boys of England*. He promised readers that it would "enthral you with wild and wonderful but healthy fiction".[16] Its pages contained serialised fiction about the escapades of rebellious and wayward public schoolboys and the adventures of heroes such as Jack Harkaway, which proved extremely popular. Non-fiction included contributions on science, nature, sports, hobbies, biography and history. Readers were attracted by competitions and free gifts. During the 1870s the magazine had a weekly readership of approximately 250,000 anxious to consume vigorous and adventurous fiction liberated from religious sermonising.[17]

The popularity of penny dreadfuls created enormous anxiety among moral entrepreneurs within the ranks of clergymen, teachers, magistrates and social commentators. They were seen as an attack upon the minds of the impressionable, particularly because authority figures such as the police and teachers were mocked or depicted as tyrannical bullies in their pages. The RTS claimed that they were "eminently fitted to train up a race of reckless, dare-devil, lying, cruel and generally contemptible characters".[18]

Although it is doubtful that penny dreadfuls caused anywhere near the moral and social damage their critics claimed, this was not what the Victorian elite and middle classes wanted transmitted to the young through their choice of reading material.[19] The children's writer Harriet Martineau warned against them reading papers and magazines containing the "Lives of bad people. . . . [T]rials of celebrated malefactors, love, crime, madness, suicide, wherever they be got in print, are powerful in preparing the young for convict life."[20] *The Morning Post* attacked penny dreadfuls and their "representations of every possible horror. The last crime, the last terrible accident, the last destruction of life, are portrayed with ghastly glee."[21]

By the late 1870s the impact of the worst of the dreadfuls with their frivolous and utterly implausible tales was being challenged by the RTS, who decided to publish an alternative that would be "sound and healthy in tone".[22] The result was the *Boy's Own Paper* (*BOP*), conceived of as a moral antidote to what was considered pernicious and melodramatic fiction judged hazardous to children's moral development. The dilemma the RTS faced was how it could supplant the attractions of the penny dreadful if it did not include content readers found appealing.

The editor G.A. Hutchinson found the answer by imitating the format of penny dreadfuls but replacing their bloodthirsty and criminal sensationalism with lively and "healthy" adventure stories.[23] While overtly religious messages were absent, the aim was to improve the moral tone of the next generation through example and the provision of role models. The *BOP* included secular content, an idea met with resistance from some within the

RTS who wanted the paper to be entirely evangelical in tone. But they had little choice but to include it; the days when a juvenile audience might have read a magazine dominated by evangelical religious proselytising were gone.

The first edition of *The Boy's Own Paper* appeared on 18 January 1879 and was hugely popular. It was bought by schoolboys (and schoolgirls) and juveniles in work, passed from friend to friend, sold second-hand, loaned out and treated with reverence until the next copy appeared. Sunday schools placed bulk orders and gave away copies as prizes for regular attendance. By the 1880s the *BOP*, together with the phenomenally successful *Girl's Own Paper* (*GOP*), first published in 1880, were the most widely read magazines for children and adolescents. By 1887 the *GOP* was reported to have "a circulation equalled by no other English illustrated magazine".[24] In 1899 *Pall Mall Gazette* was claiming that the *BOP* had a "grip on British youth that no competitor has yet been able to loosen".[25]

The quality of the paper's contributors won the approval of parents and teachers. W.H.G. Kingston, Jules Verne, R.M. Ballantyne, G.A. Henty, Arthur Conan Doyle, Gordon Stables and George Manville Fenn all wrote for the *BOP*. W.G. Grace wrote on cricket, John P. Cheyne on arctic exploration, John George Wood on natural history and John Scoffern on general science.[26] The artists and illustrators who contributed were among the most respected, including Stanley L. Wood, known for his drawings of American cowboys and Indians; R. Caton Woodville, a prolific painter of battle scenes, most notably the Zulu Wars and the Boer War; and Alfred Pearse, who contributed for nearly fifty years.

As the magazines were part of the RTS's broader educational programme, self-improvement figured prominently.[27] Content included articles on geography, history, science, natural history, literature, poetry and sport, a letters page, puzzles and competitions. John Hammerton was a fan and remembers preferring the *BOP* to the penny dreadfuls he read because

> in addition to the excitements of such stories as the Prairie Chief, by R.M. Ballantyne, Talbot Baines Reed's A Dog With a Bad Name, Jules Verne's Clipper of the Clouds, David Kerr's IIderim the Afghan, and Lovett-Cameron's Tom Saunders, my awakening curiously about nature, vanished civilizations, inventions, famous personalities had more satisfaction than in The Boy's Standard, The Boys of London, Ching Ching's Own, or any of the other "bloods".[28]

Between 1870 and 1885 the number of children receiving an elementary education trebled and throughout the 1880s and 1890s this rapidly growing audience was served by the appearance of further magazines. *Chums*, published by Cassell and Company between 1892 and 1927 and then by The Amalgamated Press until 1941, rivalled the moral tone of the *BOP*. Writing in *Chums* in 1893, George Manville claimed, "a book for boys should possess plenty of good, stirring adventures, without any preaching. Boys don't like being preached at."[29] In 1900 Mee wrote an article for *Chums* extolling the virtues of Robert Baden-Powell, one of his personal heroes.[30]

Other papers included James Henderson's *Young Folks* (1871-1897), in which serialised editions of R.L. Stevenson's *Treasure Island*, *The Black Arrow* and *Kidnapped* appeared. Cassell and Company published *Little Folks* (1871-1937), written for young children, which included short stories with a moral and ethical core, poetry, articles on science, technology and crafts and a section called "Little Facts for Little Folks".[31] *Young England* (1880-1937), published by the Sunday School Union, was praised for never offending good taste. *The Captain* (1899-1924), published by George Newnes and aimed at an audience drawn largely from public school boys, included school stories by J.P. Wodehouse and John Buchan.

Alfred Harmsworth added to this list. In 1885 he told his friend Max Pemberton, "The Board Schools are turning out hundreds of thousands of boys and girls annually who are anxious to read. . . . They do-not care for the ordinary newspaper. They have no interest in society, but they will read anything which is simple and sufficiently interesting."[32] Whenever one of Harmsworth's juvenile weeklies appeared it promised to crusade against "unwholesome" literature. *The Halfpenny Marvel* (1893), *The Union Jack*, re-published in 1893, *Pluck* (1894) and *The Boys' Friend* (1895) were launched with spirited attacks on penny dreadfuls. *The Boys' Realm* (1902) announced that it would "wage a continued and persistent opposition to that pernicious form of literature, the penny dreadful!"[33] Together with *The Gem* (1907) and *The Magnet* (1908), with its Frank-Richard-inspired stories of Greyfriars School and Billy Bunter, Harmsworth's papers continued the tradition of adventure fiction, non-fiction, jokes, competitions and prizes. The fictional detective Sexton Blake appeared in *The Halfpenny Marvel* and then in *The Union Jack*. Selling approximately 150,000 copies per week, these papers depicted a world of the heroic and civic-minded individual, brave, honest and fearless, where right eventually triumphed and the villain was always defeated.

This was the context within which Mee worked as he set himself towards writing and editing for children. The *BOP* and the *GOP* were widely read and *The Children's Companion* had a market, as did *The Sunday at Home*. *Little Folks*, *Young England* and *The Captain* all had their devotees and the Harmsworth magazines reached a wide audience.[34] But what Mee was thinking of was something quite different; he wanted something original. His view was that if he found the world a fascinating place, thousands of others must do as well. He wanted a magazine that proved to children and parents who would buy it that the world beyond the fictions contained in story papers was worth exploring and that the journey could be an exciting adventure. His aim was to colonise progressive ideas about education by promoting the idea that learning could be stimulating and fun.[35] Mee wanted a non-fiction publication that would break the distinction between an education that took place within the classroom and one that took place within the home. It was to be a magazine that was educational, informative *and* entertaining.

The Children's Encyclopaedia

Mee struggled to think of a title he felt captured the uniqueness for which he was searching. The magazine began life as "The Child's Book", before, having considered alternatives, he and Harmsworth reluctantly settled upon *The Children's Encyclopaedia*.[36] Mee disliked having "children" in the title, thinking it placed a restriction upon the magazine's market, while Harmsworth thought that calling a children's magazine an encyclopaedia was a mistake.[37]

Mee's blueprint for the magazine was similar to that of the *Self-Educator*; it was thematic, with content divided into topics, added to which were chapters on "Things to Make" and "Things to Do". Articles on practical tasks and the learning of new skills were included, as were sections on literature, poetry and art, science and technology, history and geography, social studies and citizenship, flora, fauna and animal life, and ethical and moral ideals. The magazine contained hundreds of colour and black-and-white paintings, drawings, diagrams and photographs. The format meant that each section could stand alone and readers could browse it at will, or, as Mee put it, "Left to wander in this field, the child will find whatever it wants."[38]

The first fortnightly edition appeared on 17 March 1908, priced at 7d. In it Mee used the device of the imaginative and curious child seeking knowledge and suggested that the magazine originated from the questions a seven-year-old Marjorie Mee asked her parents.[39] In a 1982 interview with Eynsford local historian Barbara Lamming, Marjorie told how her father gave her a specially bound set of *The Children's Encyclopaedia* with her name on it as a thank you because it was her questions that had given him the idea.[40]

As with all his publications, Mee was a consummate publicist, and the magazine's educational potential was aggressively marketed. When, as a child, Pamela Travers, later famous for writing *Mary Poppins*, was sent an issue from relatives in England, it included a letter from Mee addressed to "Dear Child" suggesting that they might like to purchase further copies. Travers thought the letter a personal one and when told that as a marketing ploy thousands of such letters had been sent out with the magazine, refused to believe this could be so. She wrote to Mee asking if he might pay her fare from Australia to London; the reply was a disappointment.[41]

The core audience for the magazine was middle-class parents ambitious for their children. Having paid rent and the gas bill, bought food, clothing and coal, and spent money on their own leisure activities, the working-class family was unlikely to have 7d left in their budget to spend on a children's educational magazine.[42] Mee knew his market, telling Harmsworth that they had tapped into a new audience including powerful and influential people.[43] The marketing strategy was manipulative; parents were told that not only would reading the magazine make their child's school life more satisfying, but that teachers would prefer to teach children who read it.[44]

The magazine got off to a hesitant start and it took a while for the public to understand its purpose; it was not, after all, a story paper, but a non-fiction magazine for children. In order to create a credible body of support, advance copies were sent out for review and four days before the first part appeared, *The Daily Mail* published a selection of letters, all of which were unsurprisingly unanimous in their praise. Letters were included from archbishops, politicians, teachers, headteachers, teacher educators, university professors and novelists, on the basis of which it was claimed with much fanfare that no work in the entire history of publishing had received such enthusiastic support.[45]

Newspapers were effusive, considering the magazine "fascinating", "wonderful" and fully deserving of the "chorus of praise" that greeted its publication.[46] *The Norfolk Chronicle* declared it to be original in content, illustration, language and tone and bound to make learning entertaining and enjoyable.[47] *The Review of Reviews* congratulated Mee and Harmsworth, claiming, "no praise is too high to be given to this amiable attempt to introduce encyclopaedic knowledge into the heads of youngsters."[48] *The Illustrated London News* described it as "A work in which the school-book and the story-book finally merge in one".[49] This was exactly what Mee had intended; Harmsworth was delighted and wrote congratulating him.[50]

Relieved and excited at this reception, Mee was convinced that the magazine would generate large profits, telling Harmsworth, "there is money in the future."[51] Unlike many part-publications, the sales of each consecutive issue outdid the previous one, making it necessary to re-print the magazine to cope with phenomenal demand. So extraordinary was the demand that it was being published in volume form before it reached the end of its fortnightly run.

The strategy had always been to sell the magazine to teachers and schools. Mee was anxious that teachers would come to see it as indispensable for their work.[52] To take advantage of this market, Mee turned to John Derry. When he left Nottingham to edit *The Sheffield Independent*, Derry and Mee had lost contact. Mee had not seen him since May 1898, when, on the day of William Gladstone's funeral, as Mee stood on the pavement watching the procession, he saw Derry make his way into Westminster Abbey.[53] In

September 1908, eight weeks after Derry resigned from *The Sheffield Independent*, Mee wrote asking that he and Rose Derry come for lunch at Uplands; he promised that together with Ernest Bryant they would reminisce about their days in Nottingham.[54]

Aside from wanting to renew the friendship, Mee had a job for Derry; he saw him as the ideal collaborator in helping to write, edit and manage *The Children's Encyclopaedia*.[55] Rekindling his friendship with Mee marked the beginning of a new phase in the fifty-two-year-old Derry's life and Mee was more than happy to provide his mentor with a regular income. One of the first tasks that Mee set Derry was to use his experience as a teacher to draft an entry in *The Children's Encyclopaedia* on education and educational systems, suggesting that he be paid thirty shillings per thousand words.[56]

Figure 9.

Marjorie Mee c. 1910. This is a montage of Marjorie placed in front of a copy of The New Children's Encyclopaedia *when it became a monthly magazine*

Mee needed Derry's connections to convince Sheffield policy makers that the magazine ought to be used in schools. His postbag told him it was widely appreciated by teachers and he wanted Derry to find a way of guaranteeing that the city's children read it as part of the curriculum.[57] Mee suggested that the Sheffield Education Committee might give its teachers a subscription to the magazine.[58] Derry did his work and Mee subsequently wrote to say how delighted he was that Thomas Quine, the senior inspector of schools in Sheffield, had sanctioned the magazine as a resource that teachers could choose to use.[59]

Reviews of the magazine sometimes assumed that because his name was on the cover, Mee produced much of the material.[60] There were, of course many writers, but Mee preferred to provide a small group of trusted collaborators with a lot of work rather than giving too many people small tasks to complete. The writing was contracted out to an ensemble of individuals, some with expertise in a particular area such as science, history or the natural world, and others with nothing more to offer than the ability to write and communicate clearly. At the core of Mee's team were John Derry, Ernest Bryant, Harold Begbie and John Hammerton, all of whom made substantial contributions to writing and editing. In addition to having edited the poetry section, Hammerton claims to have written about 400,000 words of original copy for the magazine, as well as assisting Mee as editor.[61]

Derry's role was significant and Mee regularly told him so.[62] He edited contributions – "cleaning it up", as Mee put it – produced book reviews and wrote introductions to new material.[63] In addition he wrote standard letter replies to readers and when Mee was ill or on holiday answered personally on his behalf some of the more contentious letters among the enormous number he received. In editing the *Self-Educator*, Mee had employed Ernest Bryant to write about scientific and technological innovation. Described as an expert on the natural world, Bryant wrote *The Children's Encyclopaedia*'s section on nature and articles on animal life.[64] Harold Begbie wrote articles on evolution, biology and Bible stories. Mee and Begbie were close friends who occasionally holidayed together. Until his death from throat cancer in 1929, Begbie remained a regular contributor to Mee's publications.[65]

Mee's sister Sarah Lois also wrote for the magazine. Lois, as she was always called, was a friend of D.H. Lawrence during their time training as teachers at University College Nottingham, where, unlike Lawrence, she got top marks for reading, poetry, music and teaching. Lois Mee appears in some of Lawrence's early writings, including the short story *The Goose Fair* (1910), published in Ford Maddox Ford's *English Review*, in which she is Lois Saxton, described by Lawrence as "tall and slender, dressed with the severe accuracy which marks the girl of superior culture".[66] The character was "A glorified Lois Mee", as Lawrence described her.[67] Lois wrote some of the "School Lessons" for the magazine.

Writing for Mee required meeting his exacting and uncompromising standards. He took a forensic interest in commenting upon, editing and returning for action thousands of entries. Obdurate and pedantic about personal and professional standards of behaviour, Mee hated inefficiency, disorder and clutter, to which he reacted with irritation. Even if he shared his opinions only with those closest, he disliked pretentiousness and pomposity and did not suffer fools lightly, particularly if they threatened to delay the work. Although, unlike Alfred Harmsworth, he had no reputation as an intimidating bully, he did become impatient and exasperated when contributors did not grasp the focus of a theme or if they wrote poorly and disregarded instructions.[68] Idleness caused by ineptitude was anathema to him and he had no time for what he considered incompetence.[69]

The magazine's reception convinced Mee that failing to build upon its success when its run came to an end in February 1910 would be madness. Protecting the market was a priority and he decided to republish the magazine with original content monthly rather than fortnightly. He was unhappy about publishing monthly, thinking four weeks between issues too long a time to keep an audience motivated. But he was convinced that a monthly magazine would lessen the financial burden for parents, increase sales and offset the disappointment of the *Great Books* series.[70] The task was to make existing readers think they were buying the same magazine while also trying to convince new readers that it was worth buying for the first time.[71]

Mee suggested to Harmsworth that to differentiate the new magazine from the existing one it be called "Arthur Mee's Monthly", on the basis that "children's" kept juvenile readers away and "encyclopaedia" failed to identify the magazine's aims.[72] Harmsworth did not like the idea of keeping "children's" in the title but was even less enthusiastic about naming the new series after its editor and rejected the suggestion, claiming that the company shareholders would never agree.[73] The magazine was re-issued as *The New Children's Encyclopaedia* on 21 February 1910, less than two weeks after the final edition of *The Children's Encyclopaedia* was published. As a result of what was said to be unprecedented demand, it was heralded as "The book that cannot be stopped".[74]

Mee wanted to close the gap between monthly editions of the new magazine by keeping in touch with his audience and on 19 February 1910 began a weekly Saturday column for children in *The Daily Mirror* that lasted until September 1911. As Mee put it to readers, "you and I can meet in this page much more quickly and frequently than we are able to do in the CE itself."[75] The page included a short homily by Mee, vignettes on points of interest, short stories and poems from children, for which they were paid, and readers' letters. Competitions offered prizes including fountain pens, watches, pocket knives and cash. The majority of correspondents were aged between eleven and sixteen; popular topics included "Should Homework Be Abolished?" (the answer was yes), rudeness, manners, thoughtlessness, looking after animals, "Should Children Express an Opinion?", child workers in factories, corporal punishment in schools, teaching health education in school and children living in poverty.

Other strategies to maintain the new encyclopaedia's market included encouraging children to send photographs that Mee could put on the walls of his office; the first edition included photographs of over 1,000 children.[76] Mee created a children's organisation, The League of the Helping Hand. Children could join by filling in an application form in which they had to pledge to be honest, helpful and trustworthy, to fight against cruelty and injustice and to make the world a happier place. Members got a membership card, a badge and a book of rules. If they wanted to keep up to date with the League's work they were encouraged to read the encyclopaedia and to form groups in schools and youth organisations. By September 1911 the League had 14,800 members in the UK, Canada, South Africa and Australia.

Mee's column never missed a chance to promote the educational aims of the new encyclopaedia; on one occasion he wrote,

> It must be true to say that the Children's Encyclopaedia is helping to educate at least a million children, and it is safe to predict that from this vast army of young people the successful men and women of the future will be chosen. The boys and girls who are reading the Children's Encyclopaedia will be the authors and artists and teachers and rulers, the men and women who will build up great businesses, who will make names that their mothers will be proud of in the years to come. . . . From all parts comes this testimony to the wonderful magazine, which is now in the hands of the rising generation, widely used in schools, as well as in the nursery. The August number is ready this week, seven pence, everywhere.[77]

In December 1910 *The New Children's Encyclopaedia* became *The Children's Magazine*, something that, had it happened sooner, Harmsworth thought would have increased sales. In December 1910 monthly circulation stood at 85,000,[78] rising to 100,000 by August 1912. But sales continued to worry Mee and he wrote to Derry,

> The Children's Magazine is very well in its foundations, but the superstructure trembles a little unsatisfactorily. It is really too good for this world. Offer the public a ticket for a music hall, or a pass for Epsom racecourse, or a cheap way of getting a new umbrella, and they will fly like mad. But open for them the gates of the Kingdom of Heaven, and you can count them in ones and twos as they creep in. It is a sad, glad, hopeless, hopeful world.[79]

A further name change was made to make it *My Children's Magazine* before in 1915 it became *My Magazine*, described as "the most loved monthly in the British Empire. No other magazine is read by so many people of all ages."[80] *My Magazine* continued to be published until 1933 when, in a climate of national economic crises, it was discontinued. Mee, who made the decision, was upset; "I have known it a month or two," he wrote to Derry, "but have not told a soul til now, for it is a sad thing to have to do, the death of the child of the *Children's Encyclopaedia*."[81] Four days later he told Derry, "I shall do a big cry at the very end."[82]

Connecting With Childhood

As sales of *The Children's Encyclopaedia* gathered momentum, Mee was constructed as a writer parents could trust, somebody who "had done more than any other man living for the education of English speaking childhood".[83] *The Sunday Times* advised that for scoutmasters or preachers looking for stories of truth and duty, "When in doubt, try Arthur Mee is a wise counsel."[84] Mee's name was manufactured into a brand used to convince the public that it stood for reliability, prudence and good sense. As Mee's reputation grew he became a celebrity and when giving talks to children found himself signing autographs for the young admirers in his enthusiastic audience.[85]

According to reviewers, the secret of Mee's appeal was that he understood what interested children and how to communicate with them.[86] This was not a novel idea; consciously attracting and maintaining a readership through editorials, competitions, prizes and correspondence columns had been a marketing strategy in children's periodicals since the 1860s.[87] In August 1903 the editor of *The Boys' Herald* wrote to his readers of a wish to become their friend: "I want them to feel, in me, your editor as I have styled myself, a real chum, a man who can feel with them in their difficulties."[88] Mee's message to his readers that he had once, like them, been a child and thus knew what it meant to think like a child was another well-established marketing ploy. In 1905, G. Andrew Hutchinson, editor of *Every Boy's Monthly*, wrote to his readers that he understood their needs because "was he not once a boy himself? [A] healthy, hearty, merry British Boy".[89]

Important in Mee's connection with the world of the child was the view that childhood was not simply an experience during which children waited in anticipation for adulthood. In the preface of *The Children's Encyclopaedia*, addressed to "All Who Love Children All Over the World", Mee wrote that the magazine had

> no sympathy with those who would set a child down at a desk almost before it can run. It believes that in its early years a child is its own teacher, and that in a right environment it will teach itself more than all the teachers in all the schools can teach it.[90]

Mee had no time for writing that took ideas and complicated them. He insisted that contributors to the magazine wrote plainly in simple and accessible English, and anything that threatened to bore or confuse readers was sent back to the writer for correction. Derry was unsure about how to write for children and Mee offered some advice:

> The great mistake that people make is in thinking that it is necessary to write down to a child. Nothing could be more fatal. Nothing could prevent a boy from reading anything you write more certainly than the feeling that you regarded him as a little boy who is unable to understand things. Put yourself on a level with him, say us and we instead of you, and use the plainest possible words, and the thing is done. There is no childishness in the CHILDREN'S ENCYCLOPEDIA: we have simply dropped the nonsense of saying that a spade is an agricultural

implement. That is all. Grown-up people read it because its language is plain; children read it because we use the words they hear every day.[91] (original emphasis)

The message was reinforced in the introduction to the magazine in which Mee claimed that it was "written in the words the children know. . . . [I]t is a book that children may read because it is simple, and that men may read because it is plain."[92]

Mee's bond with his childhood audience was a part of a wider attraction to idealisations of innocence and imagination. In writing about the world of imagination in Barrie's *Peter Pan*, Mee said,

> Out of imagination come the tender sentiments that make life gracious, the heroic sentiments that make it noble, the aspirations that give it distant aims, the loyalties that endow it with stability, the wonder that brings humility, the poetry that gives a glow to all creation, the reverence that reaches out to God.[93]

He had an affinity with the experience of childhood and was among those writers, including Lewis Carroll, Kenneth Grahame, James Barrie and Rudyard Kipling, who wrote about the tensions and problems of stepping out of childhood into adulthood. The world of the child provided adults with a retreat from a reality that had seemingly lost touch with the purity embodied within the symbolism of childhood.[94] A retreat into the fantasy world of the innocent child represented an escape into the comfortingly familiar and a way of expressing disquiet with aspects of modern society. Hammerton claims that Mee "was always a child himself in his cast of mind"[95] and that his friends affectionately referred to him as Peter Pan.[96]

Mee enthusiastically joined the romanticised framing of childhood as a time of innocence and wonder. Throughout the pages of *The Children's Encyclopaedia* are line drawings and paintings of infants or young children, reflecting the idea that the younger the child, the more innocent they are. Mee's idealisation of childhood drew upon Wordsworth, for whom the imaginative interaction with nature taught children valuable lessons. The encyclopaedia romanticised this idea with drawings and colour plates of quasi-angelic young children within an Eden-like paradise where they played in an atmosphere of idyllic harmony, happiness and peace among spring flowers in sunlight meadows.

In the final pages of *The Children's Encyclopaedia* Mee returned to the theme of innocence in a double-page spread, "Goodbye to the Book of My Heart". The illustration is an evocative representation of childhood purity; there are birds in the sky, rabbits in the grass, flowers and trees in the wood, fairies, elves and cherubs, winged angels familiar from church frescoes and the work of Raphael. The scene is full of religious and spiritual symbolism and associations with peace, goodness and innocence. Posed in the centre of the illustration are three young children with the sun, symbolic of God, life, heaven and warmth, as a halo lighting them from behind.

Mee's sentimentalised constructions of childhood helped define who he was and as he approached middle age he encouraged readers to "*Keep young. . . . We are as old as we feel, whatever the calendar may say, and the age of our feelings is much more under our control than most of us imagine.*"[97] He was ever conscious of time passing and reluctant to admit that the older he got, the further removed he was from the world of his childhood audience. He wrote to them, "I have thought myself a boy; I have tried to forget that Time goes on and we go on with it; I have pretended that I belong to you and your age, and not to the grown-ups and theirs."[98]

On his fiftieth birthday he gave expression to a melancholy awareness that his childhood was behind him. Writing to Derry two weeks after his birthday party, he said,

> I am fifty. We had a lovely day in my long, green walk, all of us. With Ern and his mother and my Dad and my sister and I took charge of a Tent from which I gave them all Lunch, Tea, and Dinner! It helped to kill the sadness of the day that marks the passing of my youth for me.[99]

On the death of his sister Annie he wrote to Derry, "I find it impossible to believe that Annie took me to school for the first time 50 years ago."[100]

The Children's Newspaper

The enormous success of *The Children's Encyclopaedia* tempered Mee's worries about his career but not his determination to produce something permanent. He wanted a project that would not be dependent upon a two-year cycle of writing before forcing him to turn his attention to a new idea. Harmsworth had his newspapers and would forever be associated with them, and Mee wanted one of his own. In February 1909, on Harmsworth's insistence, Mee spent a week with him in Pau in the French Pyrenees where he had gone for a holiday and to recover from illness.[101] Wilbur Wright was completing his first European demonstration flights and Harmsworth wanted Mee there.

In Pau the pair discussed the idea of a penny weekly paper perhaps to be called *Boys and Girls*. A newspaper magazine called *Boys and Girls* had been included within the "Wonder Box", a companion to *The Children's Encyclopaedia* that was literally a box containing booklets and educational material. The practical difficulties associated with its production were

MOTHER NATURE AND HER LITTLE ONES

MERRY AND CHARMING ARE THE WAYS OF SOME OF NATURE'S SMALL WILD CHILDREN, AND
HERE MISS PEARSE HAS PICTURED MOTHER NATURE WITH A GROUP OF THEM ABOUT HER

Figure 10.
"Mother Nature and Her Little Ones"
from The Children's Encyclopaedia, *Volume 1*

EVERY CHILD'S GOOD THINGS

I, NATURE, give to you, to be yours for ever and ever, the right to the free enjoyment of this world. I give to you the years that are before you, and the world that is about you.

I GIVE to you the Sun by day and the Moon and stars by night, with the power to wake as the Earth rolls into the light of the Sun, and power to sleep when the night comes.

Figure 11.
"Every Child's Good Things"
from The Children's Encyclopaedia, *Volume 1*

insurmountable and it was a failure. But Mee was anxious to hold on to the idea of publishing a weekly newspaper for children and by May 1909 was writing to Harmsworth suggesting that he pursue the idea.[102]

His excitement was palpable and he very much wanted Harmsworth to be as enthusiastic as he was about the project. Mee thought that a children's newspaper would give The Amalgamated Press enormous influence as a medium through which children could be educated to care about nation, Empire and the wider world.[103] Mee ensured that Harmsworth knew that the motive behind the project was as much economic as educational, claiming that if the marketing was right it would become a "gold mine".[104] He wanted it to be something that, like *The Children's Encyclopaedia*, parents would buy for their children and something that could be sold to teachers and local education authorities.[105]

From October 1910 *The New Children's Encyclopaedia* included an experimental supplement, "The Little Paper", which Mee hoped would lead to the publication of a weekly newspaper. Prior to the first edition he sent out a note explaining that its purpose was to develop a sense of citizenship among the young.[106] It was endorsed by Surrey and Staffordshire County Councils, who agreed to provide it for any teacher that asked.[107] Mee pursued his own efforts at getting it into London schools.[108] Negotiations saw the London County Council (LCC) ask him to send quotations for ordering between 25,000 and 30,000 copies.[109] "The Little Paper" continued until June 1919, by which time the first stand-alone edition of the weekly *The Children's Newspaper* had appeared on 22 March 1919, priced at 1½d.

The publication of *The Children's Newspaper* (*CN*) was Mee's response to the trauma of the First World War, which had shattered dreams and ruined millions of lives. Mee was a public moralist who felt that after the war a sense of private and public morality, optimism and duty needed to be re-established within a society faced with fundamental social and economic challenges. Mee knew change was inevitable but wanted it underpinned by moral principles central to his nonconformist conscience, without which he thought the world would fall into a quagmire of vice and corruption. The "CN", as Mee called it, provided him with a medium through which he could express his values and opinions. Described as "from the very beginning a viewspaper as much as a newspaper",[110] its every page had Mee's stamp writ large across it, and, according to Hammerton, it became "his preacher's pulpit, his reformer's platform".[111]

The didactic moralism Mee favoured could already be found within the world of religious publishing. Mee's work was not of that genre, but his writing always contained a robust moral and religious tone. The most widely read religious magazine was *Christian World*. Though it was originally edited by Jonathan Whittemore from 1860, its circulation increased significantly under the leadership of the energetic, innovative and influential James Clarke. During its heyday as a leading nonconformist paper of serious and popular journalism, *Christian World* had a circulation approaching 120,000.[112] Other titles included *The Christian Age* (1871), established by John Lobb; *The Christian Globe* (1874); *The Christian Herald* (1876); *The Christian Commonwealth* (1881) and *The Christian Million* (1885). In 1891 this became *The Independent and Nonconformist*. In 1900 it was acquired by Congregationalists, who published it as the weekly *Examiner*. It then became *The British Congregationalist* until 1915 when it closed. For fourteen years *The Baptist* (1872) was edited by G.A. Hutchinson, who also edited *The Boy's Own Paper* from 1872 to 1912. In 1910 it was acquired by the Baptist Union and amalgamated with *The Baptist Times and Freeman*. Other publications included *The Methodist Recorder* (1861), the voice of the Wesleyan Conference which enjoyed a wide circulation, and the Anglican newspaper *The Church Times* (1863).

Of religious newspapers, the most influential was *The British Weekly: a journal of social and Christian progress*, published by Hodder & Stoughton and edited until his death by William Robertson Nicoll (1851-1923). Nicoll was a gifted journalist and editor who intended that *The British Weekly* would become the principle organ of liberal nonconformist opinion. Each issue contained news, comment and reviews and a front-page religious homily written by Nicoll. At the height of its popularity it claimed a readership of over 100,000.

In 1891 Nicoll launched *The Bookman*, a monthly magazine also published by Hodder & Stoughton. It was a catalogue of current publications, reviews, advertising and illustrations designed to encourage literature with a religious and moral focus to it. *The Bookman* published stories and poems by a wide variety of writers of distinction, such as Nicoll's friend J.M. Barrie. Nicoll became a figure of enormous authority; of his influence it was said,

> Every Thursday, in the British Weekly, Sir W. Robertson Nicoll addresses an audience far more numerous, far more responsive, far more eagerly in earnest, than that controlled by any other living critic. He praises a book – and instantly it is popular. He dismisses one, gently – and it dies.[113]

Mee read *The British Weekly*, as did John Hammerton, although he read it not so much for its religious sermonising as for its literary interest.

Mee saw *The Children's Newspaper* as a voice for peace, reason and progress. He had a tendency to be captured by the spell of his own rhetoric and in a typically florid editorial four weeks after the first edition appeared, he set out its aims:

> The Children's Newspaper will build up such a manhood and such a womanhood in this country as shall make it like the very gate of heaven. We shall love the Flag so much that we shall see that it never

flies over a slum. We shall love law and order so much that we shall see that law has no taint of injustice. We shall love health and strength so much that we shall see that the poor do not sell them for bread. We shall love knowledge so much that ignorance shall not dare to hold up its head.[114]

The Children's Newspaper included topics that appeared in adult newspapers as well as original articles. Its scope was eclectic, including history, geography, science, politics, geology and zoology, as well as serials, competitions, cartoons and photographs. Within the first four issues were stories of a channel tunnel, the wireless telephone, air travel, space flight, the League of Nations and child miners, as well as an editorial critical of conditions in which miners' families lived.[115]

It was marketed as an educational resource, and *The Times* declared that "When the CN came, education came out of its text books and down from its shelves and became a living thing."[116] Teachers enthusiastically endorsed it as a source of teaching ideas.[117] Again Mee's name meant something, with *The Western Daily Press* claiming, "That it is edited by Mr Arthur Mee is a guarantee of the excellence of its tone."[118]

Who bought it? Like that of *The Children's Encyclopaedia*, *The Children's Newspaper*'s readership was largely middle-class. The BBC journalist and author John Simpson was unmoved by it, remembering later that it "exuded a middle-class confidence and security, as though everything was going to continue exactly how it had done for decades: even though you only had to look around to realise that it wasn't".[119]

Readers included the entertainer Harry Seacombe; it was bought for him by his parents and he claims to have been an "avid reader". He also read *True Confessions* and *The Magnet*.[120] The parents of the broadcaster and one-time editor of *The Daily Mail* William Hardcastle bought it for him but he seldom read it, preferring *Rover*, *Wizard* and *The Boy's Magazine*.[121] It was bought for Roy Hattersley but put aside while he read *The Magnet*, which he then swapped for *The Beano* and *The Dandy*.[122] Author and journalist Hunter Davies wanted to like *The Children's Newspaper* because "it seemed to convey high status. People talked about it in such glowing terms, especially adults, but it struck me as dull and grey."[123]

The historian of children's literature Gillian Avery remembers it as an "up-market" publication:

Those of us for whom it was bought in the thirties and forties, were mostly bored by it although we loved the Children's Encyclopedia. We did not bother to read the news, found the marvels of nature tedious and the jokes even more so. Most of us wanted fiction. Parents no doubt bought it hoping that it would deflect their children from comics. Private schools would have taken it for their pupils.[124]

Figure 12.
"Life as it Will Be Some Day"
in The Children's Newspaper, *31 May 1919*

The Marxist historian Eric Hobsbawm, who had it bought for him by relatives, found it "boring and incomprehensible".[125] Bob Bartholomew, who was a sub-editor on the *CN* at one time, admitted, "Kids would never have been seen dead with *The Children's Newspaper* but parents thought it was worthwhile."[126] A 1948 review of children's magazines claimed that it was too serious to be entertaining:

It is the kind of periodical that parents and well-meaning friends think their children ought to read, but do they really read it from cover to cover, or do they only pick out the lighter bits? As a news-sheet of information it is excellent, but the production and layout would need to be more attractive to make it a favourite.[127]

Nevertheless, it proved a huge success and at its peak during the 1920s and 1930s sold 500,000 copies a week across the Empire.

As well as editing *The Children's Encyclopaedia* and *The Children's Newspaper*, Mee also edited a range of other part-works, including *Harmsworth Natural History* (1910-1911), *Harmsworth Popular Science* (1911-1913), *The Children's Treasure House* (1921), *The Children's Pictorial* (1924), *Lands & Peoples* (1926) and *I See All: A Pictorial Encyclopaedia* (1928-1930), none of which captured his enthusiasm.[128] *Harmsworth Natural History* was not Mee's idea; because it was intended as a specialist magazine for those with an interest in natural science, he was unsure how well it would sell. As natural science was a school subject, the marketing strategy was to advertise it to parents and teachers.[129] *Harmsworth Popular Science* was Mee's idea and from the outset he was determined that it should have a strong educational focus. While he wanted it to be a serious magazine, it had to be entertaining in emphasising what he thought was the excitement and wonder of scientific and technological discovery.

From the outset Mee disliked the *Children's Pictorial* project. It was not his idea and he wanted nothing to do with it. On 2 January 1924 he wrote to Derry about the circumstances the magazine found itself in:

> The situation is not made easier by the fact that my misgivings about the C.P. were right. It is not a failure – yet; it may be a success eventually; but it is not very promising, except that it has not taken <u>one reader</u> from the C.N. I am worried by it, the more so because I have allowed my name to be associated with a paper which is not my own conception.[130]

In November 1924 Mee voiced a private frustration at having his name associated with a publication he considered neither one thing nor another. He was convinced that it had no place in the market and that he ought not to have agreed to be associated with it. But to have rejected the idea would have subjected him to the accusation that he was not prepared to support the company.[131] He was not prepared to voice such views in public, writing to Derry, "<u>Who wants it?</u> I don't know. I have no interest in it (though God forbid it should be said aloud)."[132]

*

The phenomenal success of virtually all that Mee wrote and edited was a consequence of his imagination, determination and ambition, coupled with the sophisticated branding of him as a product. Mee and Harmsworth were skilled publicists who knew their audience; their magazines were marketed as being indispensable to anybody who cared about education and improving themselves. Implicit in much of the advertising copy that Mee wrote was the suggestion that if parents failed to buy *The Children's Encyclopaedia* or *The Children's Newspaper* they were complicit in letting down their children. They were being disadvantaged by being left unsupported to cope and compete in a complex and demanding world minus the knowledge and competencies they needed to succeed. What was more, why wouldn't parents purchase them? After all, they were exciting, colourful and educational and made learning enjoyable.

Mee knew how to connect to the world of his readers on an emotional level and how to create the perception that he and they enjoyed a friendship. His brand worked because he manufactured a deep empathy with readers and was constructed, not unfairly, as a sympathetic personality who cared about knowledge and learning. This deliberately linked key ethical, moral and cultural ideas with Mee. He was symbolic of what Robert Bellah has called a "representative character", an individual allocated a public image "that helps define, for a given group of people, just what kinds of personality traits it is good and legitimate to develop".[133] He was considered serious but down-to-earth, crusading and enthusiastic, responsible and trustworthy.

Mee's writing was a source of comfort in its references to a valued past coupled with eager anticipation for an exciting future. Readers could become enthralled by technological and scientific innovation and learn about the natural and human world in an engaging fashion. This was achieved within a framework of values that emphasised enduring stability and continuity with the traditions of God, England and Empire, that trinity of ideas which for many of his middle-class readers defined the nation and Englishness.

4.

God, Faith and Evolution

The Meaning of Life

By the beginning of the twentieth century, many of those living within industrialised towns and cities had disconnected themselves from the teachings of the church that had once forged such a resilient connection between lifestyle and faith.[1] While they remained inexactly and vaguely committed to belief in a Christian God, many became indifferent and antagonistic towards organised religion.[2] The intellectual and social challenges of the day caused a re-evaluation of commitments to theological principles. Long working hours, the emergence of a class consciousness that drew people to the Labour Party, organised sport, the music hall and modern literature all challenged the communal solidarity of religion.[3] While the rituals of the church remained a reminder of the institutionalised nature of religion, behind this lay powerful inconsistencies. It was apparent that there were contradictions between the culture of self-sacrificing obedience preached by the church and the practical compromises individuals were forced to make in their everyday lives.

This scepticism had absolutely no influence upon Mee, who had no doubts regarding biblical authority – his faith governed and explained everything. In a biography of his friend Thomas Carlyle, the historian James Froude wrote, "The secret of a man's nature lies in his religion, in what he really believes about this world, and his own place in it."[4] This is true of Mee; the faith he inherited from his father and the values Henry Mee vigorously championed formed the indestructible bedrock upon which his eldest son built his life.

Mee's faith provided him with a compelling justification for the way in which he lived. He thought of himself as a vehicle for his God's purposes, and that through God's creations and humankind's ingenuity, the second the product of the first, his role was to ensure that God's will was fulfilled.[5] Living a life based upon a faith embedded within a nonconformist conscience enabled him to connect the social crusades he chose to his interpretation of the scriptures. What Mee thought and wrote, the decisions he made, the positions he took on political and social issues, how he behaved at work and home and how he treated people – all were based upon his conception of doing what he interpreted as his God's work.[6] His very being was based upon the absolute certainty that everything charitable, honest, just, good and right had been placed within the individual mind and soul by God.[7]

Mee understood that as inquisitive beings, humankind would ask questions about who they were, why they were here and what happened when they died. For him the answers rested entirely upon accepting the proposition that his God had a purpose and that, whatever it might be, the future would unfold to a timetable in line with God's aims for humankind. For Mee the whole point of faith was that it could not be questioned or doubted; there was no point in asking why God did what "he" did. Even if God made interventions that seemed beyond reason and understanding, there must always be faith because "Greater even than knowledge is faith".[8]

While faith shaped Mee's life, once he reached adulthood and moved to London he exercised it outside a known commitment to any particular religious community. There is nothing to suggest that he regularly attended a local church or chapel, although he believed that prayer and worship were important for keeping faith alive and when travelling he visited churches and attended services.[9] Mee saw faith as a matter of individual conscience and a nonconformist rejection of bureaucracy and officialdom saw him opposed to the rituals and authoritarian control fostered by the church. He had no difficulty in separating faith from the church as an organisation. In a letter to Derry regarding what they might include in the *Great Books* series, he wrote,

> I think we shall have to leave the Church out. That, of course, does not mean leaving out religion, because religion certainly animated many and probably most of these twelve men. This point did occur to me, and I thought it over and decided that, while religion has contributed to the greatness of these men, the Church itself has not produced a man worthy to stand among them.[10]

Mee judged religion as a spirit best seen outside the church.[11] In *Arthur Mee's Letters to Boys* (1913), a series of essays on living a healthy and moral life, he told his audience not to make the mistake of thinking that religion was

> something to do with a particular Church, or a particular form of worship, or a special form of words in which we must believe. There is no particular Church or creed to which we must bow down.[12]

For Mee faith was political and practical; it was meant to inspire, not discourage; to provide hope, not anxiety; and to bring "honour and beauty and courage and justice" into people's lives.[13]

Like many nonconformists, Mee was scornful of the Roman Catholic Church, feeling that it exercised a tyrannical control by refusing to allow freedom of conscience in how its canons were followed. Mee wrote to Derry, "As a rule the opinions of Roman Catholics are not worth anything, because it is the curse of Romanism that it vitiates a man's judgment and unfits him for independent reasoning."[14] In March 1925 Percy L. Parker, a Wesleyan scholar, editor and owner of the magazine *Public Opinion*, died.[15] Parker was a colleague and collaborator and Mee, who had known him for twenty years, was upset by his death. But what distressed him more than "P.L.P." dying was that on his deathbed he converted to Roman Catholicism. Mee's anger and frustration was tangible; the idea that a devout nonconformist had on the eve of his death become a Roman Catholic at the dogged insistence of his wife, a convert to Roman Catholicism, was a "lie" and a "fraud". So real was Mee's anger that he refused to go the funeral service or to write Mrs Parker a letter of sympathy.[16]

Darwinism, Evolution and Faith

Edwardian England was a society of conflicting ideas and a kaleidoscope of opinion. Efforts to manufacture a coherent system of values and beliefs became problematic in the face of tensions between science and religion, reason and romanticism, morality and public fashion, society and the individual. Mee travelled through these days intrigued, fascinated and excited by much of what he witnessed and entirely secure in his values, what he knew, what he believed and what he prized.

So confident was Mee in his faith that he had no difficulty in integrating within it a commitment to Darwin's work on biological evolution. Although evolution was a process Mee considered incomplete and not fully understood, he believed in Darwinian explanations for the origins of humankind.[17] He accepted as obvious that evolution was predicated on the view that organisms adapted themselves to environments and to the changing nature of those environments. In linking scientific discoveries to the Bible, Mee was comfortable making his faith in science religious and his faith in religion scientific. He did so by claiming that biological evolution was a device purposefully created and employed by God to fashion and explain the universe.[18]

For Mee, the more humankind came to understand the world of science, the more obvious it became that it was his God's work. Natural selection may have been a scientifically proven fact but it was not a matter of chance.[19] Every lifeform was God's creation, made with precision and meaning, and it made no sense to see the world in any other way. He wrote, "The science that forbids you to believe your pen-knife came by chance to your pocket forbids you to believe that Earth came by chance the home of life."[20]

When Mee wrote about faith and evolution, he used ideas and justifications gleaned from William Paley's *Natural Theology* (1802) to suggest that each scientific discovery was proof of a divine creator and evidence of design in the natural world.[21] Paley is best known for his metaphorical use of the watch-maker as explanation for the claim that such is the complexity of the natural world that it had to be the work of a designer. Paley's well-trodden argument is that a watch is designed, therefore it must have had a designer. The fact that we do not know how it was designed or by who does not mean the absence of a designer. The fact that we may not understand how parts of a watch work does not mean there was no designer, and what is true of a watch is true of the natural world. Just as the complexity of a watch implies a watch-maker, so the complexity of the universe implies the existence of a creator.

This seemed a reasoned, logical and intelligent argument to Mee, who, in his writing, used the watch metaphor, as well as paraphrasing other aspects of Paley's explanations of how life originated.[22] Mee thought evolution extraordinary and complex; so elegantly did it integrate countless forms of life that "There is not one chance in a myriad millions that it could have happened without a controlling mind".[23] There was nothing within his faith that allowed him to consider any alternative explanation. How was it possible to conceive of the intricacy of the universe unless you believed in a God? Mee suggested that if "men should say to us that it is impossible to conceive a Creator behind the world, let us ask them by what possibility they conceive the world *without* a mind behind it!"[24]

In enthusiastically endorsing a belief in intelligent design, Mee recruited the writings of iconic figures of nineteenth-century science and philosophy. He claimed that Charles Darwin, Herbert Spencer and John Tyndall believed in the controlling mind thesis and that no serious scientist would argue otherwise.[25] Thomas Huxley can be added to the list, along with Spencer and Tyndall; Mee and Hammerton discussed his thinking.

Darwin, Huxley, Spencer and Tyndall had far more sophisticated views than Mee suggests; all were agnostic to different degrees and, as scientists, struggled to come to terms with the idea of religious faith. Mee claimed that Darwin refused to see evolution as blind chance, preferring to view it as "the result of a creator's work".[26] Yet Darwin's views on faith were ambiguous and the scientist within him never successfully reconciled evolutionary biology with his fluctuating religious views.

Thomas Huxley was more agnostic than Charles Darwin – he invented the concept; writing to Charles Albert Watts in 1883 Huxley claimed ownership of the term from the 1860s. In a critique of dogmas held by theists and atheists he described agnosticism as a position held by those who were entirely ignorant about issues that theologians and their opponents professed to know about and understand with assurance. For Huxley it was impossible to declare unequivocal support for a set of beliefs not substantiated by scientific evidence.[27] Within a framework bounded by logic, reason and evidence, faith in the existence of a God was beyond analysis. Huxley concluded that neither he, nor anybody else, was able to answer any questions about it. In a series of articles in *The Nineteenth Century*, Huxley made the important point that agnosticism was not a dogma or a faith but offered an approach to critically exploring the condition of humanity and its values, beliefs and ideas.[28]

Hebert Spencer was a resolute agnostic and, unlike others who may have found themselves turning away from a belief in God, made no such journey, for there was never any God in his consciousness. While young he distanced himself from what he called "the creed of Christendom", finding the doctrines of religious observance and claims for the existence of God not credible.[29] Never having known God intellectually or emotionally, Spencer found it problematic to make any intelligent statement about the existence or non-existence of a God. In a letter to his father he wrote, "My position is simply that I know nothing about it, and never can know anything about it, and must be content in my ignorance."[30]

Mee claims that John Tyndall saw in evolution a clear sense of purpose and direction, all under the guiding control of a benevolent God who fashioned the Earth, prepared it and then created humankind to inhabit it.[31] But as with Huxley and Spencer, the scientist within Tyndall rejected notions of blind faith.[32] He did not believe it possible, outside faith, to claim to know about the origins of life or the existence of a controlling force because evolution was an unfathomable mystery.[33] Having at best exaggerated the views of these thinkers, Mee continued to claim that while there were many things about evolution that were unknown, one thing beyond doubt was that it was the work of an intelligent mind.[34]

Mee's faith would not allow him to contemplate that life ended with the arrival of death. It was inconceivable that with everything that humankind had achieved it was simply "marching through the centuries to a grave of dust and ashes".[35] Arguing that humankind was incapable of understanding the purpose of his God's creations, Mee believed that a lack of scientific proof that life continued after death was no reason for rejecting the idea.[36] He had no doubts, and, in a series of statements outlining his personal philosophy, wrote, "I believe that I shall not die; that I shall sleep to wake; that all that is good and pure and noble in me shall live again; that all that has been has been but a building-up."[37]

Mee saw death as a stage in human evolution. It was a transition to something unknown, but it was undoubtedly progress and a move to something better; death was "but the passing through a gate between two worlds".[38] This was a view from which he never departed. In 1934 he returned to the controlling mind thesis in a series of articles for *The*

Children's Newspaper in which he expanded upon the theme that evolution was always progressing and that God was daily intervening in the lives of humankind.[39] Telling readers that they must simply admit that God was omnipotent, he wrote, "It is not for us to expect to be able to understand so great a mystery; we must accept it."[40] In 1942 Spencer, Tyndall and Darwin were again presented as believers in an intelligent creator and Darwin is said to have rejected the notion of evolutionary chance. Mee makes the questionable claim that "He believed in God if any man ever did,"[41] despite the fact that after the death of his favourite daughter, Annie, Darwin decided to have nothing to do with any deity that could take her life.[42]

Mee was an incurable optimist. The alternative was pessimism and doubting that God had a plan for humanity, and that was never a possibility. For him, "Faith wins through; the laughing-stock of all the ages is the pessimist, the weakling, and the coward."[43] His faith and optimism went hand-in-hand and he found it impossible to believe in a benevolent God without being optimistic about the future, writing, "We are not to allow the disappointments of life to blind us to the incalculable glory of it all."[44]

Optimism provided Mee's work with relevance and purpose. His faith meant that even in the worst of times, during war and economic and social crises, he could argue that the world was always improving. In spite of injustice, inequality, misery and disease, it was in a state of constant improvement.[45] In June 1922, during a time of significant social unrest, he urged readers that in a "world of chaos" they should remain confident and optimistic because "Tomorrow the sun may rise on a cloudless world come to its senses".[46] In March 1929, on the edge of a decade that for millions was to be characterised by despair, crises and war, Mee's idealism knew no bounds as he offered readers a faith-based oration of hope:

> We believe that there was never so good a time as now. . . . War is dying out and Hate is dead. Ignorance is ashamed of itself. Disease is losing its power. Ugliness is going. Selfishness sneaks about like the skulk that it is. Drink and Slums and Poverty will vanish in a lifetime. All that we believe.[47]

In 1938, the year the Nazis began opening more concentration camps, the year of Kristallnacht, the year German troops marched into the Sudetenland and occupied Austria and the year Neville Chamberlain returned from Munich to announce "peace for our time", Mee was continuing to write about progress.[48]

Mee had enormous faith in humankind's achievements and the forces of evolutionary progress that for him made everything possible.[49] Writing in 1919, he posed questions about life in 1950:

Will every house be on the telephone? Will railways and motorways run everywhere? Will every cottage have electric light? Will heat and power be carried into every house as water is carried now? Will every house have a garden round it? Will chimneys disappear and smoke be utterly abolished? Will a stream of water run all day and night down every street? Will men read of the plague of flies, and the lives that flies destroyed, and go to a museum to see what a fly was like? Shall we talk from anywhere to anywhere, and shall we see the distant friends we talk to? Will every child have enough to eat, and a warm house to live in, and clothes to wear?[50]

He was right about some things, predicting in 1941 that

You will carry telephones in your pocket. You will see anywhere across the world as easily as across a street. You will have the sense of touch at a distance. You will go where you like in a day. You will fly like a bird. You will switch on power and heat as we switch on light.[51]

Yet, amongst this progress and optimism, why did poverty and destitution remain a feature of millions of lives? Why did inequality remain a powerfully institutionalised feature of society? Why did economic crises, unemployment and the spectre of war continue to scar humanity? For Mee the answer was that with faith, when society had evolved sufficiently, these blights would be defeated. The fact that they continued to persist was the product of the gradual process of a God-driven evolution. Even war Mee unconvincingly argued was a product of the freedom a benevolent God had given humankind to make wrong choices.[52] "God allows a free race of men to inhabit the Earth and do their will," he wrote, including allowing them "to do good and evil too".[53]

A Eugenic Society

Mee's generation was gripped by the perception that not only was their world confronted by internal and external threats, but that the national capacity to meet them was damaged by the mental, physical and moral condition of the population.[54] Prompted by the mediocre state of recruits to the army during the Boer War (1899-1902), a 1904 government inquiry into the condition of the populace concluded that poverty, disease, poor diet and alcohol consumption were major causes of degeneration amongst the urban poor.[55] It became axiomatic for many that the English were experiencing a challenge that only "hard-nosed, coolly implemented scientific measures could repair".[56] Geoffrey Searle writes of how a "mood of hysteria" was created as "journalists and politicians discussed the problem of physical deterioration in language which often bordered on panic".[57] That mood was characterised by a national pre-occupation with "decay", "decline and fall" and "decadence".[58]

Motivated by a fusion of class and racial prejudice, eugenics seemed to offer a solution.[59] Eugenic theorising originated in part from Herbert Spencer's thoughts on how Darwinian evolution might be applied to the way in which societies functioned. Spencer was convinced that the natural evolution of society was inevitable, provided people adapted to their environments. He posed the question that if you could apply Darwinian ideas to the natural world, why not to the human world? Through a struggle between competing groups and individuals, why could the evolution of human society not be allowed to proceed without interference?[60] Some of Spencer's writing echoes thoughts that were to become important in eugenic theorising. These included the claim that it was right to encourage childbirth among the most able members of society; not to do so would produce "an increasing population of imbeciles and idlers and criminals".[61]

Francis Galton, Charles Darwin's half cousin, combined Darwinian and Spencerian views of biological and social evolution to construct a eugenic theory defined as "the science that deals with all influences that improve the inborn qualities of a race; along with those that develop them to their utmost".[62] So committed was Galton to the pursuit of eugenics that he aspired to see it introduced into the public consciousness as something analogous to a religion.[63] He looked forward to the day when "a Jehad, or holy war against customs and prejudices that impaired the physical and moral qualities of our race" could be announced.[64]

Edwardian eugenic theorising claimed that cognitive and physical abilities were inherited and that disability, mental illness and immorality were individual characteristics; thus the problem of racial degeneration was biological, not socio-economic.[65] A poverty-stricken urban life was said to be responsible for physical and moral erosion as people failed to avoid the temptations of smoking, drinking, gambling, immorality, lethargy and apathy.[66] In the struggle for survival within a harsh world, the more able, fit and superior would win over inferior classes of people. But the difficulty eugenicists faced was that natural selection appeared not to be functioning as they saw poorer elements of urban society reproduce more rapidly than the middle classes, leading to what some thought was racial debasement.[67]

For eugenicists, state action was necessary to improve the physical and mental condition of successive generations. Eugenics, defined by *The Times* as "the science of race building",[68] was not an obscure intellectual exercise in scientific and philosophical theorising located on the fringes of public debate. Although in 1900 few expressed any interest in eugenic theorising, a decade later it had significant support amongst those whose opinions covered a wide social and political spectrum.[69] Often ridiculed by the populist press, who reported it with a mixture of speculation and sensationalism that stretched public credulity, eugenics became important in the search for reforms in public health, social welfare and education.

In 1912 T.P. O'Connor described eugenics as a phenomenon that excited passionate interest from a generation that was "profoundly interested in all the many momentous considerations that are involved in the future of the race".[70] G.K. Chesterton detested eugenic thinking, but in a withering denunciation admitted that the years before 1914 were "a time when this theme was the topic of the hour",[71] adding that in 1913, "Eugenics was turned from a fad to a fashion".[72] Karl Pearson, Marie Stopes, Sidney and Beatrice Webb,[73] Virginia Woolf, H.G. Wells,[74] W.B. Yeats, Bertrand Russell, D.H. Lawrence, George Bernard Shaw[75] and Winston Churchill all endorsed elements of eugenic thinking with varying degrees of sincerity. Former Conservative Prime Minister Arthur Balfour saw developing a scientific approach to social issues through eugenics as a pressing national concern.

Readers of daily newspapers were regularly treated to reports on a range of eugenic issues. Topics included whether people should have a physical examination before marriage; how to select a eugenically appropriate partner; who ought to be allowed to have children; whether sterilisation ought to be introduced for those suffering from mental illness or disability; and whether eugenics should be taught in schools. It was a time when the names of prominent eugenic theorists became as well-known as those of music hall performers.

Mee developed an enthusiastic interest in aspects of eugenics, which he defined as "the love of pure minds and healthy lives".[76] So popular was eugenics that Mee suggested to Alfred Harmsworth that they publish a magazine about it, but the idea came to nothing.[77] Like Galton, Mee believed that health, intelligence and moral character were to some extent genetically determined and that eugenics could speed the progress of human evolution and social reform. He knew some of the movement's most prominent figures, notably Caleb Williams Saleeby and Ronald Campbell Macfie, who were friends and wrote for him.

Early in his career, Saleeby was an enthusiastic Social Darwinist, believing as Herbert Spencer did that the same laws of evolution applied to the natural and human world.[78] He was a founding member of the Eugenics Education Society (1907) and has been described as "one of an elite band of middle-class professionals with sufficient private income to devote their lives to the eugenic cause".[79] Saleeby and Mee appeared on the same platform speaking in support of temperance and eugenic issues.[80] On at least one occasion, Saleeby stood in for Mee at a temperance meeting.[81] It was Saleeby who proposed a distinction between positive and negative eugenics. Positive eugenics, his preferred option, suggested manipulating human heredity to increase the birth rate among the professional classes and skilled artisans. Negative eugenics involved improving the quality of the race by preventing reproduction among the least healthy and capable members of society.[82]

A doctor and poet, Macfie, like Mee, rejected notions of evolutionary chance, and, proclaiming Darwinism a "spiritual disaster", was on the whole persuaded by the intelligent mind thesis.[83] Unmarried, eccentrically independent and leading a lonely, troubled and often poverty-stricken life, Macfie wrote for *Harmsworth Popular Science*, *My Magazine* and, throughout the 1920s, *The Children's Newspaper*.[84] A regular visitor to Eynsford Hill, he dedicated one of his poems, published in the *CN*, to Marjorie Mee's Guides group in Eynsford.[85] Mee was shocked and distressed by Macfie's death on 9 June 1931; describing it as "tragic and terrible", he was appalled that his friend's demise had gone unnoticed.[86]

Saleeby's work on eugenics and public health appeared in several of Mee's publications. He wrote articles for *The Children's Encyclopaedia* on evolution, biology, physics and chemistry in which he claimed that sunlight and fresh air were critical if children were to fulfil their physical and mental potential.[87] Readers were urged to make sure they avoided the fate of Grace Darling, who, it was said, died of consumption because she slept in a small room with the window closed.[88]

Mee ensured that eugenics appeared in *Harmsworth Popular Science* by asking Saleeby to write a section called "Eugenics: Man Creates a Future", in which it was described as the youngest and greatest science of all. Volume 15 of *The World's Greatest Books* (1910) includes a chapter called "Essays in Eugenics", edited by Francis Galton. In the introduction the editors said that they hoped the chapter might "serve in some measure to neutralise the outrageous, gross, and often wilful misrepresentations of eugenics of which many popular writers are guilty".[89] As late as 1920, readers of *The Children's Newspaper* were being told that eugenics was "One of the most hopeful branches of science", being "the science of making better lives".[90]

Mee robustly colonised aspects of Galton's and Saleeby's eugenic thinking. He was at home with Galton's claim that a healthy community was peopled by responsible, hard-working and vigorous individuals who took pride in their work. When that work was over for the day, they sought to improve themselves through education. In a "decadent community", people were lazy and idle and avoided work, relied upon others to support them, sank into drudgery and failed to enjoy life.[91]

For Mee, adaptation to environments and the development of individual character went hand-in-hand towards the construction of a better society. His thinking was shaped by Saleeby, who in turn had been influenced by the French philosopher Henri Bergson, the "Philosopher of Optimism", as *The Children's Newspaper* called him, and his conception of *élan vital*.[92] Bergson's ideas fitted with Mee's on the need to be creative and imaginative and the overwhelming sense he felt that spiritual intuition guided life. Through the struggle to survive and succeed in life, those with energy and character who adapted themselves achieved more than those who, as the world changed, remained passive. Character developed through working industriously at coping with the struggles of life, its hardships and its pains. Character involved maintaining resolve in the face of adversity. Mee did not see how it was possible for individuals or society to develop without struggle.[93] In a letter to Derry he wrote, "The only thing that counts in the world is character, and education matters only so far as it helps to shape character. If it leaves character untouched it is useless."[94]

Within a society in which character was valued as the epitome of the moral individual, Mee was not alone in this opinion.[95] In 1904 the Board of Education claimed that the aim of elementary schooling was to form and strengthen character.[96] In *Character Forming in School* (1907), Florence Ellis, headmistress of Warley Road School in Halifax, wrote, "Every book on education asserts that character building is the chief function of the teacher . . . and every thoughtful teacher endorses the statement."[97] In a 1908 inquiry into moral instruction in schools, Michael Sadler claimed that the most important task of the school was to assist in the formation of character, together with moral and spiritual ideals.[98]

Individual character, physical health, a strong work ethic and social obligation figured prominently in Mee's writing for his young audience. This fitted his commitment to positive eugenics and his Saleeby-inspired belief in the benefits of fresh air, sunshine and staying active as the route to living a healthy life.[99] In the pages of *Arthur Mee's Talks to Boys* and *Arthur Mee's Talks to Girls* he delivered a number of moral homilies on what is involved in living a healthy, moral and active life.

In narratives that might otherwise have been written by Saleeby or Baden-Powell, he argued that staying healthy, energetic, alert and open to new ideas and experiences was fundamental to living a full life.[100] He told male readers that playing a sport for fitness was acceptable but watching others play was a shiftless waste of time.[101] From a position of wealth and security he encouraged them to accept that "It does not matter what a man has, but *what he is*. . . . If we look at other folk in this way we shall see how little our social divisions mean."[102] Readers were told that having or not having power, wealth or status mattered little when set against the influence of a good character.

Mee employed simplistic distinctions to account for individual success or failure. Writing to a female audience, he argued that success in life rested upon distinctions between the hard-working and the lazy, the courageous and the cowardly, the educated and the ignorant, the moral and the immoral, the honest and the dishonest and the good citizen and the bad citizen.[103] An editorial in *The Children's Newspaper*, somewhat incongruously given that some of Mee's writing said exactly the opposite, suggested,

Instead of saying to ourselves We must work hard at school to pass examinations and earn a good salary, we should say we must work and play in such a way as to be real living persons destined for the eternal purposes of God. Money is the last thing we should think of, and Character the first. Money may come to us as the result of Character, but our first duty is to be something worthy, and to regard what we have as of secondary importance.[104]

Becoming "something worthy" required demonstrating courage, stoic endurance and forbearance.[105] In a manner typical of eugenic thinking, Mee wrote, "Nobody drifts into the first eleven. . . . Or, if we want to put the same truth in another way, character is *won* in this life; it is not given away to those who will not fight and work for it."[106]

Temperance and the Evils of Drink

Mee's nonconformist faith saw him utterly opposed to the consumption of alcohol, the culture of the pub and everything it represented. But he was more than just teetotal; he was a temperance militant who never missed an opportunity to preach and moralise on the alleged evils of drink. Eugenic theorising on race and evolution linked neatly with his faith-based battle against what he thought were the destructive impacts of drinking alcohol. Claiming that drinking alcohol was a moral sin had no impact upon a society for whom the pub was a social institution, and Mee campaigned against it on the basis that it was a danger to public health. From a eugenic perspective, drinking alcohol was said to result in hereditary defects and deformities such as epilepsy and insanity, as well as high rates of child mortality.[107]

Once more the hand of Caleb Saleeby can be seen in Mee's writing on temperance. Saleeby was also a temperance militant; he was a member of The National Temperance League and wrote for *The British Journal of Inebriety*. Mee had him write for *The Children's Encyclopaedia*, in which he claimed, "We all know that alcohol is a poison. There is no form of life, animal or vegetable, that it will not destroy."[108] A *Children's Encyclopaedia* section called "Alcohol, the enemy of life" told readers that it was a threat to health, hygiene and bodily growth, injured the nervous system and lead to madness and an early death.[109] Mee mirrored Saleeby's thoughts; in *Letters to Boys* he demands,

You will be too manly to do things merely because other boys do them; and of course you will never touch alcohol, the enemy of every boy who ever lived, and of every good chance he ever had. . . . It will empoison your mind and enfeeble your body.[110]

So combative was Mee that anything that threatened to associate his environment with alcohol was immediately altered. When he moved to Hextable he found that the post office was in an off-licence selling beer and spirits. He purchased a plot of land, built a tea room and a lending library and persuaded the authorities to let it become the new post office. Looking for somebody to run it, he turned to George Byford, who, having left Stapleford, had gone to Canada but had returned in 1892 to work as a school attendance officer for the London County Council (LCC). Mee persuaded Byford to move to Hextable and, while he worked for the LCC, his mother Emma and sisters Jessie and Lucy ran the post office and the tea room. Byford lived there until his death on 11 January 1920, aged sixty-three.

On a visit to Eynsford, John Hammerton commented that the design of a fireplace in Mee's library reminded him of bars he had seen in American homes. Mee's reaction was to have the fireplace redesigned so that no other visitor would ever make the same mistake. Alcohol advertising also came in for his attention. Having moved to Eynsford, he wrote to Derry,

> On your first travel journey to Eynsford I pointed out to you a big brewer's advertisement which spoilt the view from the old bridge and I excited your merry laughter and poo-poohing by promising you it should be down with six months. The six months is up and the board is down.[111]

In June 1916 Mee formed the Strength of Britain movement, a pressure group that lobbied for the prohibition of drinking alcohol in order that it could be used to support the war effort by diverting cereal crops used in making it towards food production. Framed as a patriotic movement, it attracted a membership drawn from the political, intellectual and social elite, and with Mee at its head and Caleb Saleeby as its chairman, it matured into an effective campaigning organisation.[112]

Not everybody shared Mee's enthusiasm and he had an unfriendly exchange of correspondence with William Robertson Nicoll. In many respects the two men were alike; although not friends, they shared similar instincts. Both were liberal nonconformists; both were prolific and highly respected journalists who wrote for Hodder & Stoughton; both were voracious readers with huge libraries; and both were members of the Reform Club and the Whitefriars Club. Like Mee, Nicoll believed that industry and hard work brought its own rewards and he had little time for those he thought idle. Both supported the aims of the temperance movement but in August 1916, when Mee wrote to Nicoll, he cannot have expected the reply he received.

Mee wrote asking if he might add Nicoll's name to the list of influential figures supporting prohibition through the Strength of Britain movement. The contents of that letter are lost, as is Nicoll's reply, but Mee's response to his reply remains. Dated 3 August, the letter is a mixture of puzzlement and disappointment. Mee's efforts to enlist Nicoll's support were met with a rebuttal, including the accusation that he had been offensive, "vulgar" and "brutal" and had questioned sixty-five-year-old Nicoll's ability to meet his professional obligations due to increasing age. Nicoll added the caustic comment that he had been working within the prohibition movement long before Mee came upon the scene. Mee's response was measured but biting; claiming that he had never written an offensive letter, he suggested an element of pettiness in Nicoll's response, writing, "Your note is incomprehensible to me and I should be pained exceedingly if it were just."[113] There is no evidence as to whether this correspondence continued or whether Mee's letter brought it abruptly to a halt.

Nicoll's attitude toward temperance and prohibition was more pragmatic than that held by Mee. He favoured prohibition during the First World War as a necessarily realistic measure rather than as an ideological or religiously inspired absolute. Nicoll's biographer writes that he had "scant tolerance for the fanatics who denounce alcohol as poison".[114] Perhaps he saw Mee, who was in no doubt that alcohol was a poison, as a mere propagandist. On the other hand, John Hammerton had a very good relationship with Nicoll; they were close friends and he admired him, enjoyed his company and considered him to be one of the "greatest of British journalists" with an influence unmatched by any contemporary.[115]

In addition to travelling the length and breadth of the country giving lectures and writing articles and letters, Mee wrote three prohibition polemics: *The Fiddlers: Drink in the Witness Box* (1917), *The Parasite* (1917) and *Defeat or Victory?: The Strength of Britain Book* (1917), to which Saleeby contributed the introduction.[116] In *The Fiddlers*, Mee accuses the government and the army of ignoring the impact that alcohol was having on the ability of troops to carry out their duties. He catalogues accounts of soldiers drunk in the trenches, officers court-martialled for drunkenness and wounded soldiers being given rum and whiskey to aid their recovery, and quotes parliamentary evidence pointing to significant increases in venereal disease among troops caused by visits to prostitutes.[117]

The books had an impact, but not one Mee sought. In Parliament the Liberal MP Joseph King asked the Under-Secretary of State for War whether because sales of *Defeat or Victory* and *The Fiddlers* had damaged army recruitment, there were plans to prosecute Mee; the answer was "No, Sir".[118] In June 1917 Mee wrote to *The Manchester Guardian* indignant that *Defeat or Victory* had been banned by the army from being sent abroad and that in Canada anybody caught with a copy could be fined £1,000 or sent to prison for five years.[119] In 1918 10,000 copies of *The Parasite* were seized by Canadian authorities under the pretext that it provided propaganda to the enemy on how the moral character of troops had been ruined by drink.[120]

In *Who Giveth Us the Victory?* (1917) Mee presents his most powerful eugenically inspired attack on alcohol, justifies and explains his faith, discusses evolutionary science and offers a moral treatise on good and evil. In keeping with mainstream eugenic thinking, he argues that consuming alcohol causes infanticide and destroys moral character. It is "like a river polluted, pouring into the future population a stream of imbeciles, epileptics, criminals, and all manner of social parasites".[121]

The Strength of Britain movement was attacked by a powerful lobby of distillers who took out front-page advertisements in daily newspapers accusing its subscribers of using false statements to obscure its real agenda that, war or no war, the drinking of alcohol ought to be banned.[122] At a meeting of licensed victuallers in Derby, Mee and Saleeby were ridiculed as unpatriotic prohibitionists intent on destroying people's livelihoods. Claims were made that their supporters included conscientious objectors and that their strategies were "unscrupulous and dirty".[123] Mee and his colleagues struck back through advertisements, calling for a national poster campaign, mass marches and demonstrations.[124]

During May 1917 Mee was at the helm of a series of prohibition meetings held across London, culminating in a mass meeting at the Royal Albert Hall on 17 May. Speakers at various venues included the uncompromising prohibitionist Liberal MP Leifchild Leif-Jones; the Rev. S.W. Hughes from Westbourne Park Baptist Chapel; Mee's co-author Dr Stuart Holden; Dr G.B. Wilson, who wrote on the dangers of drinking alcohol; W.D. Bayley, the Canadian author of *Labour and Liquor* (1915); the Wesleyan preacher Rev. E. Aldom French; and Lt-Col Sir Alfred Pearce-Gould, the Baptist Dean of the Faculty of Medicine of the University of London. A packed meeting at the Albert Hall heard speeches by John Clifford, the controversial Bishop of London Arthur Winnington-Ingram, Caleb Saleeby, the music hall entertainer Harry Lauder, who was a fan of *The Children's Newspaper*, as well as members of Parliament, bishops and Mee himself, who attacked a "cowardly government" for their refusal to ban the sale of alcohol.[125]

But by August 1917, Mee and several others had resigned from the Strength of Britain committee, and his departure was acrimonious.[126] He was disillusioned with the management of the movement and wrote to the committee explaining that he could not remain a member while funds collected from the public were, to his great shock, used to pay fees to committee members for the work they did. Mee considered this unacceptable, almost amounting to fraud.[127] R.H. Stephens-Richardson, the honorary treasurer of the movement, hit back, rejecting Mee's allegations as "grotesque".[128] He claimed that Mee was forced to resign because his attendance at meetings was poor and he acted independently of the committee. This saw Mee write to *The Daily Mail* arguing that he had become accustomed to being abused in his support for prohibition but that it was not true that he had been forced to resign.[129]

*

Mee embraced what seems at first sight to be a somewhat eclectic range of ideas and values, some a product of his nonconformist faith and others emerging from wider philosophical and social concerns. His faith came first – all else followed – and it gave him the certainty to argue that the scientific and biological evolution of the natural and human world was integrated, inter-dependent and controlled by his God. Life was part of a longer journey towards eternal life in an unknown but better place. Mee saw this as an entirely reasoned position to occupy and one that a combination of faith and science had proved to be true.

Rooted within Victorian ideals of progress and optimism and influenced by the likes of Caleb Saleeby and Francis Galton, Mee colonised aspects of positive eugenics which he linked with an agenda of social and moral reform. Individual character, abstinence, living a healthy life, rejecting anything that harmed you or your race, avoiding temptation in doing God's work – all were features of Mee's moral framework. His view of the world was that he lived within a society filled with opportunities in which ability and effort counted for more than privilege or status. This attitude is similar to that described by Richard Tawney when he claimed that the principles of a meritocracy invite everybody to come to dinner knowing that circumstances will prevent the majority from ever being able to attend.[130]

There is a powerful ingredient of providential certainty in Mee's views of his world, characterised by a conviction that what he knew was "true" and what he understood was right. From this position he was able to express a joyful enthusiasm for an unknown future. But although the future was unknown, his faith-based optimism in a God-managed world produced a firm confidence that whatever was to befall him and the world, it would always be progress. His faith allowed him no other conclusion.

5.

A Matchless England

Literature and Heroes

Mee's Victorian education and its identification with all things English did its job well. Throughout his life he passionately and dogmatically endorsed an ideology of Englishness and remained an unreconstructed Englishman. He thought of himself as English first, with being British a poor second best. When planning *The King's England*, he was clear that the "motherland" was England pure and simple, writing to Derry with a mixture of mischievous sarcasm and no little impatience:

> Also remember that this is a book of our Motherland, and as you are not a Scot I will whisper ever so softly in your ear that I think of it (without actually saying so) as England. There is too much sinking of England at the bidding of these northern tribes beyond the Tweed, and I think it a capital stroke to call this book Motherland because it enables us to centre it on England, putting Ireland and Scotland and Wales in their places with Fiji and Jersey and Australia. What about that my Giovanni? It pleases me to have a dig at these Johnnies who have worried me for twenty years if ever I dared say England.[1]

England and Englishness were powerful sources of emotional wellbeing for Mee who was convinced that those born English had been privileged by God.[2] So complete was his devotion that he told Derry, "If heaven is half as good as England I shall be satisfied; an everlasting curse rest on all those who injure her."[3]

Mee judged England as unique. There was no nation that could compare with it and no people that came remotely close to emulating the spirit, character and achievements of the English. England was "matchless among the nations, the envy and wonder of the world".[4] He catalogued an eclectic list of what he claimed were the gifts the English had bestowed upon the world; after civilisation, democracy and liberalism he listed the Post Office, the Scouting and Guides movements, the thermos flask, the refrigerator, the "kinema", television, photography and cricket, obviously an English game because of its rejection of "narrowness and pettiness and selfishness".[5]

Mee was convinced that God had a particular affection for the English and that more than anything the Bible had shaped English identity and language.[6] The certainty of his faith enabled him to argue that the Bible was a book that had "wrought itself into the very heart of our race".[7] He saw the Bible providing the English with a perception of unchallenged exclusivity and a conviction that their lives contained a spiritual mystery that was beyond explanation. Mee was convinced that within the English psyche and temperament was an awareness that God had bestowed upon them the role of liberating and civilising the world.

In an age when everybody seemed to be able to quote something from Shakespeare, classic texts, the romantic poets and the Bible, Mee had a particular affection for English literature. He believed it instrumental in shaping how the English saw themselves. It was universally superior to the literature of other nations, more profound, richer and more beautiful, and England had given it to the world.[8] In his personal literary tastes, Mee had no time for anything that was twentieth-century; Wordsworth, Shelley, Milton and Keats were some of his heroes, but at the heart of defining Englishness lay the "majesty of Shakespeare".[9]

Mee judged Shakespeare a towering and emblematic figure whose dramatic and poetic inventions were indispensable for understanding what it meant to be English.[10] He considered Shakespeare's work infinitely finer than "the rubbish that passes for English drama today".[11] He considered that Shakespeare's writing represented artistic genius; so powerful was his love of Shakespearian plays and sonnets that they became a secular faith for him on a par with biblical narratives. Within Shakespeare's work Mee saw the character, values and traditions of what made England, writing, "We come to Shakespeare for the things that make us what we are, for the spirit of England and the English-speaking race; and he does not fail us."[12]

The depth and breadth of Shakespeare's understanding of the lives of young and old, men and women, low and high in society, and rich and poor attracted Mee. He wanted children to know and enjoy the writing and to empathise with the man as well as the author.[13] In commissioning articles about Shakespeare, Mee insisted that his humanity shone through. The story had to be one of a man who had overcome adversity on the way to greatness; he wrote to Derry, "[I]t really is wonderful to think of the beautiful things that have come out of garrets and poverty and bitter struggle."[14]

To his romanticised imagining of England Mee added English heroes, many of whom appeared in the weekly part-publication *Arthur Mee's 1000 Heroes: Immortal Men & Women of Every Age* (1933).[15] Heroism is an ideological and political weapon and it is through the actions of those allocated heroic qualities that the history of nations is constructed. Inevitably mythologised and embellished, the hero and the narratives that surround them are focal points for building a national community and a sense of identity. The hero is symbolised as part of a larger culture and emerges to save, defend and protect not merely the people of a nation but also a way of life and what that nation values.

These themes had an endless fascination for Mee, who allocated to heroes ideals he thought lay at the heart of Englishness. Among these was "fair play", something he declared could be seen in how the English played sport and in the character of her youth.[16] Writing to a male audience, he told them,

> You will not lose your love of fair play when the stakes are higher than they are at school. You will want fair play for great ideas, for honourable motives, for right causes, for rich and poor, for strong and weak you will play the game though your team should go to pieces.[17]

To "playing the game", Mee added what he deemed to be English characteristics: integrity, honesty, compassion and a love of freedom and justice.[18] For Mee, equity was central to English justice and English tolerance was such that an Englishman "may disagree with every word you say but he will die for your right to say it".[19] Sacrifice was at the core of his rhetorical imaginings of heroism; for him heroes were

> a beacon of light in a dark place, a voice in the silence of a wilderness, a strong arm raised against oppression, a beckoning hand to a faltering host, a willing prisoner that others might be free, a life laid down that truth might spread and knowledge grow.[20]

Lessons about being English were to be learnt through Mee's heroes, all of whom were presented as people of moral fibre who struggled to overcome obstacles on their way to success. Audiences were introduced to Francis Drake, said to be just, courageous and imbued with a character that was "in the woof and warp of England".[21] Predictably he included the dissenters who sailed on the *Mayflower*, describing them as "pioneers of faith and founders of civilisation in a strange land".[22] For his chivalry and "fair dealing", James Cook was presented as one of the greatest Englishmen since the beginning of time.[23]

Few politicians appear within Mee's pantheon, but Robert Peel finds a place. In his description of this liberal hero of free trade and tariff reform, Mee allocated to him what he claimed were the distinctly English values of honesty, morality, truthfulness and selflessness.[24] Readers were also told of the burglar Walter Greenway, who transformed his life by becoming a spy in defence of the realm before dying fighting the Turks in Mesopotamia. Mee pleaded that Greenway was just the kind of role model needed to set an example for the building of a patriotic love of nation.[25]

Moving beyond the lauding of iconic national figures, Mee claimed that anybody, including those who could be shown to be ordinary, flawed and thus like us, could demonstrate heroic qualities. He employed heroic narratives as inspiration and democratised heroism by turning to "The Everyday Folk". This included those he angrily thought the nation had abandoned to live in poverty and ignorance who had given their lives in the First World War to protect freedoms and liberties that few of them enjoyed.

Mee's aim was to illustrate to readers that in demonstrating a patriotic devotion to England, they had the potential to do extraordinary and memorable things with their lives. He urged readers to remember that they could show their commitment to England and what it meant to be English – all they had to do was join the Boy Scouts or Girl Guides.[26]

Character, courage and selflessness, qualities Mee thought integral to being English, appear in his account of the sinking of the hospital ship *Britannic* on 21 November 1916. On board were six boy scouts; aged sixteen or seventeen, they were used as signalers, lift operators, servants and messengers. When the ship was torpedoed, Mee writes, "those little fellows in their knickers and wide-awake hats went respectfully to the bridge of the doomed ship and demanded that they should not be counted with the children, saying: 'We claim to be treated as men, sir!'"[27] Girl Guides could not be placed in such danger but they also had their role to play. Their qualities included striving for peace against war, rejecting hate in favour of love, building not destroying, believing in liberty and service to the community, being truthful and patriotic and, because of their gender, representing the "hope and promise of this race".[28]

"The Most Beautiful Land on Earth"

The depth of Mee's attachment to England through its language and literature was matched by a profound connection to the English landscape.[29] As a response to industrialisation and growing urbanisation, many of Mee's contemporaries felt that while towns and cities were sites of cultural and social transformation, hamlets, villages and the natural landscape were enduring reminders of a historical and cultural continuity with the past that desperately needed protection.[30]

Writing in 1904, a sceptical Charles Masterman, convinced that the values that underpinned rural patriotism were fragmenting in the face of the magnetic pull of urban life, claimed that the nature of England was found in its villages.[31] Masterman's pain was shared by the journalist and historian Robert Ensor. Vegetarian, teetotal and an Edwardian progressive, Ensor was troubled by the abject squalor and destitution of urban life. In 1904 his response was to write poetically that England's achievements had been nurtured by the timeless qualities of its rural communities and their natural landscapes.[32] The grotesque horror of the First World War enhanced the appeal of rural myths. In 1915 Ernest C. Pulbrook, that chronicler of a mawkishly romanticised vision of rural life, wrote of the peace and harmony of the landscape and the lessons in patience and hope it taught.[33]

In a 1924 speech appealing to a suburban middle class fearful of social unrest and the perceived threat of Bolshevism, Stanley Baldwin commented, "To me, England is the country, and the country is England." He then went on to evoke romanticised images of the sights, sounds and smells of a rural England to which he attached an ageless and nostalgic simplicity.[34] In 1927 the flawed but enormously popular travel writer Henry Morton declared, "The village and the English country-side are the germs of all we are and all we have become."[35] Writing in the summer of 1940 in what was intended as a wartime version of Priestley's *English Journey*, Vera Brittan described her England as one of

> the fields and lanes of its lovely countryside; the misty, soft-edged horizon which is the superb gift to the eyes of this fog-laden island; the clear candour of spring flowers; the flame of autumn leaves; the sharp cracking of fallen twigs on frosty paths in winter.[36]

These deeply nostalgic eulogies for an idealised world of peace, tranquillity and aesthetic mysticism found a ready ally in Mee. He was simply enthralled by pastoral landscapes; they were integral to his sense of belonging and to how he imagined England. He had an intensely emotional attachment to the countryside, ascribing to it a spiritual and magical beauty as a miraculous, eternal and earthly paradise.[37]

Mee saw rural landscapes as infused with restorative qualities; they were a source of inspiration, reassurance and renewal. Immersion within the beauty of the natural world was for him a pathway to personal growth and refinement. For Mee the Englishman (his gendered term) valued "the loveliness of simple things – his garden, a little wood, the glory of our oaks and beeches, the beauty of a country lane, the village church that draws the people to it in their joys and sorrows".[38]

The natural landscape was an environment of mystery and imagination. Mee writes, "Our valleys are like so many secret places, with their hidden treasures, murmuring streams, old mills, sleepy hollows, green meadows, deep gorges, mysterious caverns, footpaths trodden for a thousand years."[39] Writing in April 1919 with the scars of the First World War fresh in mind he told readers that they had fought for

> the most beautiful land on earth. . . . There are lands with vaster spaces than these little islands; there are lands with nobler landscapes, broader rivers, greater heights. But there is no land so homely as this, so comfortable, so friendly; with all the dignity of a thousand years of greatness and all the closeness of a brother.[40]

Mee's thoughts about the natural landscape encompassed a sense of collective ownership and he democratised it, referring to it as "our" countryside. The landscape was a sacred possession; it was an inheritance to be passed on, and he encouraged people to believe that conserving and protecting it was in everybody's interest. A May 1920 editorial in *The Children's Newspaper* told readers, "We are trustees for the beauty of the earth; we owe it to our country, the land we are growing up in to rule, to keep it rare and sweet and beautiful."[41] In a *CN* editorial two months into the Second World War, he returned to the theme:

> We live in an ancient and beautiful house; our country is our home, our garden, and our workshop. But what are we, owners, or tenants who have a lease for a time? Some of our people act as if it were their own and they could do what they liked with it. They do not remember that it was here before they were and will remain after they have gone. They did not make its beauty; neither are they free to destroy it. . . . We might make this our aim, to leave these islands with no beauty lost, and with a new beauty added.[42]

Mee's imaginative invention of England was heavily influenced by the past and its symbolism in landscape and architecture is ubiquitous in his writing.[43] He staged contrasts between his "Old England" of tradition, confidence and stability and the England of new technologies, mass consumerisation and creeping urbanisation, of which he was far less certain. The theme is evoked in *Enchanted Land* (1936), the introductory volume of *The King's England* series. Mee surrendered the book to capturing what he thought was the custom, mood and spirit of England. In an excess of relentlessly florid and elaborate narratives, the volume assaults the reader's senses with idealistically romanticised vignettes of villages, towns, landscapes and architecture as unchanging scenes of warmth, security and timelessness. Included is a Betjeman-esque adoration for gothic churches known to have reduced Mee to tears.[44] Ancient track ways are used to further a sense of historical continuity as readers are told of journeying along them down corridors of time into villages filled with scenes of "wondrous beauty where time seems to stand still".[45]

Visions of a strong, unique and unchanging landscape are elaborated in Mee's descriptions of his gardens at Uplands and Eynsford Hill. For centuries the imagining of Englishness through the metaphor of the garden has been a pervasive cultural practice.[46] As a bounded territory representative of a secure and sheltered space, drawing comparisons with the biblical paradise of Eden, the garden is an icon of English national consciousness.[47] For those that had one, the garden came to represent an alternative and more tranquil way of life and a place that counterbalanced a perceived sense of loss brought about by the challenges of socio-economic change.[48]

Gardens can say a lot about the character, aspirations and wealth of their owners. Writing in 1909, F.E. Green suggested that

> In the making of a garden rather than in a collection of books do we get the reflection of a man's soul. The appearance of the house he cannot help, if he did not have it built for himself; but in the garden, with its summer-house, its pergola, its pools, its statues, in its wildness or in its formalism, in its seclusion or in its ostentation, will be seen the maker's sense of beauty or the want of it.[49]

What Green meant was found in Mee's gardens. He saw them as sites within which he could unleash his imagination and so he lavished money and attention on them, particularly the one at Eynsford Hill which, under his supervision, was created from a bare hillside.

In "Five Acres of England", a piece about the garden at Uplands, Mee wrote, "He who has a garden has the most precious thing in the world."[50] Although he knew little about the names of the trees, shrubs and plants in his garden, Mee used them as a template for creating scenes of historical continuities that for him shaped England; he wrote,

> The bluebells come up in the wood, and the carpet of anemones and violets that for generations have never missed a spring. The handsome jays come screeching where their ancestors planted oaks a hundred years ago. The moles burrow in the same old paths, the bees hive in the same old tree, the rabbits and hares have been home for centuries.[51]

So central to his being was Mee's faith that wherever he looked he saw evidence for the existence of God.[52] For him, gardens were more than just aesthetically pleasing physical spaces; they were spiritual places.[53] For those searching for evidence of how God intervened in the natural world, Mee suggested they look no further than a garden, in which everything was the work of an intelligent creator.[54] He thought this obvious and that nobody with any understanding of the world could argue differently. Those who had a garden had "no need to die to go to heaven".[55]

Eynsford Hill was a "paradise of beauty"[56] and Mee described it as his personal "little kingdom of delight".[57] He was happy to share his gardens and periodically opened them to the public, who could walk through them and buy tea for a shilling and a small charge which was collected for the Queen Alexandria Nursing Association.[58] Each visitor was given a four-page leaflet describing the building of Eynsford Hill and its gardens. Mee was far from pleased when in 1941 service personnel visiting the garden at Eynsford Hill trampled it down, damaging several of its features.[59]

Mee's gardens were designed and enjoyed as a wistful "Neverland"; like the original Arcadia of Greek mythology, the home of Pan, nymphs

Figure 13.
A view of part of the gardens at Eynsford Hill with Arthur Mee's summerhouse, in which he did much of his writing, and, behind, his wood.

and spirits, they were constructed as environments untouched and uncorrupted by the material world.[60] They were his psychological refuge from the problems and anxieties of work as well as a metonymy for his emotional veneration of England.[61] The garden provided Mee with some certainty in an often uncertain world and he had a compelling affinity to the landscape of Eynsford Hill and beyond to the hills and valleys, woods and rivers of Kent.

A Principled War

Like nearly everybody, Mee was horrified by the outbreak of war in August 1914, writing of it as "the most terrible day in the history of the world".[62] It was as if a hideous and utterly inconceivable nightmare had become a shockingly terrifying reality. Mee thought that the world as he knew it was about to plunge into darkness, meaning things would never be the same again, and that war was the ultimate expression of utter political stupidity. What made his distress more disturbing and profound was that he had lived through a decade of what he considered progress and wanted to believe that no nation would ever risk such a cataclysmic conflict.

He was not alone in his thoughts. Prior to 1914, nonconformist leaders had joined pacifists, trade unionists, socialists, members of the Labour Party and others in viewing with alarm increased militarisation and the onset of tensions between England and Germany. There were demonstrations against going to war until the day it was declared.[63] Even after the outbreak of war H.G. Wells was arguing that Germans were an artistic and intelligent people, who, like a naïve and gullible child, had been led astray by an alien political and military culture.[64] This message was re-enforced by Lloyd George: "We are not fighting the German people. The German people are under the heel of this military caste, and it will be a day of rejoicing for the German peasant, artisan and trader, when the military caste is broken."[65]

Once war was declared, Mee's deep-seated patriotism saw him without question accept and endorse the official narrative that blame did not rest with the German people or with a Germany that for centuries he felt had been a beacon of art, literature and civilisation.[66] But while he had a nuanced view of Germany, it was not one shared by Alfred Harmsworth, who, for five years prior to 1914, had ensured that the pages of his newspapers dripped with virulent anti-German sentiment.[67] Harmsworth was adamant that Germans could not be trusted and wrote to Mee that in his view envy and suspicion were core features of the German character.[68] Mee tried to convince him otherwise and before the war suggested that Harmsworth use his political influence to improve Anglo-German relations, rather than contributing to their decline and failure.[69] Harmsworth was unimpressed and came close to telling Mee that he was talking nonsense.[70]

War tested Mee's nonconformist conscience and when it came he had a choice to make. He could oppose it, as many nonconformists did, or he could put conscience to one side and contribute to the crusading rhetoric that the war was a fight for Christian civilisation against barbarism and tyranny. He needed no persuading to take the latter course and, if his decision needed easing, it found justification in his enthusiastic agreement with the torrent of popular patriotism that engulfed the country following the German invasion of Belgium.

Day after day, vicarious accounts, speculation, rumour and accusations appeared in the print media describing the most brutal and shocking inhumanity.[71] Atrocity propaganda provided fuel to both exemplify the righteousness of the English cause and confirm the populist ideology of an unfettered brutal enemy. Horror stories of outrages swept the country and to doubt their authenticity was considered unpatriotic and traitorous.[72] Germany was presented as an acute threat to a civilised way of life and as a vicious and sadistic enemy who systematically flouted the conventions of fighting war in an ethical and principled manner. Many, including Mee, came to share the view of the British ambassador in Paris that "I began by not believing in German atrocities, and now I feel that I myself would, if I could, kill every combatant German that I might meet."[73]

Initial hostility towards the war from nonconformists disappeared. John Clifford stressed the moral justification for war and claimed that the nation had been forced into it and that it was a fight for freedom against oppression.[74] Mee adopted exactly the same stance. He had no difficulty in putting aside the principles of individual freedom and conscience in support of a patriotic duty towards community and nation. The war was manufactured into the moral crusade it had to be if a generation of young men and women were to be convinced to die for their country, and Mee gladly helped shape that crusade.

Like everybody else he joined in the demonisation of Germany that swamped the nation.[75] He described Kaiser Wilhelm II as a dishonourable man who had broken his word; he was a "brigand", a "pirate", a "criminal", an "assassin", the "new Attila" who had "flung open the gates of barbarism" by sending out his "ruthless butchers" to murder the innocent.[76] In a letter to Derry written on 12 October 1914 he vented his rage:

> You remember the last time you and I set foot on foreign soil together? It was in Antwerp, and I have been thinking about it during these days. You remember the nice little hotel off the square in which we had tea? I expect it has gone, and at this moment, if the world were in my hands, the one thing that would please me would be that the Prussian beast, and everything that is Prussian, except the women and children, should be flung into the flames of Antwerp.[77]

Belgian war refugees were housed in Eynsford and their children attended the local primary school. On hearing that a German woman was living locally and serving on a committee helping them, Mee told Derry, "as for the German, either she will leave the committee, or everybody else will. She lives at the Vicarage!"[78]

In promoting the idea that war could be fought in a civilised fashion, commentators claimed that although it was cruel, pitiless and tragic, the English fought within a clearly defined set of rules. Mee's education and the cultural values of his generation had indoctrinated him into this mythology. One of his most stinging reproaches was that Germans fought in ways alien to an English sense of fairness and justice. Using the culturally ingrained metaphor based around an ideology of athleticism and "manliness", he attacked Germans for failing to fight within the rules:

There is no objection to Germany using her submarines, only she must keep the rules, and the submarine cannot keep the rules. There is no objection to playing cricket, only one side must not bowl with a bomb for a ball. We must play the game and keep the rules, and the submarine can do neither, because it must make haste to be gone, and cannot wait to make sure of its ship and it has no means of saving the lives of the crews.[79]

Two months into the war, so intense had Mee's loathing of Germans become and so complete had been their populist demonisation that he felt able to tell Derry, "I would not mind the least if people said I murdered my mother, but to be called a German is perhaps the ultra-limit that a human man can be expected to stand."[80]

Spy fever swept the country and Mee found himself an unlikely victim. William Le Queux's stories of invasions and plots sold extremely well. Some were serialised in national newspapers including *England's Peril* (1899), *Spies of the Kaiser: Plotting the Downfall of England* (1909) and *The Invasion of 1910* (1910), all emblematic of a national sense of decadence, complacency and decline. Spy films included *Huns of the North Sea* (1914), *The Kaiser's Spies* (1914), *The German Spy Peril* (1914) and the D.W. Griffiths film *Hearts of the World*.[81]

Consequently, by the outbreak of war the English had been convinced by propaganda that anything which at any other time would be quite insignificant might actually be very suspicious. With Mee still a relative newcomer in Eynsford, some locals became suspicious of the man that lived in the big house on top of the hill. Mee wrote to Derry,

As for me, if you will come up into Kent and ask anywhere within ten miles of Eynsford, you will learn that I am a German spy. The only safe thing is to believe nothing in these days, so you need not believe me, and I will not attempt to deny it. Most extraordinary stories are about proving it up to the hilt, and I hear it by telephone, letter, and word of mouth. I have just built a house on a hill, near a fort, overlooking the lines to Dover, with a terrace that happens to be flat, with some concrete about, and with electric lights that flash up and down suddenly and have even been on at midnight. And there is the red lamp – my little bit of Florence – which shows through the window and can be seen four miles away. And then one day I took down my flag for a little while, and another day I had a bonfire in the wood.[82]

Mee got close to war on a supervised visit to France. When in December 1917 he took an escorted tour through the battlefields of France and Belgium, he wrote of the destruction in Arras, a visit to Vimy Ridge, Bapaume, the

Somme battlefields and Ypres. In the streets of Ypres, Mee came closer than he wanted to battle when a shell landed behind him in the ruins of the Cloth Hall. It was, he wrote, "as near as a man need wish to get to this war that is devastating our cities and saving our liberties".[83]

*

Mee's spiritual link to England provided him with a profound sense of pride, hope and optimism. While he was conscious of its mistakes, these paled into insignificance against what he considered to be its glorious past and the contribution it had made to civilisation and the spread of democracy and freedom. While Mee's view of England was romanticised and excessively partial, it was not fictional or irrational; for him and many of his generation it was sincerely felt, common sense, taken for granted and simply true. It was a view of England within which tradition occupied a critical space as Mee sought to persuade readers of how important it was that the nation, revered in all its splendour and glory, retained a continuity with its past that saw its population prepared to sacrifice all for its protection.

6.

An Accidental Empire

An Empire of Good Intentions

Through its Empire England enjoyed authority over more than 450 million people, providing the nation with unparalleled power, prestige and political control. But the processes of imperialism and imperial expansion had been extraordinarily complex and how the Empire was perceived varied greatly. In November 1899 Henry Campbell-Bannerman claimed, "[E]veryone nowadays appears to cultivate some peculiar species of his own of what is called Imperialism and to try to get one qualifying adjective of his own before the word."[1] One distinction was between those who saw the Empire as a critical source of markets and investment opportunities and those saw in it the prospect of bringing English social and political culture and Christianity to indigenous populations.

It has been argued that the Empire meant little to most people, who reacted to it with occasional pride mixed with doses of indifference and ambiguity.[2] Writing in 1941 George Orwell observed, "[I]t is quite true that the English are hypocritical about their Empire. In the working class this hypocrisy takes the form of not knowing that the Empire exists."[3] More recently Bernard Porter suggested that "The empire made no great material demands on most people . . . and did not need their support or even their interest. All that was needed was a minimum of apathy."[4] But although the impact of the Empire upon public consciousness may have been understated, through a range of influences it was systematically internalised and a familiar and often mundane part of everyday life.[5] The Empire was part of what Michael Billig called a "banal nationalism".[6]

The Empire was central to how the English were encouraged to imagine themselves. It may have been pedestrian and clichéd but it was in their lives through ceremony and celebration, music, theatre, art, fiction and, later, film.[7] Even children could not avoid it as imperialistic discourses dominated schooling through curriculum and pedagogy, textbooks and class readers. For children both in and outside school, becoming literate meant reading heroic narratives of imperial adventure. At the core of this was indoctrination into nationalist and imperialist civic values designed to manufacture an explicit identification with Englishness as well as a distancing from the undesirable "other".[8] The purpose was to ensure that individuals, regardless of status, social class or gender, could view themselves as citizens of an imperial family tied by birth, duty and heritage.[9]

In the classroom of George Byford, Mee had been introduced to narratives of English imperial greatness; it had its impact and he retained an unswerving commitment to the Empire. While over time what the Empire meant transformed in the face of changing national and international circumstances, Mee's view remained consistent. He was inordinately proud of the Empire and even the most cursory glance through his writings on the subject reveals constant reminders to readers that millions of the world's inhabitants ought to be grateful that they enjoyed the benefits of English rule and governance.

Some of Mee's contemporaries had a very different view. The liberal John Hobson mounted a withering attack on imperialism as an immoral process of exploitation through the military subjugation of indigenous populations.[10] The critic John George Godard saw it as a product of pride and greed acquired by brute force and a self-interest that disregarded the principles of liberty and freedom.[11] Frederick Harrison attacked what he saw as the "cancer" of the Empire and the damage he felt it did to the nation.[12] Others described it as "Emporialism", nothing more than a source of new markets designed to enhance trade and profits.[13] In a climate of growing hostility with Germany in 1913, Winston Churchill claimed that the nation had all the territories and colonies it wanted and simply asked to be left alone to enjoy its "vast and splendid possessions", which were "mainly acquired by violence, largely maintained by force".[14]

None of this convinced Mee, who was never opposed to imperial expansion. He combined his Englishness, his faith and his nonconformist conscience to manufacture an image of Empire as a humanitarian project designed to carry civilisation to "backward" races.[15] In *The Doctrine and Discipline of Divorce* (1643), one of Mee's favourite poets John Milton wrote, "Let not England forget her precedence of teaching nations how to live." Mee would have agreed. He never moved from the conviction that the Empire was a wellspring of Christian righteousness and a force for universal good.[16]

Mee's writing is drenched in the ideology of imperialism and colonisation. The Empire is cast as a gloriously romantic enterprise, a miraculous and wondrous thing. It was thrilling and nothing that humankind could ever create would be able to match it. Throughout his youth and into maturity, central in his thinking was the belief that the uncivilised world could consider itself fortunate that the English were there to tame it. His personal mythology of imperialism saw it as a liberating force provided by a collection of England's immortal heroes who had sacrificed themselves to bring peace and freedom to the world.[17]

Mee saw English imperialism as entirely philanthropic and the acquisition of the Empire as an honourable and ethically motivated enterprise.[18] With the Bible as the basis of its principles, all the ideas, values and morals, everything that really mattered in the world, flowed from England to its Empire. With a conviction that was absolute, he claimed for England the credit of having brought independence to every continent on the globe, writing, "All over the Earth our British freedom has made its way, conquering disease, spreading knowledge, giving liberty to captives, bringing light out of darkness, overthrowing tyranny."[19]

A century after its publication, Kipling's poem "The White Man's Burden" (1899) is judged to be symbolic of Eurocentric racism, but in the early decades of the twentieth century its theme of benevolent imperialism was widely accepted, and Mee supported it without question. In "The Rise of Britain Overseas", he writes,

> [O]ur race has spread itself all over the world. It has not only made itself rich and powerful – which is a small thing after all – but it has made itself the guardian of the welfare of hundreds of millions of people who had less knowledge, or skill, or courage. It has taken upon its own shoulders what has been called the White Man's Burden. We must answer for it that we have striven honestly for their welfare.[20]

With the responsibility of Empire came the paternalistic obligation of ensuring that the English managed it responsibly. Mee considered justice and liberty the foundation of imperial expansion and that the principal aim of Empire was to ensure that all within its borders were able to prosper, free from exploitation or subjugation.[21] It was, he claimed, English justice that enabled the maintenance of the Empire. In *Why We Had to Go to War* (1939), he wrote, "If the Pax Romana was a peace of power, the Pax Britannica is a peace of justice."[22] In September 1939, on the eve of war, he wrote a contemptuous denouncement of Hitler's expansionist ambitions which he contrasted with the growth of the Empire:

> Through many centuries we have built up our freedom, the liberty under which every man can live his own life, think his own thoughts, go his own way. We have spread the love of it about the earth and given the chance of happiness to hundreds of millions. We have built up an empire on which the sun never sets and in which none need be afraid. We have terrorised no people, have destroyed no country's freedom. The aim of the British Empire is nothing less than the building up of free nations throughout the world, domineering no man, coveting no territory, envying none.[23]

Mee continued this argument in *1940: Our Finest Hour*, written in some of the darkest days of the war. In a clarion call to resist the threat of the "brutal Juggernaut of Barbarism", he characterised the Empire as an unselfish bastion of Christian civilisation working for "the right of every man to be free and every nation to be independent in its homeland".[24]

Writing in 1883, the Victorian historian and imperial apologist J.R. Seeley claimed, "We seem, as it were, to have conquered and peopled half the world in a fit of absence of mind."[25] Mee voiced an identical view; not only did he accept without question the claim that the Empire was one of good intentions, he judged that it had been obtained accidently. He had no time for accusations that the acquisition of the Empire took place against a background of economic ambitions, conquest and indigenous oppression.[26] There had been no planned rationale behind it; he writes, "The fact is that we did not seek an empire, and that it has come to us almost against our will."[27] Over time, argued Mee, the Empire grew somewhat spasmodically, often engineered by non-government private trading companies and missionary colonisation; as such it was attained justly.[28]

Mee rejected the idea that imperial expansion involved economic, industrial and military subjugation. He thought the opposite the case, writing, "It is not true that it is an empire made by war. It is not true that it has oppressed small peoples. It is not true that it has been built up by selfish ambition and national greed."[29] The only things conquered in his imagining of the Empire were poverty, ignorance, savagery and slavery. Mee's interpretation of the Empire saw it as a compassionate mother giving birth to, raising and nurturing its children before, having proved they could survive unaided, they left home and made their own way in the world. Then, having replaced paternalistic benevolence with partnership, like a dutiful child, when called upon they returned the favour in economic and military support of the motherland.[30]

This perspective enabled Mee to write that India had never been conquered militarily but had become part of the Empire by "peaceful means".[31] Once the country had been integrated into the Empire, the English had provided stability and order within a society scarred by ethnic tensions between a "dark race and a fair, Aryan, race", Hindus and Muslims, and by a caste system he considered brutal and intolerable.[32] England had saved India from itself and needed to continue doing so: "The truth is we have to guard this mighty eastern empire not only against its frontiers but against itself."[33] Mee took the idea of England as the self-appointed guardian of India's affairs and arbiters of its future very seriously; independence, when it came, would be the gift of the motherland.

He did not live to see Indian independence and never thought that India was capable of governing its own affairs, considering such a move to be a dangerous act.[34] He had no time for Mahatma Ghandi, telling Derry he thought of him as "a good man on wrong lines". Indian independence was beyond Mee's comprehension and Ghandi was "a well meaning religious dreamer", a "simpleton" and a mischief-maker attempting to lead a country riven with internal strife, wars, famines and religious and political contradictions.[35]

Emblematic of social cohesion and indoctrination into the imperial family, Empire Day was a vehicle through which the English were reminded of their obligation to civilise the world. Instigated in 1903 by the imperial apologist Lord Meath, Empire Day's aim was to tell the English of the "crushing sense of the overwhelming nature of the responsibilities and duties which God in his providence had thought fit to place individually upon [their] shoulders as citizens, or future citizens, of this greatest earthly State".[36]

In claiming with typical hyperbole that it was "perhaps the greatest day in the annals of human freedom",[37] there was no English reserve or bashful understatement in Mee's commitment to Empire Day. As far as he was concerned it was a time to celebrate the remarkable achievements of a noble people and their heritage.[38] It was a day of national joy and pride, symbolising a glorious past and a hopeful future provided for the world by an extraordinary people.[39] Readers of *The Children's Newspaper* were reminded that

> It is fitting that there should be an Empire Day on which British boys and girls are reminded of their splendid heritage. Not only of the glories of their world-wide empire are they reminded, but of the responsibilities it involves, and of the great service and duty to which all are called.[40]

While not universally supported by all local authorities, especially those with socialist or Labour majorities,[41] Empire Day was celebrated enthusiastically by most children, who usually saw it as a respite from the tedium of school with its rigid discipline and authoritarian training in morality.[42] Being granted a half-day holiday from school no doubt helped.[43]

A Darwinian Empire

Within the cultural and ideological environment in which he lived and worked, Mee was racist. There is nothing surprising in that claim. In contemporary society such views are utterly intolerable, but inside Mee's Victorian and Edwardian world of eugenic theorising, questions of race and racial superiority were routine and taken seriously and they permeated the public psyche. As Catherine Hall and Sonya Rose point out,

The colour of skin, the shape of bones, the texture of hair as well as less visible markers of distinction – the supposed size of brain, capacity for reason, or form of sexuality – these were some of the ways that modern metropolitans differentiated between themselves and others.[44]

Within the context of a claimed racial supremacy, the English were gripped by the fear that their dominance was under attack. One response had been eugenic; another was to re-emphasise the cultural and biological superiority of the English race.[45] The English saw the Empire in terms of racial hierarchies borrowed from understandings of an English society that was inherently unequal. Brutalised urban environments provided opportunities to draw distinctions between the lifestyles of what some thought of as the "undeserving poor" and other more respectable sections of the community. Contrasts of superiority and inferiority were employed in the construction of similar distinctions between the English and indigenous populations within the Empire. The cultural and social structure of England was understood in terms of class, status and race, and so were its imperial possessions.[46]

Mee joined a widely-held Social Darwinian consensus that had stepped across the boundary from the biological into the social. A flourishing and prosperous Empire required an imperial race, and Social Darwinists, in asking the same questions they wanted answers for at home, shared a widespread interest in how best to re-produce that race.[47] This was a commonplace view during the years that Mee was at his most successful and a strong thread of racial paternalism runs through his writing about Empire. Central in Mee's construction of "backward" races was that when contrasted with European Enlightenment philosophies of logic, science and reason, they possessed child-like qualities and lacked agency in developing their culture, society and economy. Mee believed that if colonised peoples living under the protection of the Empire were to become civilised, they required guidance from a morally inspired, capable and benevolent English race. Although he expressed it mildly in comparison to some contemporaries, Mee's readers were left in no doubt about what was thought to be the biological and racial superiority of the English.

The Children's Encyclopaedia included an account written by Caleb Saleeby on craniology. With origins linked to eugenic theorising regarding hereditary characteristics, craniology, the theory of measuring skulls for an index by which to analyse individual personality and intelligence, was a fashionable pursuit, part-science for some and more a hobby for others. As it was a populist theory, in the 1880s and 1890s, many parents took their children to have their skulls examined, thinking it would provide them with information about how intelligent they were.

By the 1890s, craniology was being treated as an amusement. You could have your head read for nothing at the Cardiff Panopticon.[48] One exponent was seeking to pitch a tent on the beach as an entertainment; it was being called "bumpology" and its supporters "bumpologists".[49] A political candidate seeking election circulated a phrenological chart of his head, leading *The Burnley Express* to suggest that other candidates might do the same and the election could then become a "grand political bumping race".[50] By the time craniology appeared within *The Children's Encyclopaedia* it had been largely discredited as little more than pseudo-science that did nothing but confirm racial prejudices. Nevertheless, readers were informed that "In the brains of some of the lowest savages we find that the vision area is small compared with that in the brains of healthy members of higher races".[51] Caleb Saleeby argued that

> We find that some parts of the Earth are inhabited by a humble kind of men and women who do not merely know less than we do but are not able to learn as much as we do, even when they get an equal chance; and we notice that these people do not have high and broad and straight foreheads as we do, but that their foreheads are long and narrow and slope sharply backwards, almost suggesting the humbler forehead of a dog.[52]

Mee subscribed to the idea that so-called "backward" races occupied a low place on a Social Darwinian hierarchy, but, unlike Saleeby, claimed that this was not inevitable. They could, with English tutelage, rise to a higher status. Until that time, however, they would remain paternalised, infantilised and positioned within narratives emphasising a lack of self-determination. In "The Head and the Limbs", Mee claimed,

> We have no more right to despise these people than we have to despise any other creature that God has made. But we must understand that they are less able to look after themselves and to protect themselves from evil things than we are, just because their brains are not so large as ours; and, therefore, a special duty falls on us, who have larger and better developed brains, to do the right thing to these people, the little backward races of the Earth, and not, for instance, to get rich by making slaves of them.[53]

Mee claims to have received thousands of letters from readers; many of them were described as "boys and girls of backward races".[54] A 1925 editorial in *The Children's Newspaper* congratulated the achievements of readers as they worked at "plodding up the hill to civilisation".[55] The editorial criticised the manner in which indigenous peoples were described; it was wrong to think of the Chinese as "Chinks" and wrong to denigrate "those splendid black citizens of ours . . . as niggers". Readers were reminded that, regardless of colour, all races "have their own good points", before being told that nobody should forget how "the black races can sing" and that those who heard Roland Hayes, "the Negro singer", would not soon forget his voice.[56]

YOUR LITTLE FRIENDS IN OTHER LANDS

Figure 14.
"Your Little Friends in Other Lands". Note the racial hierarchy from back to front moving through African, Asian, Islamic and finally white European races with a Marjorie Mee look-a-like complete with parasol. This illustration appeared in the first edition of The Children's Encyclopaedia *in 1908. By the time of its re-publication in 1922 and in volume form into the 1930s and 1940s it had disappeared.*

In *Arthur Mee's Book of the Flag*, first published in September 1941 and re-printed four times before the end of the year, Mee labelled the Empire's population in terms of their racial characteristics. White settlers in Australia, Canada, South Africa and New Zealand were placed at the pinnacle of a racial hierarchy, with indigenous populations positioned at the bottom. At the lowest point stood the Australian Aborigines, "the most primitive race of all mankind, vanishing from the earth before the eyes of men".[57] In contrast, the New Zealand Maori, said at one time to have been savages and cannibals, had evolved to become civilised and came to be known as "the Britons of the south".[58] Next in line were African Bushmen, "the most lowly of all the native races in Africa",[59] said to be marginally more civilised than African races from Zululand, Kenya and Uganda.[60]

Africa was described by Mee as a continent of backward and primitive races that had been civilised; what conflict there had been was the consequence of "misunderstandings and the limited vision of Nature's backward children".[61] For Mee the development of South Africa rested entirely upon the expansion of the British Empire; the Boer War was described as a tragedy for both sides, although the Boers were credited for "taming" the "barbaric Zulu Race" accused of standing in the way of civilisation and progress.[62] As for the West Indies, the colonies were growing and progressing, although Jamaica less so because of "the natural laziness of the Negroes, who need little to live and can satisfy it with little labour".[63] Outside the Empire, backward peoples were to be found among the Slavs of the Russian Steppes and the indigenous populations of the Middle East, the Far East and the Pacific.

Being English, White and Australian

Within the English imagination, Australia has always been a magnificent enigma. Familiar and unfamiliar, understood and misunderstood, close and yet distant, it is a land of stark contrasts and contradictions that has historically captivated, bewildered and intrigued their English cousins. Since the earliest days of European settlement, the idea of Australia has been exotic, mysterious and quite extraordinary.[64]

The Children's Newspaper rarely missed an opportunity to include something about Australia, ranging from short factual statements about the number of apples exported or the number of sheep there, through a miscellaneous variety of human interest stories, to detailed articles on diverse aspects of Australian life. Readers could expect to be informed about Don Bradman and Ashes cricket, Christmas at the beach, Australia's Flying Doctor Service, the opening of new railways, airways and roads, the building of Sydney Harbour Bridge, the new capital in Canberra, the construction of Parliament House, described as "probably *the ugliest Parliament House in the Empire*"[65] (original italics), and Sir Isaac Alfred Isaacs, Australia's first home-born Governor-General.

The extraordinary and exotic nature of the continent's flora and fauna, which presented such significant challenges to botanical, zoological and biological categorisation, was a particular fascination. This reinforced in the imagination of English readers the idea that Australia was a land of contradictions where the natural order of the universe was inverted. Australia was "the real Ultima Thule, the end of the world"; it was "a topsy-turvey continent, where so many things are different that it is bewildering".[66]

Australia was established to be a white nation on the other side of the world, one that replicated the kind of society left behind in England. In articles spread over four decades of reporting, *The Children's Newspaper* enthusiastically claimed that Australia had to remain undeniably English and exclusively white, a view that Mee supported. Within its pages, Australia was culturally and ideologically constructed through a racial bond of whiteness that provided a hierarchy of identity, social structure, privilege and entitlement. Being Australian and living within a white nation was a hegemonic, taken-for-granted assumption that underpinned Mee's view of the kind of migrants Australia required.

Social Darwinian views on racial hierarchies in Australia emphasised that Australians were really English. Various letters published in *The Children's Newspaper* reflected the view that "There is no doubt that England is the finest country in the world";[67] they were supported by statements on Australia reminding readers that "No part of the Earth is more purely British. No part is more proud of its parent stock",[68] and claims such as "I was born in this country, but still I am English".[69]

During the 1920s and 1930s the context of Australian growth was of a white nation under siege from the perceived threat offered by the developing economic maturity, power and progress of Asian states. White Australia looked anxiously to the north, worried that it might find itself challenged by peoples looked upon as being grossly inferior. Mee shared that view and vigorously supported the idea that Australia had to be populated by white migrants from the motherland. Throughout the 1920s, *The Children's Newspaper* campaigned for increased migration to the Empire's colonies and particularly to Australia. An article in 1925 suggested that

A difficulty which many leading countries are feeling strongly today is the inflow from other countries of people who are not wanted. . . . Canada, Australia, and New Zealand are being equally careful in preserving their country for people who can be safely and wisely admitted as citizens.[70]

The aim of English migration was to avoid "the lowering of our native stock by the admission of undesirable foreign elements".[71] An un-named correspondent asked,

How can the teeming millions of a go-ahead race like the Japanese be withheld by an all-white policy in Australia if the British and Australians cease to breed enough virile colonists to till and defend that vast country?[72]

Mee believed that Australia offered endless possibilities that were being woefully ignored by an incompetent government who failed to see the potential on offer.[73] Frustrated, he wrote to Derry with the somewhat extreme solution of sending a "second fleet" 137 years after the first:

I am sending you something about Australia and its great empty spaces. This to me is one of the great tragedies of the world. We must not say it bluntly, of course, but it is time this great farce ended. If we had anything like a conception of our duty we should send out a great fleet crammed with unemployed, and set them to work in this Australian wilderness. If it is true that the Empire is going, and the poor little Motherland, bowed down with the burden of the world, is to be left alone, it will be an excellent thing for the Japanese to land on Australia and show us what we might have done.[74]

But Australia was no longer prepared to accept the detritus of English society. Populating it with youth of good character, promise and potential became an important objective of migration policy. *The Children's Newspaper* played a role in advertising migration schemes for children, juveniles and young men containing narratives of how they would be found paid work on farms or as apprentices.[75] These claims were supported by effusive and romanticised accounts of the benefits that could accrue through fulsome descriptions of Australia and the potential it offered to build a healthy, successful and prosperous life. Potential migrants were told that they would be able to pick fruit from trees in a land where the sun always shone, swim in warm oceans and play with kangaroos and koala bears.

The aspirational attractions of migration were exemplified in letters and reports from migrants who, through a discourse of exploration, adventure and excitement, informed readers of *The Children's Newspaper* that, provided they worked hard, Australia offered them unparalleled opportunities.[76] Australia was a land that said, "Please come and live in me."[77] Readers were told of James Joynton Smith, who, born in the East End of London, migrated to Australia, started his own business, earned a fortune and became Lord Mayor of Sydney.[78] Claims were made that "given the right kind of boy a good future, and possibly a fortune, is waiting on some of them".[79]

The Children's Newspaper enthusiastically endorsed child and youth emigration schemes, particularly the Big Brother Movement and the

Fairbridge Farm School. The Big Brother Movement, acclaimed as "a splendid idea", sought migrants from juveniles aged sixteen and above of good character, rather than orphans or those with criminal records.[80] The *CN* told readers that those interested in the scheme would have to be "clean living" young men who wanted to "make good" in Australia, rather than those looking to escape from past failures.[81] Applicants were selected based upon their level of education, references and an interview. There was an expectation that they would be sober and thrifty, attend church and write home regularly. Upon their arrival in Australia they were allocated a "Big Brother" to welcome them; after a few days they were sent to a farm to live and work and it was up to them to remain in contact with their Big Brother.[82]

The Fairbridge Farm School at Pinjarra, thirty kilometres east of Mandurah in Western Australia, was a favourite topic of *The Children's Newspaper*; it described it as a "splendid training-ground for the men and women of Australia's tomorrow".[83] Many of the children who arrived at Pinjarra, some as young as four, had been institutionalised in the care of charitable and religious organisations; some were wrongly described as orphans while others had been born into poverty. Child migration to Fairbridge Farms was unequivocally praised as a philanthropic attempt to rescue children from destitution and neglect. It received royal patronage when the Duke of York, later King George VI, visited Pinjarra in 1927.

The Children's Newspaper claimed that places like the Fairbridge Farm School provided "a way out for the fortunate few".[84] It was reported that children were happy, living comfortably in family groups, being well looked after by a foster mother and being educated.[85] For the *CN*, child migration was about populating "the open spaces of all the lands where the British flag flies. Thus alone can they make those lands safe for British people."[86]

While Fairbridge had its success stories, for too many children the reality, as opposed to the rhetoric, was tragically different. With staff poorly trained in child welfare, many children found the isolation, loneliness and solitude of a largely rural and alien existence traumatic. For others their experience was characterised by sexual, physical and psychological abuse, ruthless work regimes and harsh punishment.[87] In August 1998 the Parliament of Western Australia passed a motion of apology to former child migrants for their "forced migration" and the maltreatment, hurt and distress that may have caused.[88] In February 2010 the British government apologised to former child migrants.[89] In 2012 more than 200 child migrants sent to Fairbridge Farm School at Pinjarra were awarded more than AUD$1.1 million in compensation for the abuse they suffered there.[90]

Being an Aboriginal Australian

As the unknown flora and fauna of Australia presented challenges to biological categorisation, so too did Aboriginal peoples. Contemporary writers considered them a race impossible to classify against the standards of known human cultures. Enlightenment ideas of progress were used as measurements, against which Aboriginal peoples were said to flout all the conventions of human development. This was particularly so to those who argued that property ownership, government and progress towards a civic society were markers of progressive and enlightened nations.

Aboriginal Australians fitted Mee's categorisation of a "backward" race on the edge of extinction. With a history stretching back thousands of years, in his eyes they were "the lowest examples of human life on the earth".[91] As far as Mee was concerned they were a race that would never be able to climb the evolutionary ladder and were beyond help. He claimed that this had not always been the case; their regression was a direct result of the arrival of colonists, who had corrupted their culture with alcohol and disease.

Mee described Aboriginal peoples as a relic of an earlier stage of human development. They were a primitive and child-like Stone Age culture, exhibiting perplexing and sometimes barbaric customs; their extinction in the face of evolutionary progress was unavoidable.[92] In the meantime, Aboriginal Australians were passive spectators standing on the edge of progress, either as an irritating hindrance or as a marginalised group with no role to play in the project of Europeanised nation building and modernisation.

By the early 1920s, this theme was being developed by Daisy Bates (1859-1951), whose accounts in *The Children's Newspaper* were instrumental in shaping the representations of Aboriginal Australians and thus the views held by many who read them. Thirty-six articles by Bates appeared in the *CN*, as well as another ten in *My Magazine* and three in *Arthur Mee's 1000 Heroes*.

Bates is a controversial and enigmatic figure in Australian history. A person of stark contradictions, she was intelligent, committed, dynamic and compassionate but irrefutably eccentric, authoritarian and conservative. She was also a Social Darwinian, a devoted imperialist and a bigamist, with a talent for self-publicity and fabrication.[93] In spite of the ambiguities in her life, the significance of Bates is in how, for a generation, she was an iconic figure who contributed to a repertoire of foundational myths that for much of the twentieth century contributed significantly to populist constructions of Australian national identity.

Between 1904 and 1951, Bates was best known for her work with Aboriginal Australians, work that brought equal measures of international celebrity and notoriety. As that rarest of things at the beginning of the twentieth century, a female self-educated anthropologist and ethnographer, Bates gave accounts of the culture, traditions and rituals of Aboriginal peoples that offered detailed insights into their lives.[94] Critical in manufacturing her reputation was the popularity of mythologised narratives of a self-professed gentlewomen of aristocratic descent living unaccompanied in a desolate and treacherous environment while she tended a race claimed to be on the edge of extinction.[95]

The story of Daisy Bates was employed by Mee to produce an authoritative and legitimising imagining of Australia and its Aboriginal peoples. He would often have Bates's reports prefaced with a contextual prologue, sometimes written by John Derry, designed to impress that she was living in a remote, godless and dangerous environment amongst people "who are perhaps more primitive than any other race on the Earth".[96] She was "living between two worlds, a world of civilised people and a world of savages, both ours under the flag".[97] Bates was hopelessly romanticised; in a letter to Derry, Stella Hancock, a member of his staff, wrote,

> A.M. finds he has never done anything with the enclosed letter from Miss Daisy Bates. Would you look through it for him and see if you can get anything out of it for the C.N. – preferably told in her own words, so that it can be headed From Our Backwoods Correspondent?[98]

Bates's writing on Aboriginal peoples emphasised the widely held view that they were the dying remnants of a civilisation incapable of being assimilated into a white Australia.[99] She considered that her task was to investigate them anthropologically and, through welfare projects, help "make the passing easier".[100] Through infantilising Aboriginal peoples she constructed their culture and traditions as a form of tragic innocence; they knew no better because they lacked the capacity to reach the intellectual thinking of a civilised adult.[101]

Readers of *The Children's Newspaper* were introduced by Bates to the most controversial aspect of her writing, the claim that cannibalism, including infanticide, was a widespread practice. Mee was convinced that Bates was right, although he seems at first to have been reluctant to include it in the *CN*. In a letter to Derry, Mee asked him to respond to one from Bates by writing it up as an article for the *CN*, arguing that

> I have changed my mind about this cannibal business in Australia, and I hope you will agree with the course I have taken. It is more than time that this blot on the flag was removed, and publicity is the beginning of the end of it. . . . [T]he fact must be known that these cannibal mobs are forever roaming about in the heart of an empty continent.[102]

Mee wanted Derry to pursue accusations of Aboriginals cannibalising their children as a "shameful story" for which Australia ought to take responsibility, writing, "I don't care what they say – I blame them for it."[103]

Narratives of Aboriginal peoples practising barbaric, brutal and savage customs were designed to both horrify and fascinate the readership of *The Children's Newspaper* and to reinforce the symbolism of a race that civilisation could not progress, living a degenerate and corrupt existence. Mee repeated Bates's claims of widespread cannibalism: "The men are immoral, the women are slaves, and both, when the uncontrollable desire for revenge drives them, are cannibals."[104]

In 1938 Bates's book, *The Passing of the Aborigines*, repeated these and other claims. *The Children's Newspaper* was impressed, claiming that the book was "one of the most astonishing books written by a woman".[105] Mee wrote the introduction, in which, in a hymn of praise, he claimed,

> The race on the fringe of the continent has been there about a hundred years, and stands for Civilization; the race in the interior has been there no man knows how long, and stands for Barbarism. Between them a woman has lived in a little white tent for more than twenty years, watching over these people for the sake of the Flag, a woman alone, the solitary spectator of a vanishing race. She is Daisy Bates, one of the least known and one of the most romantic figures in the British Empire.[106]

Mee did not disappoint Bates, who wrote to a supporter, "Dear Arthur Mee will say many kindly things I know and his foreword will reach many readers of the CN and so help the book."[107]

Bates never witnessed any act of cannibalism but it was a short step from reading her accounts to generating the populist assumption that all Aboriginal peoples were, by definition, cannibals. Her claims generated controversy with those who disagreed and who saw cannibalism as ceremonial and rare.[108] Some anthropologists claimed that Bates's stories were lurid and embellished fictions for public consumption that had little evidence to substantiate them.[109] Contemporary reconstructions of her work have offered cautious re-appraisals. Richard Hall has argued that a capacity for self-delusion caused Bates to manipulate Aboriginal peoples to serve her own ends;[110] Ann Standish is unambiguous in condemning her as "a racist and a liar",[111] while Rowena Mohr has claimed that her representations of Aboriginal traditions were "outrageously inaccurate" and "sensationalist".[112] But for Mee and those reading *The Children's Newspaper*, Bates was a courageous and heroic voice of truth resonating from the deserts of Australia.

*

Mee's view of the Empire was wholly conventional and paternalistic and powerfully shaped by his upbringing, education and nonconformist conscience. His views were racist in the sense that an uneasy mixture of cultural and biological racism was an everyday feature of English society during the decades Mee was at his most popular. He was not alone in this, nor did he lead debate; rather he reacted to and followed an already well-established path that saw the world in hierarchical terms.

For Mee a compassionate desire to civilise the uncivilised defined the aims of Empire. He believed in and contributed to the view that the Empire was a humanitarian enterprise in cultural progress; unwillingly foisted upon the nation, it brought untold benefits to "backward" peoples. It was for Mee obtained and governed without force and with co-operation from indebted indigenous populations. The alternative view that the Empire was the product of brutal oppression and naked greed, calling into question the very idea of a benevolent Empire, never featured within Mee's system of beliefs. To have accepted such a view would have denied not only his faith but everything that he claimed to believe about England and the English.

Contemporary descriptions of the Empire as a religiously and morally inspired benevolent project are now looked upon as being perhaps naïve, partial or at worst simply not true. But during Mee's life it was quite obvious that humanitarian self-sacrificing individuals had left the motherland and travelled into the hostile lands of "backward" peoples with the aim of saving, educating and enlightening them. The fact that the Empire granted vast wealth, power and prestige to the English was for Mee an incidental outcome of their moral work in bringing liberty, justice and civilisation.

Mee saw no contradiction in his views of a compassionate Empire and his attitudes towards Aboriginal Australians. The evolutionary nature of his world was biologically and sociologically based upon a God-given natural order that could not be challenged. Faith was not to be questioned; the world evolved in tune with natural laws and while some indigenous populations grew and matured, others withered and died. What made Australia different from other parts of the Empire was the alleged primitive nature of Aboriginal society. While in good time and with support, indigenous peoples in other colonies might replicate the cultural and social hierarchies of the English, this would never happen in Australia.

7.

Society, Humanity and Order

At War with Poverty and Ignorance

Throughout his life, Mee remained wedded to the doctrines of liberalism taught him by his father. Like many nonconformists, his faith and politics were closely integrated and in any discussion of his social values and beliefs it is impossible to separate the two. He was committed to the view that the role of liberalism was to remove obstacles to individual liberties. In a 1922 editorial in *The Children's Newspaper* he wrote,

> The glory of a nation is individualism, the self-reliance and driving power of the individual citizen. . . . Happiness goes hand in hand with high endeavour. The man who measures his strength against difficulty is happy; the man who slouches through life on the arm of State help is discontented. Therefore we shall always proclaim here the gospel of *earnestness*. We believe in working hard and playing hard. We believe in effort, struggle, and growth.[1]

To this Mee added the belief that social institutions and political arrangements existed to promote evolutionary and progressive social reform. This blend of classical individualism and social amelioration saw him champion limited government, the lowering of taxes, voluntary approaches to education, free trade and state investment in social welfare projects such as health, housing and employment *only* for those unable to fend for themselves.[2]

Mee was always more committed to the politics of liberalism than to the politics of the Liberal Party, but he was thrilled at its landslide victory in the 1906 general election.[3] Following the election of 200 liberal nonconformists, the government embarked upon a social reform agenda.[4] This included the Education (Provision of Meals) Act (1906), introducing free school meals for the poorest children. The Probation of Offenders Act (1907) provided courts with a way of dealing with first-time offenders without sending them to prison. The Old-Age Pensions Act (1908) provided a non-contributory pension for persons over the age of seventy. In 1909, labour employment exchanges were established and the National Insurance Act (Part I) (1911) gave workers rights to sickness benefits and health insurance. Mee was elated, writing to Derry, "The big things that the Government does are simply heavenly, but the little things it does belong to another hemisphere. I could rave against it for weeks, but I could praise it for years."[5]

At the time Mee began his career, towns and cities across the nation were places of acute contrasts between rich and poor, where affluence and poverty were starkly discernible within patterns of geographical, social and cultural segregation. Local railways and the Underground in London enabled members of the more prosperous working and middle classes, like Mee, to migrate to newly built suburbs and further afield. Many who remained found themselves living in a brutalised material and social environment which gave birth to a new stereotype, the "slum", parts of cities where families lived in congested squalor in homes unfit for human habitation.

In 1898, no more than a year after he arrived in London, Mee conducted his own investigation into the London slums for *Temple Magazine*. This involved interviewing the colourful Arthur Osborne Jay, Vicar of Holy Trinity Church in Shoreditch. Jay had read Arthur Morrison's *Tales of Mean Streets*; the two became friends and after several visits to the area, Morrison wrote his relentlessly bleak *A Child of the Jago* (1896). The Old Nichol, the neighbourhood around Holy Trinity and the most renowned slum of its time, became "Jago" (from "where Jay goes") and Jay was used by Morrison as a template for the High Anglican vicar Father Sturt.

Reminiscent of the sensationalism of much slum literature, Mee's article opens with a description of the squalor and horrors of Shoreditch as a "sink of iniquity without parallel in the whole of England". It was an alien and barbarian environment riddled with poverty, crime and disease. Mee's narrative turns to the work of the argumentative Jay in providing a social club for the area's youth, his efforts to keep them from crime and his work in the community. As is typical of much of Mee's writing and his continual search for heroic role models, Jay is mythologised and transformed from the flawed and contradictory individual he was and his work provided with an almost mystical religious grandeur.[6]

Mee's reforming zeal was a genuine element of his character and this visit to the Old Nichol marked the beginning of lifelong attacks on poverty and ignorance.[7] For the next forty years he took every opportunity he could to campaign against destitution and slum housing and the social and moral problems they generated. Much of what Mee said and wrote is a reflection of Caleb Saleeby's eugenics-inspired assaults upon poverty, disease and physical degeneration, and the Christian socialism of John Clifford.

Writing for the Fabian Society, Clifford expressed outrage at the hardship and deprivation he saw in the streets of London before arguing that it was a Christian duty to eradicate poverty, vice and inequality.[8] Although from different generations, Mee and Clifford knew each other well and Clifford thought him a "dear friend".[9] In *The Children's Newspaper* three weeks after Clifford's death in 1923, Mee tellingly wrote,

> He was the rarest friend and the rarest fighter and the rarest man. Many times a note of affection and good cheer has come to our desk from John Clifford, and if his spirit is not in this paper nothing is in anything. . . . Men wonder how the world is to be saved. There is one way only; it is John Clifford's way.[10]

Mee's writing about social reform mirrors Clifford's ideals, the best example of which is *Who Giveth Us the Victory?* Written in 1917, it is a passionate polemic of anger and hope that the First World War would spiritually purify the nation. The book contains a searing indictment of politicians and systems he thought had abandoned millions to lives of misery and hopelessness. Mee endorsed the widely held opinion that the experience of war required new beginnings, social change and a mindset that abandoned what he considered to be the selfishness of pre-war society, writing that "*the callousness of our social system has inflicted on our own people a cruelty as ruthless as the German cruelty in Belgium*" (original italics).[11]

If, he asked, it was possible to allocate huge resources to fighting a war, could the nation not find the same resources for creating a new society in which the "horrors of peace" threatened to move beyond the horrors of war?[12] In an impassioned denunciation of church and government, who he claimed had closed their eyes and shut their ears, Mee wrote of two Englands: one worth fighting for, the other worth nothing.

> Two Englands there are, the heavenly England that leads the world in liberty and humanity and good government, the England of Alfred, Drake and Cromwell and Gladstone; and the appalling England at our doors, with a hundred thousand taprooms thriving on misery and ruin and disease, with landlords growing rich on slums, with children creeping hungrily to school – the England that would make a worthy ally of Dahomey. It is for the nobler England that our armies fight and die; the baser England is not fit to die for. [13]

Mee raged against what he called the slavery of industrial labour and the exploitation of children in factories and mines.[14] He offered the following approach for the creation of a new national sense of unity, purpose and direction:

1.   Let us declare war on the poverty from which our people perish. Under the Minimum Wage Act it lies already within the power of the Government, by a stroke of the pen, to declare a minimum wage for any trade.

2. Let us destroy the foul slums in which our people lose their joy of life, their strength of body, their peace of mind, and their eternal hope.
3. Let us appoint a Headquarters Staff to make war on disease and establish the conditions of a healthy people.
4. Let us make war on ignorance and put the means of knowledge, the chance of education, within the reach of all.
5. Let us organise the forces of the State to produce the greatest happiness for the greatest number, and utilise the natural and mental resources of the kingdom to build up our unparalleled powers.
6. Let us lay the foundations of patriotism and justice for all, abolishing injustices admitted by all, controlling the evils that sap the moral strength of youth, spreading equality of opportunity among the people.[15]

In statements that would have won applause from Fabians, Christian socialists and members of the labour movement, Mee suggested a redistribution of wealth from rich to poor.[16] Rhetorically he asked, "What has the war done for us all?", before suggesting that

It has shown us that at any time we could have abolished poverty and hunger, and distributed wealth with something like justice.

It has shown us that we could accomplish in a night things that we were afraid of for a generation – nationalisation of railways, conscription of excessive profits, the taxation of wealth, and the establishment of a living wage.

It has revealed the dangers at the heart of the State: the peril of private enterprises operating against the national interest; the powerful element of unpatriotism possessed with greed, selfishness, and indifference; and the unspeakable treachery of the liquor traffic.[17]

Mee's voice grew louder throughout the 1920s when, during times of profound economic crises, the tragedy of mass unemployment became a catastrophic feature of millions of lives, destroying communities and producing unprecedented levels of poverty and anguish. Between December 1920 and June 1921, unemployment doubled to two million and for the remainder of the decade stayed at an average of one million. In towns and cities, groups of shabbily dressed and gaunt-looking figures huddling on street corners became an iconic sight.

From the early 1920s until the outbreak of war in 1939, Mee mounted a campaign against the waste and heartbreak of unemployment. Editorials in *The Children's Newspaper* were sympathetic to the plight of those who could not find work; it was a national disgrace made worse by incompetent

The Shadow

There are two million breadwinners in the
United Kingdom with no work to do

❀

Figure 15.
"The Shadow" in The Children's
Newspaper, *21 September 1935*

governments unable to find a solution.[18] Mee wrote to Derry, "it is a scandal and a foolishness that civilization has no way of allowing men to work when they want to. . . . The whole situation is intolerable, and we have no right to call ourselves civilised."[19]

Mee's campaign against poverty raised an ethical question: what was of greater importance, Herbert Spencer's view that welfare interfered with natural selection and social evolution, or Clifford's opinion that Christians had a moral duty to help those disadvantaged by a system that marginalised them? These were points of view that Mee never fully reconciled and his support for the eradication of poverty and inequality was nuanced.

Committed to social justice and equity he may have been, but only for those who earned it. The genuinely unemployed were one thing, but he had no sympathy for those who, in receipt of unemployment benefit, avoided work. Writing from his sick bed at the Goring Hotel, he told Derry of his irritation at not being able to supervise work being done in landscaping the gardens at Eynsford Hill, before turning to the frustration that

> Scouring the country for men I managed to get one from the Labour Exchange. He had done no work for two years, and he crawls about by day, and gets drunk on my money at night, starving three little children, and sending his wife into the workhouse to have another. The State has been maintaining this gentleman out of your Income Tax for two years, and he longs for the day when I shall kick him down the hill so that he can get his money for nothing once again. Pray for a little sanity for a nation outraged and betrayed.[20]

The Children's Newspaper offered a familiar solution to what Mee believed was an epidemic of unemployed men deliberately abusing the system, paying unemployment benefit for work on community-based projects. While the unemployed received benefits, an editorial proposed that in return they *"may be called upon to **work it out**"* (original italics and bold).[21] A scheme was suggested whereby groups of unemployed men could work on local projects for which there was no funding. The advantages as *The Children's Newspaper* saw them were that they could earn their benefits, make a contribution to society and re-gain self-respect through work.[22] A front-page article in February 1939 claimed, "Our plan simply turns unemployed pay into wages; when the State gives a man a pound it gives it to him for doing something instead of doing nothing."[23]

There is no doubting the substance of Mee's anger, but as John Hammerton suggested, he let his enthusiasms and frustrations overwhelm the practical implications and consequences of his ideas.[24] The outcome was a tendency to suggest what he thought were obvious and uncomplicated solutions to what were demanding and intricate problems. Beyond the crusading spirit, which in Mee's case was largely about critique, he found it difficult to deal with the complexities of social problems in a practical way. He also found it problematic to come to grips with the idea that significant parts of society were moving from individualist to collectivist ways of thinking and that, having won a war, millions were now looking for a very different future.

"This Civil War"

The First World War had interrupted a pattern of widespread social unrest that between 1909 and 1912 saw the nation engulfed by industrial action. After the war, as thousands returned from the battlefields and the nation held its breath, unsure what was to follow, turmoil re-appeared in the form of widespread strikes. A 1919 police strike in London and Liverpool during which nearly 50 per cent of the force withdrew their labour sent shock waves through the nation. Troops with machine guns and tanks patrolled parts of Liverpool, warships sailed up the River Mersey, the city was placed under military control and the army patrolled the streets. Bayonet and baton charges brought to a swift end demonstrations by what *The Daily Mirror* described as thieves, looters and rioters.[25]

On Friday 31 January 1919 pitched battles broke out in the centre of Glasgow between strikers and the police. In what became known as the "Battle of George Square", police baton charges were met with a hail of bottles and stones. Newspapers reported that the strike was fermented by anarchists intent on promoting class warfare.[26] Disturbances were placed at the door of Bolshevik agents accused of funding "revolutionary rumblings" designed to overthrow the government.[27] The perception of change was palpable.

It was fed by the fear that, like Russia two years earlier with its 1917 Bolshevik Revolution, England faced the possibility of a rebellion that would sweep away democracy. In his autobiography, the socialist journalist Kingsley Martin wrote, "The only time in my life when revolution in Britain seemed likely was in 1919."[28] Calls for patriotic dogma to be replaced by the "language of class"[29] gathered pace and the growth of labour politics amongst what Lloyd George called "a great inflammable industrial population"[30] promised the potential of changes that would be wide, deep and inevitable.

Mee's reaction to this mayhem was one of anger and alarm. Schooled in the history of duty, self-sacrifice and service, he thought that those who went on strike ignored the obligations they owed England and committed acts of shameful humiliation.[31] His commitment to freedoms and liberties did not extend to a point where individual rights eclipsed those of the wider community. His liberalism was based upon the premise that the individual and society ought never to be in competition and that people ought to recognise that their interests were not served by opposing community expectations.

The role of individuals was to work for the benefit of all and to abandon sectional interests in pursuit of national unity. It was for Mee the height of selfishness for anybody to exercise their rights in ways that impacted adversely upon others and upon the dignity and integrity of the nation. Workers had a duty to maintain England's reputation and, in his view, "no workers are more worthy in any nation than those who quietly and steadily maintain the even tenor of its ways".[32]

What Mee meant was that those with faith and patience in evolutionary gradualism should never disrupt society in pursuit of their own interests and should simply accept that in time life would incrementally get better. During the 1920s and 1930s, this was not a consideration for many whose faith in progress, so badly damaged by war, was political, not providential. It is easy to see why looking out from his world Mee could interpret the politics of class not as attempts to widen equality, but as attacks on England. It was an argument that cut no ice with those millions who believed they had put the nation first and were now seeking something in return.

Viewing social and industrial disruptions as he did from a position of security, wealth and influence, Mee's commitment to freedom and justice did not extend to those who went on strike. *The Children's Newspaper* saw the national rail strike of 1919 as a danger every bit as serious as the First World War. Had the strike continued, it would have been "little short of revolution" as workers "victimised a friendly nation".[33] While sympathetic to the rail workers no matter the circumstances, Mee thought strikes unlawful and morally dishonest attempts to hold the nation to ransom and he condemned them utterly.[34]

With crippling unemployment, economic crises and social unrest dangerously significant problems, Mee thought it timely to remind his readers that if workers sought to settle disputes outside the "rules of the game", they became "a traitor to us, a traitor to the rest of the team".[35] What *The Children's Newspaper* called "political communism" based upon the fighting of a "class war" was what Mee feared most. Agitation for social

Figure 16.
"John Rides the Sure Horse"
in The Children's Newspaper, *15 November 1919*

reform had to be lawful – it was never acceptable to force change through coercion.[36] At the prospect of a miner's strike in September 1920, a *CN* article suggested that if a miner wanted more money he should "work a little harder, as hard as he did before the war".[37]

As the politics of the labour movement gathered momentum, the political landscape changed. The December 1923 General Election saw the Liberal Party and James Ramsay Macdonald's Labour Party poll enough votes to produce a hung parliament, and Macdonald become the nation's first Labour Prime Minister. His administration, which shocked and disturbed Conservatives to the core, was short-lived. For much of the populist press, Macdonald's government was radically socialist and impregnated with agitators, and it was relentlessly attacked for its allegedly close connections with Russia.

On 25 October 1924, *The Daily Mail* claimed that Macdonald's government was in the pay of communists and was planning to terrorise the people, commit treason and fight a class war. Macdonald was labelled a communist puppet and the paper's readers urged to vote Conservative.[38] On election day, 29 October 1924, the front page of *The Daily Mirror* urged readers to "Vote British, Not 'Bolshie'".

With Mee's Liberal Party in terminal decline, the general election was an unmitigated disaster. The campaign was an amateurish shambles and, with 158 seats before the election, the party was reduced to 40 after it. The Labour Party lost 40 seats while the Conservatives, under Stanley Baldwin, gained 149 and a landslide victory. Mee thought the Labour-led government incompetent and infiltrated with communists; he was happy to see the back of it, writing to Derry in November 1924 four days after the election,

> I say nothing except that I abandoned Ramsey after his Glasgow speech and have utterly severed myself from any shred of Sympathy with a party that has proven the truth of Winston's sense that they were not fit to govern. They are fit for Standard Five. They are ready to sacrifice the country for a party any day.[39]

An article in *The Children's Newspaper* endorsed its editor's view, welcoming the defeat of a Labour Party it suggested was politically subservient to Russia:

> One thing there is no doubt about that the country has sent back to power, deliberately, an overwhelming majority against the wild men who would introduce the Russian system here, and it is hoped that we may now look forward to a period of security and freedom from anxiety under a Government so firmly established.[40]

Changing the government was one thing but changing the national mood was another, and Mee was far from confident that Balfour's Conservatives could check the social unrest he thought had produced such a menacing climate.[41] The spectre of communism, anarchy and revolution remained in his thoughts.[42] On 12 August 1925 he wrote to Derry,

> Everybody wants to make the world a better place. The wise man, the extremist, the fool, will all declare that this is their intention. The difficulty is that some of them want to do it slowly and surely and steadily, while preserving what is good and educating people for better things; while others believe they have a dramatic way of building up millenniums quickly. . . . The only safe way of doing things is Evolution not Revolution.[43]

LABOUR WILL STAND BY THE FLAG

The greatest patriot is the man who works, and the workers have decided to stand by the flag. Labour has rejected the idea of a "Direct Action" strike against the State ; it will pursue its aims towards a nobler life by worthier means.

Figure 17.
"Labour Will Stand by the Flag"
in The Children's Newspaper, *30 August 1919*

His anxieties were heightened when in the spring of 1926 the miners' union stated their intention to strike in defence of better wages and conditions. The response of the mine-owners was to lock them out of the workplace. With neither side prepared to give ground, the dispute escalated into a general strike and between 4 and 13 May, miners, together with workers in transport and other industries, withdrew their labour, bringing parts of the nation to a standstill.

The reaction to the strike was one of fear, indignation and anger. Newspapers that managed to keep publishing condemned it, with *The*

Daily Mail's readers being told it was a "foul blow", an illegal revolutionary act co-ordinated by extremists intent on wreaking havoc and suffering on an innocent public – it had to be smashed.[44] *The Manchester Guardian* declared the strike indefensible; there could be no bargaining with the strikers and the TUC and the government were in "A Fight to a Finish".[45] The symbolism of warfare, battle, hostilities, struggles and crusades was instilled in the public consciousness by a media who rallied their readers with a call to arms. Reports of troops on the march, pleas for calm, the issuing of hourly bulletins on the BBC and packed crowds in the streets searching for news added to a perception of crisis.[46] But life went on and, juxtaposed against reports of what was professed by some to be impending revolution, readers of *The Daily Express* were told that the Australian cricket team had scored 532 for 8 against Essex with Woodfall scoring 201 not out.[47]

Mee was outraged by the strike; the idea that it could prevent him and others from going about their daily business greatly offended him. It impacted upon his personal liberties, it upset the organised balance of his life and work and he saw it as an illegitimate challenge to individual freedoms. Like many liberal and conservative commentators, Mee pushed the claims of the strikers into the background and his nonconformist conscience had little to say about their plight. What was at stake now was not the pay, conditions and dignity of workers but the very survival of English democracy.

On 7 May, four days into the strike, Mee vented his anger in a long handwritten letter to Derry that roundly condemned the strikers and their leaders:

> Was ever such a set of Brainless Idiots as the controllers of the Trade Union Movement that you and I have all our lives supported? England is what she is to me but I would rather she should perish off the earth than that she should give one inch to those three million Tsars. I pray every hour that these men are beaten to their knees and shown no mercy. If they were fit to rule a hen roost they would have seen that such a challenge to the very foundations of liberty must fail.

The miners came in for particular criticism:

> The miners are fighting against the eternal law that if a man shall not work neither shall he eat (every miner brings up 100 tons a year less than his father) but even the miners, lazy as they are, might have won a bad case by themselves. But who with the brain of a tadpole could imagine this sort of thing to succeed.[48]

Figure 18.
"A Better Way Than Striking"
in The Children's Newspaper, *18 September 1920*

With road and rail transport disrupted, all work in his office stopped and publication of *The Children's Newspaper* was halted for a week when the issue intended for 15 May could not be prepared. Mee saw the strike as a form of personal betrayal whereby the support of nonconformists for social reform had been abused. He asked Derry, "have a John Derry or Arthur Mee put Trade Unionism above the law and sown the seeds of this? Have we been right or wrong to follow in the wake of that movement which gave Power <u>before</u> Education?"[49]

Seen as absurdly overblown now, but at the time constituting a genuinely perceived threat, the strike was interpreted by most as a prelude to a revolutionary coup designed to devastate the nation and destroy its freedoms, and Mee was no exception. The role of Baldwin's government was to unambiguously crush it:

I rejoice that the fight is on. . . . Baldwin saw that the challenge had come and he acted like a man. He would have been a worm to do otherwise. Those idiots fighting for freedom are to tell you what you shall write, what you shall say, what you shall think. Even in Russia under the Tsars Tolstoy could write what he liked, but under our Tsars there is no room for free opinion. Must we be ruled by a class which is ruled by a Committee as in the days of the doges of Venice. We are in sight of the chamber again, and the dungeons.[50]

He saw no reason why strikers should receive benefits or why those who wanted to work could not get compensation from their unions:

Two things occur to me: don't you think the dole should stop now? Why pay a million men to be idle? Why not give them work instead? and also there is a great chance for another Osborne Test Case.[51] These unions are often bound by rules to ballot their men before striking, and more of them do so. Should not some men sue the union for his wages of which he has been robbed in breach of the rules?[52]

The thought that the strike might succeed was unthinkable, and there was only one possible outcome:

I expect the men to be mercilessly beaten, the decent half to go back in a week as a feeling of shame creeps over them, and there is a great smash up of Labour and a grand culling of leaders, and I predict that in three weeks it will be over and England will own its soil again and feel that a terrible surgical operation has given it a new lease of life and a new sense of its own freedom. I can hardly endure the thought of the infamy of it all, the impudence of these ignorant fools playing with fire in God's England; but I refuse to believe that England can give way, or that she can go down. If Trotskyism could not crush her, if Drink has not destroyed her, if she has survived the bitterness and hardship of these ten years, she will survive this civil war.[53]

Life in the sheltered security of Mee's hilltop continued almost undisturbed. With the post not being delivered, the family were using the telephone more than he wanted and he was finding it difficult to get a haircut! The biggest inconvenience was the absence of newspapers and not being able to get hold of the government propaganda newspaper *The British Gazette*.[54] But there was always the "wireless" to fall back upon, something Mee thought a "providential blessing, a wonderful example of the working of Evolution".[55] His letter to Derry ends with a re-statement of a core aspect of his values:

[R]emember that it is liberty which is challenged; that it *is* the most precious possession in the world that is at stake and that whatever else on Earth may happen this conspiracy must fail. Even if I believed in the object of it I should wish it to fail, for I would rather not live at all than live at the bidding of the T.U.C. or of <u>any</u> class whatsoever.[56]

Given the industrial unrest of previous years, the government had experience of managing strikes and they reacted ruthlessly.[57] It was never total, with patchy impact, and while some Labour politicians were in support, it was always going to fail.[58] It alienated popular opinion and the exaggerated moral panic of a Bolshevik conspiracy created an environment in which perception was manufactured into truth. While the miners continued to strike for a further six months, outside their ranks too few believed that a national strike was an appropriate or justifiable way of pursuing their cause.

After the strike, commentators like Mee used the defeat of the strikers to promote the idea that the nation had avoided revolution by forcefully rejecting the politics of class. On 13 May *The Financial Times* claimed that "freedom from tyranny has been won for those countless thousands of working citizens who were never in the slightest degree favourably inclined to the pernicious principle of the sympathetic strike".[59] *The Illustrated London News* ran a series of pictorial essays focussing upon how volunteers had kept the country running.[60] *The Daily Mail*, which had kept up its vitriolic "civil war" rhetoric throughout, declared "Revolution Routed", claiming that the spirit of a proud English people had seen off "reckless extremists".[61] In a front-page editorial in *The Children's Newspaper*, Mee interpreted the end of the strike as a victory for the nation:

> If there is one thing that has been made clear in these wonderful nine days it has been the solid loyalty of that great mass of people who are the backbone of our nation. There cannot be a Class War in England; the marvellous way in which all classes rallied to the Government is everlasting proof of that.[62]

While confident enough to write privately to Derry that "lazy miners" and others who had joined the strike should be "mercilessly beaten" and union leaders "shown no mercy", publicly Mee demonstrated a more conciliatory tone:

> In the midst of it all the miners and their claims to justice were forgotten; it was one of the tragedies of this act of folly that this magnificent body of men, entitled to all the humanity and respect that we could give them, were made use of to help on a conspiracy with which they had no natural sympathy. All good people hope that, in spite of what has happened, the Government will see that ample justice is done to the miners.[63]

Predictably Mee saw public reaction to the strike as evidence of national character, and *The Children's Newspaper* carried headlines such as "Carry On", and "Patience of a Much Tried People", claiming,

The British temperament is always a good deal maligned. We are called stolid, heavy, and so on. But when we are up against it we know how to behave. Millions of people have had their daily lives disorganised, have had to put up with extraordinary inconveniences, and have laughed about it and gone on. . . . There has never been anything like it for bringing out the good humour and kindliness that are part of the rock of British character.[64]

Mee saw the strike as being peculiarly English, writing, "In no other country could so great a strike have been maintained for nine days with so little disorder."[65] The private Mee saw it as an irresponsible, un-English attack on stability and order, an affront to the national character, a strike led by foolish and ignorant people who had deceived naïve and gullible workers into believing that they could improve their lives. For him, liberties and freedoms had been restored, what was right had prevailed and the politics of class had been routed. The natural order of things had been restored.

The Angel in the House

Mee spent his life surrounded by women he relied upon: those who managed his home and life and those who managed his work. His relationships with them were never based upon an authoritarian or puritanical misogyny; had he been accused of sexism the concept would have meant nothing to him. But he would have been horrified to have been charged with treating women oppressively. He cannot be blamed for the fact that he grew up within a patriarchal society in which education, custom and the law provided males with authority over females, husbands over wives, brothers over sisters, and parents over children, in the home and in the workplace.

Mee's world was far from democratic. Many of the thousands of young men who had died in France and Belgium did so never having been allowed to vote. No female could vote until the 1918 Representation of the People Act gave women over thirty the right, provided they or their husband met a property qualification. In the 1918 general election at age forty, Amy Mee was able to vote for the first time because of her husband's property ownership, but about 22 per cent of women aged thirty and above were excluded.

The other women in Mee's life could not vote until 1928 when equal franchise became law, an event that went largely unnoticed by *The Children's Newspaper*. Marjorie Mee was twenty-eight and Lena Fratson forty-six before either of them could vote, which they did in the May 1929 general election. Prior to 1928, any female servant living and working for the Mees was denied the vote. Two of Mee's closest female professional associates could not vote until 1929, by which time the unmarried Margaret Lillie was fifty while Stella Hancock was twenty-nine.

Opponents of female suffrage thought women had no need for a parliamentary vote. The argument was that they already voted in local council elections in districts that had responsibility for health and education issues. These were spheres in which it was believed a women, tied to notions of being a homemaker and a mother, could perform their duties in a non-political way.[66] From this viewpoint the world was gendered and in their public and private relationships, men and women occupied a God-given place not to be contested.[67]

Mee's attitudes towards women were entirely Victorian.[68] He never fully came to terms with why women, who he thought were lynchpins of domesticity and family life, would want to take on responsibilities such as voting and earning a wage. There is nothing to suggest that he took the suffragette movement seriously; he had little to say about it apart from poking fun at how during Derry's 1910 election campaign Rose Derry might have a strenuous time "when her husband spends his days keeping off suffragettes".[69] Mee thought women influential but not in political terms; their power rested upon a moral authority he thought more significant than casting a vote.[70] Writing to a female audience, he suggested that

> It is a common mistake to measure our power in the nation by our vote, and to imagine, therefore, that we have no power as long as we have no vote. The truth is that it is the moral force behind the vote that the Statesman fears or craves.[71]

Mee never directly opposed female suffrage, but he seems to have been ambivalent about it, suggesting that if women active in seeking the vote gave as much energy to pursuing issues where their moral voice could be heard, they would make a very substantial contribution to shaping social opinion.[72] Like Caleb Saleeby, he believed that women had more significant things to do than enter the world of politics and business, telling a female audience,

> Remember that your greatest pride is to be womanly, and not manly, and, whatever work you may do, scorn to let it be said that you, with all the glory of womanhood about you, were so blind to it that you slipped from your throne to the lower level of a man.[73]

Mee venerated women; they were idealised and transformed into ethereal beings who were the epitomes of graciousness. Women were chaste, selfless and unsullied by the material world, and expected to remain so. They occupied a pre-eminent position as custodians of a civilised world; it was to them that society looked for stability, strength and resourcefulness and for the moral guardianship of the national conscience.[74]

Sex and sexuality were secrets that everybody knew about but nobody ever mentioned. Mee encouraged his female readers to remain feminine and completely asexual. His nonconformist dislike of pretension and posturing is found in his encouragement that they avoid all signs of sexuality. He felt women should be reserved and modest and should reject vulgarity, vanity and ostentatious fashion.[75] In their dress, females were to demonstrate "neatness", "good taste" and "maidenly ways". Make-up was to be shunned; "paint and powder", as Mee called it, was said to hide the natural complexion of a woman and was to be avoided as poison was.[76]

On marriage Mee reflected the eugenic theorising of Caleb Saleeby, Mary Scharlieb, Elizabeth Sloan Chesser and Henry Havelock Ellis. In pursuit of what he called "eugenic feminism", Saleeby claimed that the role of women was critical because the future of the English race depended upon their ability to reproduce.[77] Motherhood was a natural state and young females should be taught that it was an ideal to which they should aspire.[78]

Mee's adoration of women also focussed upon their role in reproducing the race. He wanted young female readers to seek what he claimed was the ideal of marital domesticity, and explicitly approved eugenic ideas of motherhood and family. In *Letters to Girls*, readers were advised that a career, study or leisure pursuits should not take the place of their principle role, which was to assume their "natural life" as homemakers.[79] Motherhood was the highest goal to which a female could aspire, and managing a home was a patriotic duty equal to anything that a man might do.[80] Having created a home, nothing they could do in life would match the respect and admiration they would receive.[81]

Mee had a Victorian attitude towards maintaining a distinction between the world of males and that of females, between a world of work and a world of domesticity. In 1924 he was telling female readers that, when married, they could expect to live a life often separated from their husband. They would each prosper within a loving and caring relationship and would cultivate rich but parallel ways of living.[82]

In managing a home, a wife's function was to recognise the needs of her husband and respond to them. She was to provide encouragement, support and understanding, take an interest in his work and what he valued and encourage him to develop his social life.[83] The home was to be a sanctuary designed to protect him from trivia and the temptations of gambling and drink; Mee wrote,

> You will take great care that you know the physical health of the man you choose to marry; you will not be afraid, at all costs, to assure yourself on this, remembering how terrible the price of carelessness may be; you will be careful of his moral health, so grave a thing to you; and you will be not less careful to see that your minds have that sympathy between them without which no home-life can bring you lasting happiness.[84]

Mee's attitudes towards the economic liberation of women seem to have been somewhat blasé. In a letter to Derry dated 22 May 1922, Stella Hancock wrote, "A.M. thinks (with a broad grin at me) that we ought to have a column on the strides women are making nowadays!"[85] Mee's role models, "shining examples" for female emancipation, as Stella Hancock wrote mockingly, were a tennis player and a golfer. John Derry's article under the headline "Two Girls Doing Things" appeared on page four of the 10 June 1922 issue of *The Children's Newspaper*. On page seven, under the headline "Girls Doing Great Things", are photographs of Kitty McKane, "the brilliant young tennis player", and Joyce Wethered, a twenty-year-old who had won the Women's Golf Championship at Sandwich.[86]

But while Mee wrote about the roles of homemaker and motherhood as the natural place for females, later in life, when it came to people close to him, he had a more flexible attitude towards women working after marriage. The suffragette movement had little tangible impact upon the division of labour. Despite the introduction of the Sex Disqualification (Removal) Act (1919), there remained significant discrimination against women continuing to work after marriage. Females could either be single women pursuing a career or married women running a home – they could rarely be both. During periods of socio-economic crisis when mass unemployment was a critical social issue, married women were frequently denied employment.

In September 1932, aged thirty-one, Stella Hancock married a solicitor, James Hawkins Palwyn. Mee was complicit in a deception on her behalf to prevent her having to make the choice between marriage and a career. Stella wrote to Derry that she was planning a honeymoon sailing down the Danube, but cautioned,

> . . . don't you let the office know about it or I shall get the sack. A.M. alone knows, and he says I must not tell the Editor. So you will remember, won't you, but I wanted you to know. I won't even tell you my married name, so that there will be no fear of you addressing letters to the wrong woman at John Carpenter House. I and my husband-to-be have spent all our spare time in the last seven years together, and it is very lovely that we can at last be married. But I want to keep on this work, and he is very keen that I should, and neither of us mind deceiving the Amalgamated Press in a good cause, so hush! sh! Only please whisper it to Mrs. Derry.[87]

Stella continued to work and to use her maiden name.

Society at Home

Mee's home life was organised around his needs and his career; it would never have worked in any other way. His family life was conventionally patriarchal but removed from the stereotypical portrayal of the dictatorial male schooled in the gender politics of Victorian and Edwardian England.

This is not to say that the subordination of females by males was a fiction; it was clearly not. But there were differing views on the role of women within society in addition to those of suffragettes and anti-suffragettes.[88]

It would be simplistic to assume, even given the nature of a society in which, for many females, oppression was shockingly real, that the women in Mee's home saw themselves as subject to an authoritarian domination. Life at Uplands and Eynsford Hill was never lacking in laughter; friends and family visited, parties took place and holidays were a regular occurrence. Mee was a loving husband and doting father, who, when he died, was greatly missed.[89]

What emerges through his letters and what he chooses to share with readers reveals a man defined by work, home and family. Where they appear in moments of celebration, happiness and sadness, Mee's relationship with his family is always loving, generous and supportive. He adored his daughter, writing from Capri to "My Dear Sweetheart" and signing the letter "Your Loving Daddie". On Marjorie Mee's twelfth birthday, he wrote to Derry of his delight because "my youngest daughter is 12 today, my first wife is younger than ever, my only Dad is up here for a week, and . . . the world goes well".[90]

An inescapable obstacle when writing a biography is that some of the actors contributing to the story will be mute, evidence of their lives scarce and their stories untold. Living almost entirely within a world of domesticity, the women in Mee's family emerge only fleetingly. We learn something of Amy Mee, Lena Fratson and Marjorie Mee from Mee's letters to Derry; they are there in the background, but they have little in the way of a voice.[91] Amy Mee managed the home, advertised for cooks and house maids,[92] made cakes and darned socks, while Lena Fratson performed her duties as Mee's home secretary.[93]

Marjorie Mee kept chickens, or at least had a hen that laid rather large eggs;[94] she went to school – we are not told where, but home tuition would have fitted her father's status – and rode her pony, Jack. Marjorie had a keen interest in the Guides movement and in the mid-1920s was instrumental in forming the Eynsford and Farningham troop. She remained captain of the troop until just before the war, organising local events and camps at places like the Isle of Sheppey. By the standards of the day, Marjorie led a privileged life. She was also the epitome of a modern women; independent and determined, she knew her own mind. She enjoyed the countryside and would tour the local lanes and villages on a Scott motorcycle with a sidecar. Later she drove around in an MG sports car bought for her by her father.[95]

Many middle-class women engaged in voluntary and philanthropic activities in local communities. There is some evidence that Amy and Lena engaged in such activities, including their involvement in helping Marjorie organise a village bazaar to raise money for the local Guides.

Figure 19.
Marjorie Mee in her Guide uniform and Arthur Mee sitting in the
garden at Eynsford Hill with the Darenth Valley behind them

Mee was anxious for it to be a success; "they have worked like Billy-Oh," he wrote.[96] In contrast to the domesticated nature of female life, Mee had his memberships of the Whitefriars Dining Club[97] and the Reform Club and his frequent stays at the Goring Hotel.

Apart from the death of Harry Mee, some details of how John Derry helped Wilfred Mee in his career as a journalist,[98] and passing references to Lois, we learn nothing of Mee's other siblings. His brothers and sisters remained in Nottingham, marrying, raising families and working in a variety of occupations, some of them with considerable success. But although he had left Nottingham and succeeded beyond that of any other family member, Mee regularly returned to give talks to various groups and to visit family, who also visited Uplands and Eynsford Hill.[99]

In the letters Mee wrote to Derry, there is no mention of his mother Mary, who died at Woodborough Road on 25 March 1919 aged sixty-six, but we do know something of Henry Mee's death. He died on 12 July 1930 aged seventy-nine and three weeks later Mee wrote to Derry about that day:

He got up on the Saturday morning as usual, moving about. In the afternoon he saw an old friend and sat down to write. This is what he wrote to my brother who looked after things down there and was to see him on the Monday.

He then copied out his father's letter, in which Henry sensed that his life was drawing to a close:

If I shall go home before I see you . . . my kindest love to everybody. I want you to take me to 237, Woodborough Road to have a service with chapel if convenient. You will find all papers about the grave in the box. I should like Hobson's to do the undertaking if possible, but use your own judgment . . . and I hope to be on the lookout for you all in God's good time. So all of you get ready for that happier and lovelier life of which I entertain not the slightest doubt. I cannot thank you all enough. Please take it for granted. Goodbye to you all, and to all my friends with whom I have travelled a very happy journey through this life. Til we meet in the morning, Dad.

Mee continued,

Then he felt sick and Lois' husband [Claude] took him to a favourite seat across the room and they sat for an hour. Claude took his hand and suddenly he fell asleep. . . .[100]

His father's death was followed four months later by that of his elder sister Annie, who, after a long illness, died in Nottingham on 12 November 1930 aged fifty-seven. Annie Mee had experienced bouts of serious illness for a number of years, including a brain tumour causing some paralysis that in May 1926 had seen her close to death, before, having drifted into a week-long coma, she recovered.[101] The funeral service was at Woodborough Road Baptist Chapel and she was buried, like other members of the Mee family, in the General Cemetery in Nottingham.[102] Both deaths provided Mee with a reminder of his mortality and he wrote to Derry, "I have never felt so much of late that Time has us all in its keeping and that we must bow to its decree."[103]

*

Mee's view of society was one of contradictions. On one hand was his anger at the social conditions that blighted the lives of millions and his commitment to campaigning against hardship, disease and ignorance. But conscience took him only so far; while condemning poverty and destitution, criticising corrupt politicians and self-interested business people, he also attacked those who went on strike to improve their pay and working conditions.

His view of society was functional; he saw it as a system of inter-dependent parts, each contributing to its smooth running. Institutions such as the family, parliamentary democracy, economic capitalism and the education system were all parts of that system. Consequently society could only function when based upon the acceptance of shared norms and values that provided stability, cohesion and equilibrium. This included the institution of marriage, in which males and females had their quite distinctive roles.

Mee accepted that societies changed but felt that people had to understand that the process was gradual, evolutionary and the product of his God's intervention in the world. His social opinions were sometimes a confusing mixture of liberal and conservative ideologies, combining social justice, human rights, compassion and equality of opportunity with duty, self-sacrifice, patriotism, loyalty, tradition and personal responsibility.

His advice was always to do your best, to have faith in God and in England, to work hard and to not rely upon the State to help you out. People needed to demonstrate character and patience and to know, when times were difficult, that in the goodness of time all would be well and problems would work themselves out. What you did not do was to hasten the natural process of evolutionary social change and you certainly did not attempt to rush this through the use of industrial or political power. What Mee failed to see or perhaps could not conceive of was that for many, optimism, patience and acceptance of the rightness of providential change in a world that would gradually get better were principles that meant nothing to them.

8.

The Challenge of the Modern

Old and New England

Post-war society faced the challenge of coming to terms with what T.S. Eliot in *The Wasteland* (1922) called "a heap of broken images", whereby venerated icons, touchstones of value and things that compelled consent became disputed. Those who fought in the unimaginable slaughter of the First World War and the millions it affected were changed forever. There was no village, town or city that was not haunted by the memories of those who had left and never returned. Within a context of grief, anger and uncertainty, it seemed impossible that society would not journey towards a very different world. For Samuel Hynes, the war "changed reality".[1]

While many elite pre-war attitudes and social conventions did not perish in the mud of France and Belgium, a less deferential society began to emerge based upon a heightened class consciousness, growth in trade union membership, a widening of the franchise and, for some, what seemed the promise of communism and fascism. For many this narrative of change presented a clear sense of purpose and direction; for those seeking continuity with the past, it was a dangerous cul-de-sac into disaster.

Where did Mee fit into a post-war society alive to the inevitability of change? Aged forty-three when the war ended, he wholeheartedly endorsed some features of the modern, including the safety razor, book tokens, the refrigerator, smokeless coal, escalators, heated corridor trains, restaurant cars and the National Trust.[2] Later he was to become fascinated by the science of television, the "wonder of wonders" that saw him make a three-minute appearance on camera during a visit to the BBC studios.[3] But he was never at any time at ease with the impact of change; even the new technologies that excited him so much caused him to ask whether society was becoming too dependent upon them. Was travelling by car as enjoyable as a walk in the hills? The record player was an excellent idea but not if it stopped people learning how to play a musical instrument, and a typewriter was no substitute for good handwriting – though Mee's handwriting could be awful.

Material and aesthetic change in post-war England spawned differing forms of public and private morality. This was a problem for Mee, and newly emerging cultural ideas and the social behaviours they produced caused him enormous unease. Modernity is not always synonymous with progress, and Mee certainly did not think so. His reaction to several aspects of post-war cultural and social change produced in him what has been called a "resurgent Victorianism".[4] This took the form of efforts to impose what he thought to be a civilising and moralising mission upon society as a counterbalance to changes he felt threatening.

For Mee this was more than a manifestation of a romanticised nostalgia, although it was certainly that; it had the purpose of repairing the national psyche. He found it difficult to come to terms with the fact that after the trauma of war society did not immediately focus upon creating a world free from inequality, poverty, ignorance and violence. Instead it seemed that at the very time they needed social and moral stability, people were radically transforming their lives in different directions as they adapted to the pleasures of new desires, technologies, entertainments, material goods and social relationships.

Change is inevitably met with a mixture of anticipation and hope, fear and despair, and Mee's reaction was no different. His concern was how to resolve tensions between the idea of an England rooted in Victorian and Edwardian cultural ideals and social standards and the relentless onset of the modern. The extent, pace and brashness of cultural and social change disturbed him, as did the assumption that because something was new it was an improvement. He preferred to cling to traditional ideals and the known as security against the turmoil that he felt making "wrong" choices could produce.[5]

Mee saw the challenge of the years after the First World War as one of managing the transformation of England in which adaptation and continuity were key issues. The dilemma was how to defend "Old England" from "the risk of being spoiled or defaced".[6] The question he asked was how could society manage social change, scientific innovation and new technologies without damaging his England of time-honoured principles, values and morals? He found this difficult to resolve as throughout the 1920s and 1930s he confronted and condemned populist cultural and social tastes he believed weakened the beliefs that had made him and England. On the editorial page of *The Children's Newspaper* he set out his thoughts on modernity:

> The idea of the people called modernists is to dismiss harmony and melody from music, and truth and beauty from painting and sculpture, while a pretentious school of poets writes high-sounding rubbish such as a child turns out in reels.[7]

Beneath the surface of Mee's enthusiasm for traditional art, literature and music as sources of spiritual and emotional well-being ran a powerful thread of conservative disapproval for the consumerisation of culture. He viewed rampant, irresistible and popular commercial materialism as anti-aesthetic attacks upon English cultural predilections and sensibilities. When in 1923 D.H. Lawrence wrote, "All this Americanising and mechanising has been for the purpose of overthrowing the past,"[8] he could have been speaking for Mee. Mee viewed the widespread enjoyment of Americanised popular culture as a conflict between an idealised image of cultural refinement set against vulgarity and artistic inferiority.[9] What millions were enjoying, but what Mee saw as declining standards in literature, music, cinema and language together with the urbanisation of the natural landscape, threatened to replace his England with something grossly inferior, and so he attacked it mercilessly.

The "Kinema"

By 1910 the cinema had emerged from its position as a sideshow at the fairground and music hall or a touring exhibition to become the nation's most popular form of entertainment. By 1917 there were 4,500 cinemas in the country, and going to the "kinema", as Mee always called it, was an established part of the leisure habits of millions. While other forms of recreation appealed to particular sections of the community, the cinema cut across all classes, boundaries and tastes.[10] It appealed to those seeking to close the gap between the reality of their lives and their aspirations. The regulated and monotonous nature of the working day and the tedium of many people's lives found a release in the escapist diversions of romance, comedy, crime and adventure films which created a world of imagination, excitement and dreams.

As a hugely important cultural phenomenon, cinema's significant place in people's lives spawned competing views on its role. There were those who thought that the cinema had enormous educational potential as an innovative learning medium.[11] Others accused it of being abused by unscrupulous film-makers and cinema owners who were morally corrupting a generation of young people.[12]

Mee was fascinated by the science and technology of moving and talking pictures; he thought the cinema extraordinary and one of humankind's most significant inventions. He was greatly enthused by its educational potential; it had grabbed the attention of children and juveniles and he was delighted that they demonstrated such interest in it. For Mee the cinema was a thrilling medium through which the excitement and wonder of the world could be bought to millions across the globe. This optimism was entirely misplaced; from its earliest days the cinema was driven by commercial interests and private profit. Any suggestion that its principal role could be educational swiftly disappeared to the margins of public concern as it matured into audience-driven mass entertainment dominated by American-produced films.[13]

There is no evidence that Mee ever set foot inside a cinema but there was no shortage of outraged opinion to help him make up his mind about whether it was a force for good or bad. An unnamed correspondent in *The Times* lambasted it for being "beneath and unworthy of any sane or intelligent person".[14] The novelist Ella Hepworth Dixon labelled American films trashy, stupid and trivial, accusing them of dulling the minds of the young.[15] *The Manchester Guardian* called much of what was shown at the cinema "abominably vulgar trash".[16] *The Daily Express* carried the Rev. Gordon McLeod's attack on cinema, in which he accused it of being "the very smoke of hell, screening God, and screening purity from the hearts and minds of our young people".[17]

After a decade of cinematic growth as popular entertainment, Mee had well and truly made up his mind that the medium's potential had been totally corrupted by banal, crude and offensive films.[18] He thought popular cinema absurdly sensationalist, entirely divorced from reality, trivial and morally subversive. Throughout his twenty-four-year editorship of *The Children's Newspaper* he made sure it returned frequently to the theme of the cinema as "the most miserably abused of all our scientific wonders".[19]

In Mee's editorials and in unattributed columns, *The Children's Newspaper* campaigned for a cinema industry that would temper its commercial interests and produce films that were morally respectable and educational.[20] In private Mee did not check his contempt for the way he felt the potential of the cinema had been ruined. In asking Derry to write an article on it, he made clear that he wanted

> something plain and grave about the way in which the mind of the rising generation is being not only Americanized but barbarized by the misuse of this most potential instrument – the kinema. It is an absolute scandal and an indescribable tragedy that we should allow all this filthy poison to be poured, night after night, into the minds of our children. It is far worse than giving them prussic acid and killing them quickly. Nor is it only a national tragedy, it is a world tragedy, for the only hope of the world is in the next generation of our race.[21]

The result appeared in *The Children's Newspaper* four weeks later; it attacked the "evil" influence of many American films and the lack of a moral and educational dimension, and demanded the censorship of film content. The "perversion of English called the American language" was targeted and the claim made that American films were an "appalling evil" responsible for youth crime.[22]

Efforts by American studios to make films of English novels were ridiculed. A version of William Makepeace Thackeray's *Vanity Fair* staring Myrna Loy which *The Daily Mirror* thought would appeal to popular tastes[23] was for *The Children's Newspaper* a "terrible American hash of what is a proud English possession".[24] A hugely popular version of *Alice in Wonderland*, staring W.C. Fields, Cary Grant and Gary Cooper, described by *The Daily Mirror* as "grand entertainment",[25] was dismissed as "dull, and stupid with its Americanisms".[26] *Punch* lampooned Mee, suggesting that "Owing to the influence of American films on children it is suggested MR ARTHUR MEE should change the title of *My Magazine* to *Sez Mee*."[27] Under Mee's leadership, *The Children's Newspaper* followed the technological development of the cinema and regularly included reviews of films it considered good, particularly those that had a documentary focus.[28] Reviews of recommended films were often prefaced with "The Editor urges his readers not to patronise picture palaces where vulgar plays are exhibited".[29] When in 1922 the London County Council prohibited children under sixteen attending films for adults or films likely to be "subversive of public morality",[30] *The Children's Newspaper* expressed its approval on the grounds that

> Nothing is more terrible in these days than the way in which the kinema, with all its possibilities for good, is being vulgarised and used for evil, and the C.N. rejoices in the efforts being made by the County Council to prevent the minds of children being poisoned by low films.[31]

The Devil's Camera (1932), a venomously puritanical attack on the cinema of Hollywood, echoed Mee's words:

> The cinema is fast sapping the people's sense of moral values. How can it be otherwise? . . . Night after night, week after week, month after month, the "talkies" are sweeping away the moral standards of their patrons as surely as the seas are crumbling the coasts of the world, and this moral coast erosion threatens all that we cherish as the finest elements of our heritage.[32]

A *CN* editorial praised the book, endorsing its conclusions and attacking "the kind of trash which fills the screens of thousands of picture houses throughout the world" and the "melodramatic sludge which floats out from Hollywood".[33]

Mee's crusade against popular cinema he thought offensive was, of course, futile. In a post-war world of mass consumption, the millions of cinema-goers were simply not interested in what public moralists like him had to say. He seemed to represent the values of a world that, if not gone, was slowly having less hold on the popular imagination. Cinema was exciting, it was fresh and modern and it was here to stay.

All That Jazz

Like the cinema, jazz's popularity grew against a background of social climates of change and uncertainty and demands for novelty and originality. After years of austerity, people let out a sigh of relief and went "jazzing" as jazz became a synonym for all that was new or modern.[34] It was the sheer excitement, abandon and originality of jazz that so many found attractive. J.B. Priestley recollects how in 1913 he discovered ragtime and what it meant to him:

> It was as if we had been still living in the nineteenth century and then suddenly found the twentieth glaring and screaming at us. We were yanked into our own age, fascinating, jungle-haunted, monstrous. . . . [H]ere was something new, strange, curiously disturbing.[35]

A writer for *The Daily Mirror* saw jazz as stimulating, electrifying and shocking; it reminded him of "the delicious moment, when in your first pair of knickers, you drove a cricket ball through the greenhouse".[36]

As radios, gramophones and records became more affordable, jazz secured a huge audience of devotees. Jazz records sold in their millions and dancing in jazz clubs became a popular pastime. During the 1920s American jazz musicians Louis Armstrong, Duke Ellington and Benny Carter played to sell-out audiences in London theatres, restaurants and clubs. Also popular were the Jack Hylton Band and the Fred Elizalde Band, which had a residency at the Savoy Hotel and played on the BBC. In a letter to *The Liverpool Echo*, bandleader Jack Hylton captured the mood of those who enjoyed jazz:

> There we have, opened out under our eyes, the gulf between the Victorians and ourselves. When the young people of to-day have finished the day's work they quite candidly set out to amuse themselves without any of the old smug nonsense about "elevating" their minds, and they succeed with an honesty which rather scares the self-righteousness of an older generation.[37]

Jazz was not simply music; it was a form of social expression whereby being "jazzy" evoked a sense of modernity in fashion, attitudes and morals. Customers could shop with jazz music playing in the background, and fashion followed jazz with dresses designed to make it easier to dance to it. You could dance with complete strangers in dance halls if, like you, they knew the steps, while others looked on bemused, amused or shocked. Advertisements invited people to learn how to play jazz at home through correspondence courses or to go to dance schools to learn the steps. You could make a "jazz salad", the virtue of which was that it was simply different, bet on a racehorse called Jazz, wear jazz stockings, learn how to play jazz tunes from music included in *Women's Weekly*, dye your clothes a "jazz red" and buy jazz shoes.

Attitudes to jazz varied; some considered it inventive, almost intellectual,[38] while others thought it a passing fad requiring little intelligence.[39] In addition there were those who regarded it as "vile", "grotesque" and "incredibly stupid".[40] In a world where racial discrimination was culturally normalised, some criticisms had race at their core.[41] The composer Sir Henry Coward, whose father had been a professional banjoist and blackface minstrel working in music halls, urged, "Jazz should be denounced and made taboo among the white races."[42]

David Lloyd George suggested that jazz was savage and animalistic,[43] while the rector of Exeter College, Oxford University, claimed that Americanisms and the jazz of the "niggers" was a threat to civilisation.[44] In December 1929 *The Guardian* invited readers to comment on the BBC broadcasting jazz. The majority wanted it banned, claiming it had primitive "negroid origins", with one correspondent asserting that it expressed "negroid emotions and ideas" that whites had outgrown.[45] Another likened jazz to the "wild orgies of the negroid".[46]

While Mee saw in the cinema potential that had been wilfully destroyed, he saw no such missed opportunity or latent promise in jazz – he simply loathed it. He did not join in racist condemnations but he did enthusiastically use the columns of *The Children's Newspaper* to attack jazz and to ridicule "jazz crooners" and dancing to jazz. Like the cinema, jazz to Mee was a destructive representation of American consumerism. In complaining that it was intolerable that the BBC were increasing its output of jazz, an editorial in the *CN* claimed, "jazz is not music. It is a noise in which every fine purpose for which musical instruments were invented is degraded and abused."[47] It was "appalling nonsense",[48] "hullabaloo" and "rubbish"[49] that threatened national life.[50] Crooning was dismissed as a "whining mockery of singing",[51] a "gurgling noise"[52] from "people apparently afflicted with advanced nasal troubles and obsessed with the moon and June".[53] Having attacked and demonised Hitler for nearly a decade, in May 1938 the *CN* published an editorial praising him for banning jazz. As for jazz performers, "The antics of these people would be sad if performed by lunatics but in people supposed to be sane they point to a monstrous perversity."[54]

Inspired by its editor, the cultural conservatism and middle-class standards of morality inherent in *The Children's Newspaper* saw it oppose anything it thought inferior. Gradual and providentially inspired evolution was meant to produce cultural and social progress, and jazz did nothing to help attain that goal. In fact, it did the opposite by promoting the use of instruments and "shriekings and howlings worthy of a savage tribe".[55]

At the heart of Mee's rejection of jazz was the view that listening to music was essentially an aesthetic experience through which individuals became civilised and cultivated. Mee's taste in music never strayed from the classics, with Bach, Mendelssohn and Handel being particular favourites. He thought all forms of modern and popular music played in music halls and in musical theatre boorish, inane and lacking in the romanticised qualities he sought. Music was not only for enjoyment; it was a force for romanticised moral enlightenment. Jazz could never contribute to that goal and, parodying it as alien, savage and barbaric, Mee considered it illustrative of a society in cultural and moral decline. Critics like Mee saw jazz not as a new and sophisticated cultural product but, together with the behaviour that surrounded the music – the dancing, the smoking and the drinking – as a further rejection of "Old England" and a pernicious attack on living in a morally grounded and civilised world.

Mind Your Language

Non-fiction dominated Mee's taste in reading; he read voraciously but had little time for novels, although as a boy he did read *Her Benny: a tale of street life* (1879) by Silas Hocking, whose books were favourite nonconformist Sunday school prizes; Hocking later became a friend and visitor to Eynsford Hill.[56] Mee enjoyed Shakespeare, Spencer, Wordsworth and Milton and was completely dismissive of modern poetry, calling it "New Tosh" or "the rubbish called poetry these days". T.S. Eliot and Gertrude Stein were dismissed as "pifflers"[57] and "idiots" whose work should be "killed with ridicule in order to save literature from the mockery of their words".[58]

Mee's disregard for fiction stemmed from his view that the world as fact was far more interesting than any world a novelist could manufacture.[59] Children's story papers like those published by his employer and enjoyed by huge audiences were "stupid", "trashy" and "so much wasted paper". Reading them was *"like taking poison"* (original italics) and a distasteful waste of time as they offered nothing more than an introduction to living an immoral life.[60] Readers of *The Children's Newspaper* were told that they would never think of spending time with "hooligans, or tramps, or burglars, or policemen", so why would they want to read about them?[61]

Mee was scathing about the quality of newspapers – or "stunt papers", as he called them – telling Derry, "In my opinion *The Times* and *The Telegraph* are the only dailies worth looking at."[62] Populist tabloid newspapers were condemned as being utterly without merit: "Often the ordinary newspaper reeks with foulness. . . . Some of them wallow and grow rich in filth, and in doing so produce the slum mind in their readers."[63] The alternative was to read what Mee called "good" books, books that were "clean and sane and true".[64] Accounts of sacrifice and loyalty, duty, hard work and conscience were recommended, as were books on history, geography, science and technology. There is a eugenic sense to a *CN* editorial arguing that reading "slum books" containing "crime and passion and sin" weakened a person's intellect and character by appealing to "the lower side of man's nature".[65]

The grammatically incorrect use of English and what he considered abusive language greatly provoked Mee. Protecting spoken and written English from the intrusion of "coarseness" and the colloquialisms of slang was a constant theme in his writing. Although he never defined what was meant by "vulgar language", it was detested, especially in places of public entertainment when practised by "some low comedian" and, in particular, when heard on the BBC.[66]

The BBC began publicly broadcasting in 1922 and Mee became an enthusiastic supporter of the "wireless". The BBC's first chairman, Sir John Reith, ran the corporation with a strong vein of middle-class paternalism. Reith, like Mee, saw culture as a vehicle for education, and moral and intellectual self-improvement. It was his view that the BBC ought not to provide the public with what was populist; its role was to shape tastes. Having decided that few of the BBC's audience knew what they wanted, Reith decided he would make those decisions for them.[67]

Programming would avoid the mediocre, the sensational and the frivolous. Instead it would promote a high moral tone and would provide "everything that is best in every department of human knowledge, endeavour and achievement and avoid the things which are, or may be hurtful".[68] Broadcast content included opera, chamber and symphony concerts, poetry readings, talks and discussions, programmes for schools and, from January 1928, a fifteen-minute daily service, a reflection of Reith's commitment to religious broadcasting.

Unsurprisingly *The Children's Newspaper* endorsed Reith's aims, judging the BBC's output to be cultured, educational and varied in offering "sound instruction" and inspiration.[69] Mee shared a middle-class prejudice that the working classes lacked a culture of their own and ought to aspire to things other than jazz or forms of popular music, drinking, smoking, gambling and professional sport. He agreed with Reith's idea of denying the public what it wanted in favour of determining what it ought to want, writing, "There are things the public wants simply because it knows no better. There are millions who want silly things."[70]

The answer was to make sure the BBC fashioned the nation's tastes by refusing to broadcast the "silly things" that millions wanted and by giving them what others decided was good for them instead. A note at the bottom of the editor's page in a February 1937 edition of *The Children's Newspaper*, headed "Just An Idea", asked, "Could the BBC invent some way of letting us know when the good items are coming so that we need not listen to the rubbish?"[71] What Mee deemed rubbish and what the listening public ought not to want was "quacks", "freaks" or "shams", "ravings" and "inanities", and certainly not jazz or "the twaddle of Steins and Sitwells".[72] What they ought to want was knowledge, beauty, classical concerts, Wordsworth, Shelley, Keats and the largely forgotten Victorian and Edwardian poet William Watson, whose work Mee greatly admired.

But while, to Mee's delight, Reith had set out to create a BBC that would be the embodiment of a middle- and upper-class view of English culture, he ultimately had, of course, to make an inevitable compromise. Throughout the 1920s the expectations of a growing number of listeners from all classes and backgrounds saw repeated accusations that the BBC was elitist in offering programming that ignored the interests of a majority of its listeners.

Change was needed and while drama, intellectual discussion and classical music met the tastes of some, programming was extended to include "Music which may please all tastes"[73] and comedians such as George Robey and Tommy Handley, together with sporting events. By 1924 listeners could hear dance band music broadcast from the Savoy Hotel and the Tower Ballroom, Blackpool. It was extremely popular, even if it was broadcast from 10:30pm until midnight, after which the station closed down for the night.[74]

Mee was not impressed. After the cinema and jazz, the BBC became the third medium of popular entertainment that frustrated him. The crux of his displeasure was criticism of its failure to censor language he considered vulgar and programming he thought morally offensive. An October 1927 article in *The Children's Newspaper* from "The Editor's Table" claimed,

> If some people like to use foul language, or language of needless violence, that is their business; we do not invite them to our drawing-rooms. If some theatres like to sink to such a level of depravity that clean-minded people are unable to go to them that is their business; we can stay away. *But we cannot escape the B.B.C.* It comes into our homes whether we will it or not, and as often as not the children are listening. We think it should be the first rule of the B.B.C. that there should be no swearing. Those who want it can pick up this vulgar habit in the gutter or in the tap-room; those who do not encourage it in their homes are entitled to ask the Postmaster-General to protect them from what has become a very great unpleasantness.[75]

Periodically *The Children's Newspaper* expressed itself as outraged that, in its view, abusive language was gaining ground in society and damaging the upbringing of children, asking,

> How can we hope to have a clean-minded and high-thinking generation, bent on raising the moral and spiritual level of mankind, if the common vehicle of thought, our daily talk, is corrupted by vulgarity and debased by coarseness?[76]

Mee's view of what constituted culture ignored that what people ought to want can never be an expansion to all of what a minority think they want. As the national broadcaster the BBC was there to educate, inform and entertain all who listened, including those without drawing rooms.

As talking pictures emerged, some considered the language used in them to be representative of a new and fashionable form of popular expression. But critics quickly surfaced. They mounted attacks on films that they claimed threatened to destroy a situation in which English was spoken and "American" was merely understood. Through *The Children's Newspaper* Mee mounted a campaign claiming that the use of slang threatened to obliterate how the English language was spoken. Slang was condemned as dangerous and symbolic of ignorance and a sluggish mind; those who used it were "never original, never *real*. They do not think for themselves. Their innermost thoughts, like their speech, are second-hand."[77]

The Americanisation of English became a target, especially "the Yeah's and Nopes, the Sure Things, the Tell the World's, the Some Baby talk, and all the rest of the vulgaritie".[78] Talking films, especially crime films, were blamed for the introduction of "American vulgarisms" into the English language, described, as were many things Mee loathed, as "an appalling evil".[79] His abhorrence of what he saw as the pollution of the English language went as far as ensuring that *The Children's Newspaper* debated whether "kinema" or "cinema" was the more accurate word, and he objected when "airplane" was replaced by "aeroplane".[80] Mee's complaint in *The Children's Newspaper* about using "cinema" instead of "kinema" brought this response from *Punch*:

O Parent of a blameless publication
O ARTHUR MEE
You fight a losing battle for the nation.
Who seek with sad restrained exacerbation
To stem the tide that brings the altercation of K to C. . . .

I like your pluck, O excellent and gifted
Good ARTHUR MEE
And yet I fear the tide too far has drifted
So now you stand alone (the rest have shifted)
A *Mrs. Partington* with broom uplifted
Beside the C![81]

Mee's views on individual freedoms and liberties often clashed with his belief that the needs of the community could never be compromised and always outweighed the needs of the individual. Unapologetic about advocating censorship in the cinema and on the BBC, he had equally strong opinions about which books ought to be available in public libraries.

What people read mattered greatly to Mee and in 1930 he campaigned for having what he called "dirt in the public libraries" removed from the shelves.[82] In praising John Galsworthy's *The Forsyte Saga*, an unattributed *CN* article claimed,

> To anyone who watches in a spirit of hopefulness the yearly outpouring of English books, the most damping effect comes from the field of fiction. Never before were novels of the circulating library type so numerous. Never have they been less worth writing if judged by their average aim and quality. British fiction is almost as trivial (if that is possible) as British drama. It seems to aim at being the sensation of a moment, without any thought of picturing life as it really is. Of a hundred modern novels, grant but five to be well worth reading and we should feel rich.[83]

In 1931 *The Children's Newspaper* was delighted to report that "trashy novels" in libraries were not as popular as educational non-fiction books; the newspaper asked whether the "newest generation of all is freeing itself from the fevered bustle and pleasure seeking which followed the war" by reading "good literature".[84] The books that Mee thought ought not to be read or purchased by libraries were described as "vulgar", "vicious", "filth", "impure", and "disgusting"; they appealed to "unclean minds" and contained "demoralising tendencies".

Worse still, some books were circulated through public libraries supported by ratepayers.[85] Part of Mee's attack was a reflection of a wider concern among middle-class moralists that because libraries were publicly funded, they ought not to be purchasing books that some thought offensive.[86] A *CN* article from "The Editor's Table" in May 1931 claimed that

> It was never intended . . . that our public libraries should supply at the public expense any volume any ratepayer wishes to read. Not only is that undesirable from many points of view, but it has become an intolerable burden on the rates, and has led to an abuse of the Library Act by its exploitation in the interests of publishers and writers who are entirely unworthy of public support.[87]

Some commentators suggested that in their choice of books, "People really must exercise a little discrimination for themselves"[88]; Mee disagreed. As libraries became more numerous and catered for a growing and diverse audience, he became disturbed by anything that saw reading tastes move in the direction of recreational fiction. Essentially he saw libraries as instruments for social reform, offering titles that aimed at utilitarian ideas of self-improvement. Books that were educational, literary and imbued with cultural significance were fine, but recreational books he thought poorly written, dissolute or immoral he felt ought to be censored. Popular demand mattered little in the choice of books to purchase; public libraries were not for meeting community expectations, they were for moulding them.

Repeating his view of some of the BBC's output, Mee wrote, "It is this idea of giving people what they want that ought to be fought; out of it has come this public supply of moral pollution."[89] Derry was asked to write a column for *The Children's Newspaper* urging libraries not to buy books that could be judged immoral, corrupt or decadent. Mee wanted to include the message that libraries had become "the handmaiden of every obscene scribbler who wants to make money out of filth".[90]

Derry's article "The Abuse of Public Libraries", published on 19 May 1930, was a forceful critique of libraries that, using Mee's words, made themselves *"the ally of every obscene scribbler who wants to make money out of filth"* (original italics).[91] Derry argued that the language of some library books was an outrage, shameful and obscene, written by "dirty writers" for "coarse-minded people" searching for "grossness" and "filth". Public demand for these books was irrelevant and they ought not to be purchased.

The answer was censorship. Readers should not have what they wanted to read. In the interests of public morality, all fiction books ought to be judged by library staff, who could reject them if they were deemed immoral. The outcome would be the protection of readers from "insidious poisons" as well as the prevention of writers from "profiteering in filth".[92] Mee felt that books currently in circulation that fitted his definition of immoral, corrupt and vulgar should be promptly withdrawn.[93]

None of this prevented *The Children's Newspaper* from publishing fiction stories and reviews of "wholesome" novels for its readers, or from advertising story magazines for boys and girls. Nor did it stop Mee and the *CN* attacking book-banning and various forms of censorship in Germany, Italy and the USA. Mee's support of Darwinian evolution led him to ridicule the efforts of some American states to ban its teaching. He saw this as a campaign led by "ignorant people who think they can sweep back the sea of human knowledge", who made themselves look ridiculous by burning a copy of *The Children's Encyclopaedia*.[94]

Saving the Countryside

Between the wars, the natural landscape became a politically contested space between land owners, the public, who sought greater access, and conservationists looking to protect it. It was changing and its function as an economic contributor to national wealth was challenged by those who saw it as a site of culture and identity, leisure and freedom. Those searching for England found it within its rural landscape; "the countryside became a playground and an imaginative space in which urban society could reconstruct itself on new lines."[95]

Touring by motorcar had been a popular pastime for wealthy middle- and upper-class Edwardians like Mee, but during the 1920s and 1930s rural England became more accessible for an urban population whose lives were invested in town and city, not village and hamlet. The consumerisation of leisure, the wider ownership of cars and the broadening of public transport meant that more people were able to explore the countryside. Walkers, motorists, campers and rural day-trippers flooded into it, colonising an England that for many had once been beyond reach.

Some may have been searching for identification with a historical England, for an Arcadian paradise or for the comfortingly old-fashioned as an emotional refuge from the grimness of urban life. But for the majority, rural England represented not much more than a journey there and back from a pleasant place to visit on a Sunday afternoon. They may have dreamt of a rural idyll as they ate their cream teas, drank a pint in a village pub or picnicked on the banks of a river, but they knew that it was just a dream.

Mobility brought with it the paraphernalia of making access to the countryside easier. This meant not just a massive new road building programme, but also everything that went with it, including guest houses offering bed and breakfast, tea shops, roadside cafes, garages and petrol stations. It also brought with it noise, pollution, litter and broken glass as hikers and day-trippers poured back into their urban worlds.

Some viewed this process of democratising the English landscape with anxiety, and the process spawned a nostalgic view of how it might be conserved.[96] In 1929 D.H. Lawrence lamented what he saw as the harmful ecological, aesthetic and moral impact of urbanisation, observing, "The country is lovely: the man-made England is so vile."[97] The writer and poet Edmund Blunden wrote of how "Old liberties are closed by new riches, peace broken by new noises, rusticity depraved into new urbanism".[98] J.B. Priestley described an England of

> arterial and by-pass roads, of filling stations and factories that look like exhibition buildings, of giant cinemas and dance-halls and cafes, bungalows with tiny garages, cocktail bars, Woolworths, motor-coaches, wireless, hiking, factory girls looking like actresses, greyhound racing and dirt tracks, swimming pools, and everything given away for cigarette coupons.[99]

Mee was one of many who complained loudly that the natural landscape was being ruined by those enjoying the material fruits of modernity and consumerism. He felt a profound sense of loss when a landscape he admired or thought quintessentially English was altered beyond recognition. It was as if he was losing something personal, something that was his responsibility, something that he, as a born Englishman, owned. As suburban England extended its reach, Mee used his writing and the columns of *The Children's Newspaper* to assault what he saw as attacks upon the countryside. He believed completely in what Trentmann called a "trinity of soil, soul and mind".[100] Vandalising the landscape damaged the soul of England.

Like D.H. Lawrence, Priestley and others, Mee raged at how what he thought to be the timeless and enduring beauty of the landscape had been scarred by ugliness. In the conclusion of *Enchanted Land*, published two years after Priestley's *English Journey* (1934), he attacks the "great white gash" of roads that cut their way through the landscape and the desecration of ancient villages by property developers. "Is there no cure for this disease?", he writes; "Is England anybodys? Are all these beauties, glories, to be thrown away for sixpences?"[101] Writing to Derry about plans to open greyhound racing tracks in various towns, he said,

> It is perfectly infamous that after we have spent a fortune in making a beautiful road, any tramp can come along and put up shanties or rubbish heaps or fried fish shops along it, and after a community has built it up after a generation any syndicate can come along and turn the town into a sink of iniquity and vulgarity.[102]

When it came to cutting down hedges and woodland and straightening roads that had existed for 1,000 years and more, he thought the cost of change too great, writing, "It breaks our hearts that our lanes are going, in all these years we have lost nothing more precious than the freedom of the lane."[103]

Mee enjoyed travelling the country by car, but fought long and hard to minimise the impact of road travel on the landscape. The increase in motor traffic not only brought more vehicles onto the roads; it also heralded the arrival of the petrol station, that "Beast in the Beautiful Countryside", as *The Children's Newspaper* described it.[104] In voicing its frustration at the ugliness of petrol pumps, a *CN* editorial suggested that they "make us sick to death of going the ways we used to love to go" and that oil companies should pay a guinea each day for every petrol pump they owned or erected.[105] A further editorial offered advice to readers on how to vote in the 1929 election:

> Let us vote for taxing out of existence the spoilers of the countryside, the jerry-builders and the litter louts, the petrol people who set their hideous pumps up everywhere, turning our lanes into a circus and ruining our landscapes. Let us vote for men and women who will keep our country beautiful and save for those who come after us the loveliest country-side on Earth.[106]

In supporting the Town and Country Planning Bill in 1932, *The Children's Newspaper* proposed its own bill. This included that no road be defaced by advertisements, "ugly houses" or "anything displeasing to the eye", including pink squares on the roofs of houses and bungalows. "Rattling and noisy vehicles" were to be banned and those who damaged the natural flora and fauna were to be fined.

Largely as a result of the litter dropped by visitors in his garden at Eynsford Hill, Mee attacked day-trippers into the countryside, who he claimed demonstrated what has been called an "anti-citizenship" consisting of "Loudness, vulgarity, impertinence".[107] He wanted litter louts fined £1 for a first offence, £5 for a second, and, for repeat offenders, the removal of their right to vote.[108] Later he was to suggest that if they dropped broken glass, the only appropriate sanction was prison.[109] The modern world was not only dirty, crowded and disfigured by unsightly new

The Litter Lout

A thousand years of love and care have made our country beautiful. This is the gentleman who is making it ugly.

Figure 20.
"The Litter Lout" in The Children's Newspaper, *8 September 1928*

developments, it was also too loud and filled with the "shrieking noise of the motor hooligan rushing along our highways like some wild beast".[110] On a visit to the Wye Valley he mourned the absence of peace and quiet:

> We came down and found ourselves at Symonds Yat, the beauty-spot no guide-book can leave out; it was a shrieking horror, with Litter Louts and gramophones enough to drive one mad. If we love our country we must save it from these things, or England will be but a rubbish heap fit for churls and hogs.[111]

In June 1930 the local electricity board wanted to run cables on poles past Eynsford Hill and Mee complained that they would ruin the view from his garden. A meeting followed with the engineer and Mee wrote that within thirty minutes the route had been changed, giving him "one of those dramatic little victories of public opinion which do come to journalists sometimes!"[112] He leapt to the defence of Darent Valley when in 1938 it was suggested that a new road pass along its length, including past the foot of Eynsford Hill. Evoking romanticised imaginings of Edmund Spenser, William Blake, John Wesley and Shakespeare, Mee wrote,

Even the village school is going with the coming of the Road, and with the passing of the school goes the schoolmaster, friend of the children. The church is less and less, and so the parson's influence is passing, and as the village loses its tranquillity, its character, it will lose the family doctor too: three pillars of country life are slowly passing from our villages. If things like these must be, it is surely for us to save what we can, to take the great road away from the village and to preserve as vital to our very life what still remains of that serenity and beauty and tranquillity which have made our countryside the inspiration of our people and the envy of the world.[113]

He was horrified at plans for a new housing development in Eynsford, writing to Derry,

[T]hey are building 500 houses on the hillside facing mine and it may turn into a slum, with straight streets and rows of mean places. That is written calmly but wait until I come to say what I think about it and where will calm be then? It is Murder and may mean that we shall give up the Hilltop after 21 years.[114]

The housing estate was built – it remains there today – and the Mees did not leave Eynsford Hill.

What was Mee seeking to preserve? His objections to the changes brought by modernity and consumerisation were aesthetic, and there is in his writing a powerful sense of bereavement. This focussed not only upon the loss of the natural landscape but also of romanticism, optimism and idealism in a world he thought polluted by speculation and profit, self-gratification and moral corruption. It is tempting to see Mee as a conservative reactionary but he was never naïve enough to believe that the forces of modernity could be halted – but did it have to be so unattractive? If new roads had to be built, could not their routes be carefully chosen to avoid scarring iconic landscapes? If ribbon development was inevitable, make it aesthetically pleasing. Avoid large advertising signs that hid the natural landscape or disfigured it, shun ugliness and if that was not, possible hide it, plan for the future and above all preserve as much as possible and make good any damage.[115]

*

During the inter-war decades, Mee's world of stability, duty, responsibility and providential evolution was radically challenged. He welcomed what he considered progressive social change as necessary and even exciting. But at the same time he vigorously championed the idea that society ought to value and preserve his view of "Old England". Mee saw in a changing cultural landscape the timeless truth of what England was to him slowly fading in a world gradually seduced by the trappings of cultural modernity, and it saddened him.

Mee was afflicted with a sense of cultural loss and the perception that his generation had lost control of a society that had abandoned values which had stood the test of time. It became easier to see the world as a collection of opposites in which those who interpreted it as he did were "us" and those with other values, aspirations and dreams were "them". "We" believed in God and unquestioned faith, moral certainties, hard work, decency, duty and sacrifice. "They" were more permissive, perhaps even lazy, listened to jazz, enjoyed "trashy" films, read immoral books, used slang, defaced the landscape and left their litter on riverbanks, on beaches, in hedgerows and in public parks.

The difficulty Mee faced was that his views on what constituted progressive social change were the largely fading preoccupations of a middle class reared on a diet of Victorian morality. Claims of a society in decline riddled with a creeping decadence and corruption that would, if not checked, see its destruction were the perceptions of a mind troubled by changes he detested.

Given his values, class and beliefs, this is predictable and understandable; the world as he knew it was transforming into something he considered beyond recognition. Yet denouncing aspects of modernity through moral homilies, rhetorical swirls and appeals to faith was never going to work. In an inter-war period struggling pragmatically to deal with deep social and economic crises, what was required was real solutions to real problems. Faith-based providence and appeals to the kind of moral conscience that for many belonged in an earlier and increasingly obsolete age were no longer seen to provide consolation, let alone answers.

9.

"A Heartbreaking World"

Shattered Dreams

The horror and destruction of the First World War convinced Mee that a peaceful and progressive future depended upon the prevention of further conflicts, and he became a passionate supporter of the League of Nations and disarmament. Despite what he saw around him, he continued to believe that nations would make binding promises to be ethical and transparent in their dealings with each other.[1] He was convinced that disarmament would ensure the abandonment of war as a means of settling disputes; otherwise Europe would drift inexorably towards destruction.[2] On New Year's Eve 1921, writing in *The Children's Newspaper* that the USA, Britain, France and Japan had signed a diplomatic treaty, Mee became overwhelmed by optimism:

> The greatest year that has ever been is dawning. We believe it. We believe the world is coming back to peace and reason. We believe this coming year will be remembered when all the wars that have ever been are forgotten and lost in oblivion. . . . It is going to be a lovely world again . . . for dreams are coming true.[3]

While he was sure that Germany had to prove it could be trusted before it could once again enter a European family of nations, he was scathing about the Treaty of Versailles and considered the policy of reparations to be completely unworkable. In January 1922, he wrote to Derry,

> The illusion that deceived the world is as clear as daylight to me, and it has penetrated even the political skull of your darling, Lloyd George. As a matter of fact, he knew it never could be paid, but he had to say so to win his election. I give you that as a piece of confidential and absolute information.[4]

Ten years later Mee was describing the Treaty of Versailles as a "crazy piece of nonsense" than which there had been "no greater stupidity in history".[5]

The re-shaping of European relationships exercised Mee and he was attracted to the idea of Europe as a federation of sovereign nations linked by common purposes. He was taken with the idea of economic, scientific and cultural co-operation within a United States of Europe (USE) as a way of outlawing wars of aggression.[6] Mee believed it not only possible but desirable that "good Frenchmen and good Italians and good Spaniards and good Englishmen would all be good Europeans".[7]

In asking Derry to come up with ideas for an article on the League of Nations, Mee wrote of it as "the foundation stone of the United States of Europe. I should like to look round and look forward and think what the U.S.E. will be."[8] Derry was unimpressed and dismissed the idea, claiming that the English and Europeans were completely different and had nothing in common. Mee's response was to scold his friend: "Come, come Giovanni, you are back in the Age of Pre-War! Now turn your telescope around and look at it the proper way. . . . I refuse to be made a pessimist even by an old and beloved master."[9]

Almost from its inception, the League of Nations found itself under attack from those who considered it unpatriotic and its stance on disarmament dangerous. Accusations were made that it was a pacifist organisation dominated by the politics of the left.[10] Mee continued to campaign for the League's aims, but from the early 1920s he did so alongside the emergence of German National Socialism and re-armament, making it impossible for supporters to claim that its work could create peace and stability.

National Socialism was born of a lost war. With a membership predominantly composed of an anti-communist working and middle class, ex-soldiers and others who felt dispossessed, it attracted its share of discontented cranks, rebels and reactionaries with nationalist and anti-Semitic views. Its political platform targeted those it believed had let the nation down, articulated in slogans such as "Down with those who betrayed the Fatherland".[11] On a platform of nationalism and rejection of the Treaty of Versailles, the election of September 1930 saw 117 Nazis enter German Parliament. Following the July 1932 election that made the National Socialists the largest party, with 230 seats in the Reichstag, Adolf Hitler demanded the chancellorship.[12] Within months he had dictatorial control over Germany.

In the early 1930s, English newspapers were already printing stories of abuse and violence in Germany as the National Socialists rose to power. In March 1933, *The Times* described the Nazi persecution of Jews as an "undeniable scandal"[13] and included descriptions of Dachau and Buchenwald concentration camps. On 10 March 1933, *The Guardian* carried a story of Jews being attacked in the streets and shops being picketed by Nazis.[14] Reports told of the sterilisation of those the regime considered misfits; the imprisonment of those showing disrespect to Hitler; the torture and ill-treatment of prisoners, described in detail; book burnings and the destruction of synagogues.[15] *The Daily Worker* urged its readers to "Fight Against Fascism", depicting the regime as murderers and terrorists.[16]

Mee greeted these events with shock and horror, and through *The Children's Newspaper* mounted a ferocious and unrelenting campaign of opposition to National Socialism.[17] Articles attacked the imprisonment of political opponents in concentration camps[18] and the abuse of Jews based upon a theory of racial superiority, equated with barbarism.[19] The treatment of Jews was "unthinkable" in a nation where "Any dog is better treated than a Jew".[20] Hitler was an "upstart", a gangster without vision or education[21] who in enslaving the German people had been "ruthless, brutal and treacherous".[22]

Although Mee wrote publicly of his optimism that National Socialism would be defeated, privately he struggled to retain faith that war would be avoided as the world seemed to spiral uncontrollably towards an apocalyptic future. He reacted with a mixture of disgust and foreboding as Hitler's control over Germany became absolute. How could it be that the very things he believed in – progress, faith, liberty and justice – were being abandoned? In March 1933 he wrote to Derry,

> Our dreams lie broken all about us, the result of a Liberalism you taught me, with the aid of my father, which has built up a Democracy unequal to its opportunity and unworthy of its destiny. God Forgive it for it knows not what it does.[23]

By 1936 Mee had become frustrated with the failure of Europe's political leaders to avoid the possibility of war and thought the world "an appalling place".[24] Though its impotence was obvious, he continued to put faith in the League of Nations. "I do believe devoutly," he wrote, "that if anything happens to prevent a plain and democratic triumph for the League we are undone."[25] Savagely critical of Hitler, Mussolini and the Japanese invasion of China, he reserved some of his invective for "Stone Age America!!" and its failure to take a leadership role, and for Vichy France, whose alliance with Germany "must make the angels weep".[26] As Europe moved inexorably towards another war, he wrote of his fear that hostilities were imminent:

> We walked about the garden to forget the strain. We switched on for the special news with beating hearts and high hopes. We magnified the little signs of peace. We thought of all the comfort of the Bible. We remembered all the happy days that we have had, the friends so far away, the dreams still unfulfilled. Most of all we remembered (those of us who were old enough) the long four years of war and the bitter end of it; and those who are young remembered that all their lives in this world there has been no peace. Must it come again? Was there no way but this to stop one man whose lust for power was bringing misery upon mankind?[27]

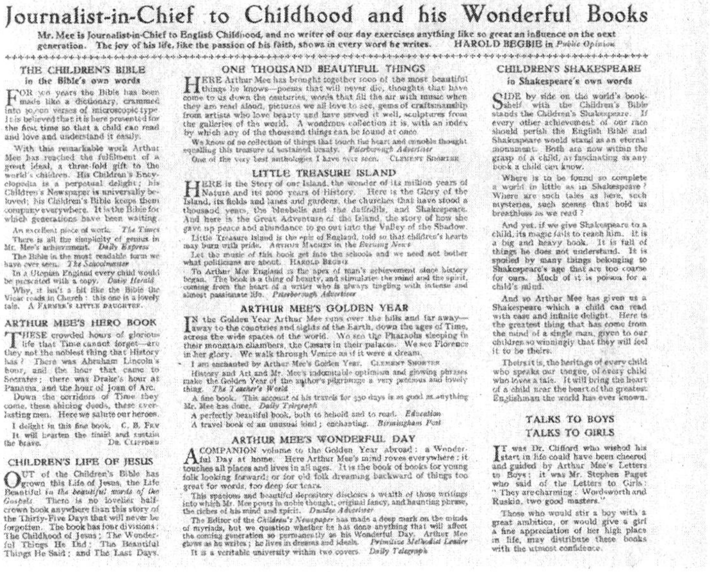

Journalist-in-Chief to Childhood and his Wonderful Books

Mr. Mee is Journalist-in-Chief to English Childhood, and no writer of our day exercises anything like so great an influence on the next generation. The joy of his life, like the passion of his faith, shows in every word he writes. HAROLD BEGBIE in *Public Opinion*

THE CHILDREN'S BIBLE
in the Bible's own words

FOR 300 years the Bible has been made like a dictionary, crammed into 30,000 verses of microscopic type. It is believed that it is here presented for the first time so that a child can read and love and understand it easily.

With this remarkable work Arthur Mee has reached the fulfilment of a great ideal, a three-fold gift to the world's children. His Children's Encyclopedia is a perpetual delight; his Children's Newspaper is universally beloved; his Children's Bible keeps them company everywhere. It is the Bible for which generations have been waiting.

An excellent piece of work. *The Times*

There is all the simplicity of genius in Mr. Mee's achievement. *Daily Express*

The Bible in the most readable form we have ever seen. *The Schoolmaster*

In a Utopian England every child would be presented with a copy. *Dusty Herald*

Why, it isn't a bit like the Bible the Vicar reads in Church: this one is a lovely tale. A FARMER'S LITTLE DAUGHTER.

ARTHUR MEE'S HERO BOOK

THESE crowded hours of glorious life that Time cannot forget—are they not the noblest thing that History has? There was Abraham Lincoln's hour, and the hour that came to Socrates; there was Drake's hour at Panama, and the hour of Joan of Arc.

Down the corridors of Time they come, these shining deeds, these everlasting men. Here we salute our heroes.

I delight in this fine book. C. B. FRY

It will hearten the timid and sustain the brave. DR. CLIFFORD

CHILDREN'S LIFE OF JESUS

OUT of the Children's Bible has grown this Life of Jesus, the Life Beautiful *in the beautiful words of the Gospels*. There is no lovelier half-crown book anywhere than this story of the Thirty-Five Days that will never be forgotten. The book has four divisions: The Childhood of Jesus; The Wonderful Things He Did; The Beautiful Things He Said; and The Last Days.

ONE THOUSAND BEAUTIFUL THINGS

HERE Arthur Mee has brought together 1000 of the most beautiful things he knows—poems that will never die, thoughts that have come to us down the centuries, words that fill the air with music when they are read aloud, pictures we all love to see, gems of craftsmanship from artists who love beauty and have served it well, sculptures from the galleries of the world. A wondrous collection it is, with an index by which any of the thousand things can be found at once.

We know of no collection of things that touch the heart and ennoble thought equalling this treasure of sustained beauty. *Peterborough Advertiser*

One of the very best anthologies I have ever seen. CLEMENT SHORTER

LITTLE TREASURE ISLAND

HERE is the Story of our Island, the wonder of its million years of Nature and its 2000 years of History. Here is the Glory of the Island, its fields and lanes and gardens, the churches that have stood a thousand years, the bluebells and the daffodils, and Shakespeare. And here is the Great Adventure of the Island, the story of how she gave up peace and abundance to go out into the Valley of the Shadow.

Little Treasure Island is the epic of England, told so that children's hearts may burn with pride. ARTHUR MACHEN in the *Evening News*

Let the music of this book get into the schools and we need not bother what politicians are about. HAROLD BEGBIE

To Arthur Mee England is the apex of man's achievement since history began. The book is a thing of beauty, and stimulates the mind and the spirit, coming from the heart of a writer who is always tingling with intense and almost passionate life. *Peterborough Advertiser*

ARTHUR MEE'S GOLDEN YEAR

IN the Golden Year Arthur Mee runs over the hills and far away—away to the countries and sights of the Earth, down the ages of Time, across the wide spaces of the world. We see the Pharaohs sleeping in their mountain chambers, the Cæsars in their palaces. We see Florence in her glory. We walk through Venice as if it were a dream.

I am enchanted by Arthur Mee's Golden Year. CLEMENT SHORTER

History and Art and Mr. Mee's indomitable optimism and glowing phrases make the Golden Year of the author's pilgrimage a very precious and lovely thing. *The Teacher's World*

A fine book. This account of his travels for 350 days is as good as anything Mr. Mee has done. *Daily Telegraph*

A perfectly beautiful book, both to behold and to read. *Education*

A travel book of an unusual kind; enchanting. *Birmingham Post*

ARTHUR MEE'S WONDERFUL DAY

A COMPANION volume to the Golden Year abroad: a Wonderful Day at home. Here Arthur Mee's mind roves everywhere: it touches all places and lives in all ages. It is the book of books for young folk looking forward; or for old folk dreaming backward of things too great for words, too deep for tears.

This spacious and beautiful depository discloses a wealth of those writings into which Mr. Mee pours in noble thought, original fancy, and haunting phrase, the riches of his mind and spirit. *Dundee Advertiser*

The Editor of the *Children's Newspaper* has made a deep mark on the minds of myriads, but we question whether he has done anything that will affect the coming generation so permanently as his Wonderful Day. Arthur Mee glows as he writes; he lives in dreams and ideals. *Primitive Methodist Leader*

It is a veritable university within two covers. *Daily Telegraph*

CHILDREN'S SHAKESPEARE
in Shakespeare's own words

SIDE by side on the world's bookshelf with the Children's Bible stands the Children's Shakespeare. If every other achievement of our race should perish the English Bible and Shakespeare would stand as an eternal monument. Both are now within the grasp of a child, as fascinating as any book a child can know.

Where is to be found so complete a world in little as in Shakespeare? Where are such tales as here, such mysteries, such scenes that hold us breathless as we read?

And yet, if we give Shakespeare to a child, its magic fails to reach him. It is a big and heavy book. It is full of things he does not understand. It is spoiled by many things belonging to Shakespeare's age that are too coarse for ours. Much of it is poison for a child's mind.

And so Arthur Mee has given us a Shakespeare which a child can read with ease and infinite delight. Here is the greatest thing that has come from the mind of a single man, given to our children so winningly that they will feel it to be theirs.

Theirs it is, the heritage of every child who speaks our tongue, of every child who loves a tale. It will bring the heart of a child near the heart of the greatest Englishman the world has ever known.

TALKS TO BOYS
TALKS TO GIRLS

IT was Dr. Clifford who wished his start in life could have been cheered and guided by Arthur Mee's Letters to Boys; it was Mr. Stephen Paget who said of the Letters to Girls: "They are charming: Wordsworth and Ruskin, two good masters."

Those who would stir a boy with a great ambition, or would give a girl a fine appreciation of her high place in life, may distribute these books with the utmost confidence.

Figure 21.
Advertising flyer for Mee's books

With the world around him drifting unchecked towards another catastrophe, sixty-one-year-old Mee continued to write and edit. He had been writing for over forty years but had no intention of slowing down. As well as editing *The Children's Newspaper*, in 1930 he had *Arthur Mee's Story Book* published, followed by *Jesus Said* (1931), *God Knows* (1935), *They Never Came Back* (1936), *Dreams Come True* (1936), *Heroes of the Bible* (1936), *Heroes of Freedom* (1936), *Salute the King* (1937), *One Thousand Famous Things* (1937) and the *Rainbow Books* series (1938). But ever the optimistic dreamer, his appetites, interests and thirst for more projects remained unabated and his attention turned to what was to be his final and, he hoped, his greatest project.

"My England Book"

At Eynsford Hill, Mee began to co-ordinate *The King's England*, the aim of which was to celebrate and immortalise the romance of the landscape, history and heritage of English villages and towns. The idea originated from his enthusiasm for motor travel throughout England and from 1925 it began to slowly emerge as a task he intended to tackle.[28] The need to work on other projects delayed its start, but in September 1929 Mee was writing to Derry, "I shall never be satisfied until I have done a big book which will give us at a glance the interesting points about every single object of interest in England."[29] He wanted to publish something for those who wished to see the country but had little time to do so, those "millions in a hurry", as he called them.[30] Given the working title of "Motherland" it took time to decide what format the work would take, and although what became *The King's England* was published as a series of individual volumes, each focussing upon a single county, it did not start out that way.

The weight of other demands meant that the project was not a serious possibility until the autumn of 1930, when Mee found himself under pressure from his employers to publish something in the form of county-based travel guides. The 1920s and 1930s saw an avalanche of travel books catering for a suburban population seduced by the attractiveness of visiting a more accessible countryside.[31] Hodder & Stoughton wanted to reach this market, but the idea of writing a travel book appalled Mee. "Big or Nothing" was his response and he decided to write something on England that would be the "Best Singular Book yet".[32]

Planning began in January 1931, and into February Mee wrote letters to Derry asking about possible formats, by which time it was clear that the scope of what he imagined could not be contained within a single volume. By the end of February, he was acknowledging that the more he thought about the project, the bigger it became.[33] Originally each county was to be covered by a general introduction describing its character followed by smaller descriptions of towns, notable personalities and then vignettes of no more than 200-400 words, what Mee called "concise little epitomes", on hundreds of villages.[34] Typically, Mee's enthusiasm was unbridled; the book was going to be his homage to England, and in March 1931 he wrote eagerly to Derry:

> This book is going to be <u>the best England book that ever was</u>. . . . I can hardly contain myself when I think of it all, for as I build it up it grows and grows. It is going to be by far the best thing I have ever done.[35] (original emphasis)

Once underway, the project became bogged down with difficulties. Mee turned to that tried-and-tested model of commissioning people to gather information on places and then turning it into copy to be edited. The difficulty he faced was in trying to get contributors to provide what he wanted. By May 1931, progress on gathering material was slow; money was being spent with not much to show for it and what was offered had to be re-written. Although his commitment to the project remained absolute, by the end of 1931 Mee was complaining that some of those trusted to collect material had let him down by providing inaccurate or badly written work. In desperation he turned to Derry to ask him to focus fully upon the project, writing, "I have wasted hundreds of pounds on useless people and hopeless copy, and my success depends on you and one other man like you tackling the thing competently and enthusiastically and without any nonsense."[36]

In a move typical of what always happened when he let impatience and enthusiasm cloud his judgment, having invested heavily in time and resources, Mee now changed tack as to how he wanted material collected. He started again and decided that a team of writers would prepare drafts of places from a variety of books, including guide books published by Murray and Methuen. What he called "rough notes" would then be edited, material would be added and, if necessary, a place could be visited to see "if things are as they are".[37]

From the outset Mee intended that Derry would play a central role in the project, but he was conscious of his friend's mortality and the question of whether, as they both got older, they could complete the task. Recovering from a winter cold he wrote to Derry, "I can get things straight and ready for my slipping out whenever the case may be. But not yet, not yet, O Lord! We have this <u>Motherland</u> to do and I want one more year with you without much interruption."[38] The demands on Derry were considerable; things were always "urgent" and needing to be done "as quickly as possible".[39] Mee was not past complaining that although he knew his requests were excessive, and although what Derry was writing was good, it was not always what was needed, reminding him how "imperative" it was that he could be relied upon.[40]

In these latter years of their relationship Mee found himself caught between worrying about Derry's health and the need for him to contribute to editing and writing. He never seemed to entirely get the balance right and often sent Derry work to do during an illness or immediately after it. He thought that this was what Derry wanted – there is nothing to suggest the opposite – and always included was the proviso that he could ignore requests if he felt unwell or if his wife Eva objected.

It was Eva Derry that managed the ageing John Derry's life. Following an illness of several weeks, Derry's second wife Rose had died on 20 July 1922, aged sixty-eight. Mee was heartbroken and stood beside his friend at her funeral. In the winter of 1924, Derry had married the then thirty-four-year-old Helena Eva Merry. If the marriage was about security for Eva and companionship for Derry, it was a great success. Mee had enormous affection for Eva and was convinced that Derry could not do without her. By the winter of 1933, Derry's health was deteriorating; Eva was sure her husband was not capable of maintaining the pace at which he was working and wrote to Mee to say so.

Greater pressure was placed upon Derry because Mee was not able to focus all his energies upon the Motherland project – he still had to turn out publications for The Amalgamated Press. With *My Magazine*, which he admitted having neglected, coming to an end, he was forced into producing a new part-publication, *Arthur Mee's 1000 Heroes*.[41] He wanted nothing to do with it but the need for profits outweighed his opinion, and so while Mee worked on the Motherland project, Derry was asked to do the bulk of the work on the magazine, the first weekly edition of which appeared on 22 October 1933.[42]

In defending himself as less of a slave driver than he was sometimes said to be, Mee gave Derry the option of doing less work, doing nothing at all, or, as he hoped, continuing to write.[43] Derry agreed to carry on, but Mee was now acutely conscious of his friend's declining health.[44] In a short and melancholy letter, he began,

> Always I am being reminded how close and how unfailing our association for 40 years has been to me. . . . [T]he thought in my mind at the moment is that you are one of the sanest and cleverest of writers I have known as well as one of the loveliest and nearest of friends I have had.[45]

By April 1934 the eighty-year-old Derry was suffering frequent bouts of illness. Mee became increasingly concerned, writing to "dear, matchless Giovanni":

> I want you for years yet, for the world is nothing to me without you in it. What I am you have made me more than any other man, and you must get well to see things through with all we have in hand. So help you God.[46]

As Derry continued to write, Eva nursed her ailing husband through the final years of his life. After a prolonged illness that caused Mee much distress, on 19 February 1937 the eighty-three-year-old Derry died at his home in Bournemouth. In an obituary on the front page of *The Children's Newspaper*, Mee wrote,

> John Derry was Arthur Mee's first Editor, and Arthur Mee was his last. He was the Editor's oldest friend. . . . He was as sane a judge of life and character as could be found. . . . He was a great optimist, and saw the best in every man who was fortunate enough to meet him; he was full of good cheer and good courage, and had the power of inspiring these high qualities in others.[47]

After Derry's death, Mee immersed himself in working on *The King's England* and invited others to help. Contributors included the novelist and journalist Herbert Gee, who wrote extensively about Yorkshire and who toured a number of northern counties;[48] the journalist and Shakespearean expert John Cuming Walters wrote on Lancashire and Cheshire.[49] Hugo Tyerman and Sydney Warner, who worked with Mee on *The Children's Newspaper*,

The King's England and Its Story

Shropshire is the newest county in Arthur Mee's New Domesday Book, the first complete 20th century survey of England, and is the 22nd volume. This unique series has now passed its majority.

Ask to See Them Anywhere

ENCHANTED LAND—A Survey of England	213 pictures	7s 6d
BEDFORDSHIRE AND HUNTS. 220 places	170 pictures	7s 6d
BERKSHIRE—Alfred's First England 170 places	120 pictures	7s 6d
CHESHIRE—Romantic North-West 150 places	117 pictures	7s 6d
CORNWALL—England's Farthest South 250 places	173 pictures	7s 6d
DERBYSHIRE—The Peak Country 226 places	134 pictures	7s 6d
DEVON—Cradle of Our Seamen 400 places	197 pictures	10s 6d
GLOUCESTERSHIRE—Glory of the Cotswolds	334 places	10s 6d
HEREFORDSHIRE—The County of the Wye 223 places	132 pictures	7s 6d
KENT—The Gateway of England 400 places	226 pictures	10s 6d
LAKE COUNTIES—Cumberland and Westmorland	217 places	7s 6d
LANCASHIRE—Cradle of Our Prosperity 250 places	185 pictures	7s 6d
LEICESTERSHIRE WITH RUTLAND 280 places	138 pictures	7s 6d
NOTTS—The Midland Stronghold 219 places	109 pictures	7s 6d
SHROPSHIRE—County of the Western Hills 242 places	109 pictures	7s 6d
STAFFORDSHIRE—Beauty and the Black Country	180 places	7s 6d
SURREY—Country Marching to Town 164 places	181 pictures	10s 6d
SUSSEX—The Garden by the Sea 300 places	238 pictures	10s 6d
WARWICKSHIRE—Shakespeare's Country 220 places	215 pictures	7s 6d
WILTSHIRE—Cradle of Our Civilisation 270 places	220 pictures	10s 6d
WORCESTERSHIRE—Land of the Heavenly Spring	189 places	7s 6d
LONDON—Heart of the Empire	200 pictures	12s 6d

THE NATION'S PRESS ON THE NATION'S BOOKS
A Sort of Light Shines all Through Them

There is a sort of light shining all through it. *Mrs J. A. Spender*

The panorama of our island home is flashed before us with a fascination which is irresistible. *Church of England Newspaper*

The book is a miracle of compression and editorial contrivance, and no phase of London's activities or achievements seems to have escaped attention. Altogether an admirable summary of London. *The Observer*

Congratulations must go to all concerned in this tremendous endeavour, a panorama of England of outstanding importance and usefulness. Romance is the only word to apply to Mr Mee's eager narrative of the building up and marching on of a nation; here is the romance of England. *Sunday Times*

No better book on Kent has been written, and it is impossible to believe ever will be written, than Arthur Mee's. *The Star*

ON SALE EVERYWHERE—HODDER & STOUGHTON

Figure 22.
Advertising panel for The King's England *series
in* The Children's Newspaper, *22 July 1939*

were employed.[50] Others included Lena Fratson, who helped Mee write about Kent, and Lois Mee and her husband Claude Scanlon, who wrote about Nottinghamshire. Friends such as Eva Derry, colleagues such as Stella Hancock, who helped with the Lincolnshire volume, and Harold Begbie's daughters Jean and Joan, who, with Derry, wrote on Hampshire and Dorset, all contributed.[51] By 1939 twenty-five volumes of *The King's England* had been published by Hodder & Stoughton. By this time England was once again at war.

Hopeful Days

With his faith in the League of Nations shattered and his England threatened, when war came Mee took up his pen and turned to hardening the resolve of his readers. His aim was to lighten the load, to make the war endurable, to enhance morale and above all to tell his readers that it was providentially winnable. 1939 saw the publication of *Why We Had to Go to War*, Mee's analysis of the war's causes and why it was absolutely necessary to fight again. This was followed by *Arthur Mee's Blackout Book: The Wartime Friend for Every Home* (1939) with its readings and entertainment for the air-raid shelter. It contained poetry, Bible stories, "A Word from Shakespeare", "Ideas that must be beaten", "Stories of fact & imagination", "Countryside tales", "Do you know these things?" and "Three minute talks", as well as puzzles, tricks, problems and mazes.

Mee's weekly editorials in *The Children's Newspaper* were filled with patriotic rhetoric infused by the principles of his religious faith. He had no qualms about describing the war as a crusade to save England, Christianity and civilisation. Readers were urged to remain strong and to have faith; defeat was unthinkable. They were fighting evil and the divine intervention of God was certain to save them – victory was inevitable.[52] While he felt a deep sadness and anxiety, there was, he wrote, no fear, just a resolute determination and "an infinite pride of our homeland and the things she has done for mankind".[53]

Mee kept working and at a time when few could have felt secure or hopeful, on 11 October 1941 he wrote, "He who writes this has this week reached his Jubilee as a writing man, fifty years of Journalism. Still feeling young and full of dreams."[54] By 1941 forty volumes of *The King's England* had been completed, at which point Mee wrote,

> It is pleasant to have given ten years of life and work to an act of homage to England, the recording in forty volumes of everything to see in her ten thousand towns and villages, our country as she was before the men of death and fire came riding through the sky.[55]

1941 also saw the appearance of *Call the Witnesses*, a forty-eight page booklet cataloguing the trials of Nazi occupation in mainland Europe.

This was followed by *Arthur Mee's Book of the Flag*, an enormously popular patriotic tour of the history and development of the British Commonwealth and its dominions, and *1940: Our Finest Hour*.

Based upon a series of articles originally published in *The Children's Newspaper, 1940: Our Finest Hour* is classic Mee as he unites his readership around king and country. Reprinted three times, the book confirms the righteousness of the cause on every page, describing the nation as a heroic community of people fighting a malevolent enemy. At the core of the book are Mee's efforts to promote a patriotic sense of identity. Mee was fighting what Angus Calder called a "People's War",[56] and what Churchill in a BBC broadcast on 14 July 1940 called "the war of the unknown warriors". The conflict was a holy one between peace and terror, justice and barbarity.[57] He wrote, "Never was a holier crusade. We fight against the attempt to overthrow the Christian Civilisation of the world."[58] He commanded readers to remember that sacrifice and denial in the cause of the common good was an act of national devotion. While troops fought, civilians also fought through their determination not to give in to despair but to work tirelessly at providing resources to win the war.

Mee had absolutely no time for conscientious objectors, "Pacifist Parsons" or anybody else who questioned whether it was morally right for those who called themselves Christian to fight a war.[59] Eynsford Baptist Chapel had a "pacifist parson" in the form of Bertram Carpenter, who had been appointed in April 1938. By October 1939 he had drawn criticism from chapel leaders for suggesting a series of debates on pacifism and was promptly warned off the topic. In September 1940 Carpenter left the chapel having been sacked. In a letter to Eynsford Baptist Church in February 2006, he claimed that his dismissal was based entirely upon him being a pacifist.[60]

With freedom of conscience a principle of nonconformity, denouncing conscientious objectors might be construed as an attack on individual liberties, but Mee dismissed this argument out of hand. The necessity of winning the war saw this principle abandoned, and conscientious objectors were venomously condemned. Mee thought them deluded and "strange creatures" with "half-formed minds". They were pagans, traitors and cowards,[61] "queer people" who "represented the gospel of the madhouse".[62] In *1940: Our Finest Hour* he tells his audience, "We are told that in the name of Christianity, too, that these people cannot support their country against its enemies. It is the most abject nonsense and the most pitiful treachery."[63] *The Children's Newspaper* had little to say about conscientious objectors; they rarely appeared and when they did were viewed as unpatriotic or positioned within contexts in which their objections to war were diluted, or, following a change of heart, rejected.[64]

Mee's contribution to the war included allowing Eynsford Hill to become a refuge for Londoners seeking to escape the bombing, and at times as many as sixteen temporary visitors stayed there. He writes of buckets of sand at bedroom doors and water pumps in the corridors, of waking up in blacked-out rooms not knowing if it was day or night and of the strain of worrying that a bomb might hit the house. The Battle of Britain was largely fought over the skies of Kent and Mee stood in his garden listening to the anti-aircraft guns, watching dogfights and burning planes crashing in nearby fields. Eynsford did not escape bombing by the Luftwaffe; in the darkness Mee watched as searchlights sought out German planes and in bed he listened as bombs fell.

Although Mee claimed that nearly 1,000 bombs fell on Eynsford and the surrounding countryside, "scarring the green hills with a line of white chalk mounds",[65] and homes were destroyed, there was no loss of life. He had an air-raid shelter constructed within the grounds at Eynsford Hill and wrote of the nights spent eating and sleeping in "our hole in the ground",[66] of learning to walk in the dark and sleep through noise and of being in a constant state of readiness.[67] Trained in first aid and nursing, Marjorie Mee served as a member of a voluntary aid detachment (VAD), which performed a variety of duties in hospitals and convalescent homes. Working alongside trained nurses, members performed clerical and kitchen duties, welfare and civil defence work; Marjorie drove an ambulance.[68]

The formulae of *1940: Our Finest Hour* was repeated in 1942 with the publication of *Immortal Dawn*. It is a typically assertive and confident account of the events of 1941, again based upon Mee's articles in *The Children's Newspaper*. Once again he introduced readers to his spiritual convictions and an idealistic and unshakeable faith that the war was being won. There is little new or unexpected within the book as he reiterates his belief that despite the tragedy, suffering and horror, God had a plan for humanity. *Immortal Dawn* was reprinted twice.

Page after page resorts to biblical imagery of duty and sacrifice, and he pleads with readers not to forget that in times of crisis and sacrifice, simple things in life give enjoyment, such as a garden, a trip through the English countryside or a visit to London. As for the future, after the war things had to change; the nation could not remain the same. Mee's words echoed what he had written at the end of the First World War. Society would have to be more democratic and egalitarian; there would have to be a national crusade against ignorance, poverty and unemployment and an end to class distinctions. In *The Children's Newspaper* he wrote,

> Everywhere there will be an end of old ideas that have disturbed the even tenor of the lives of men. There will be an end of the idea that a State can be safe without being just – that a nation can endure half-rich and half-poor, that some of us can live in fine houses with lovely gardens, while our brothers perish in mean streets. . . . Let there be

no more of the talk that a man is any worse because he is poor. Let us have an end of snobbery and class divisions, and let the only dividing line among men be whether they are just and true, the dividing line of character.[69]

Mee's war diaries continued into 1943 with the appearance of the meditative *Wonderful Year*, in which he claimed that the moral character of the nation's people would be decisive in winning the war. During a time of hardship and sacrifice for many, he returned to familiar targets in stinging attacks on modern art, modern poets, who wrote like "village clowns", and "jazz crooning" on the BBC, described as an offence "against good taste and spiritual sensitiveness". On crooning Mee lost all perspective in writing, "We may doubt if in all our history, so great an insult has been paid to our race."[70] Other targets included the wasting of food, petrol and coal, and the "extravagance of those who do not care". But his most powerful attack was upon those he accused of living lives of ostentatious contentment and consumption in comparison with those from poverty-stricken backgrounds who were fighting for king and country. He expected that everybody should be "willing to live hard", writing,

We must be content to go without. We must not expect an easy life. We must be glad to lend our money as readily as others give their lives. We must say to ourselves that we will not be anybody's burden, that we will lighten the load of our fighting men by giving or lending all we have.[71]

Mee did not live to see the end of the war. On Thursday 27 May 1943, he was admitted to King's College Hospital, London, for an operation that, although serious, was not life-threatening. Maisie Robson suggests that it was for a facial gland that had become infected.[72] There was no suggestion that he would not come through and be discharged in a few days. There was much he still wanted to do and he had enthusiastically sketched out plans for a number of writing projects. There were volumes of *The King's England* in progress; plans for another book on the war had been made; he intended to write about Eynsford Hill; and the possibility of writing an autobiography, tentatively titled *Setting Sun*, had been mooted.[73]

Mee woke from the anaesthetic and was returned to his private room. But to everybody's enormous shock, he died that evening; he was two months short of his sixty-eighth birthday. He was cremated in a private service at Golders Green Crematorium and in his will asked that his ashes be scattered at Eynsford Hill. He requested that well-wishers, rather than buying flowers, make a donation to a children's hospital with the words "For Arthur Mee",[74] and he left a message for his readers:

> I leave my love and goodwill to the multitude of unknown friends throughout the world who read the "Children's Newspaper," and the "Children's Encyclopaedia," whose devotion and sympathy have made Journalism a pleasure and an inspiration for me.[75]

Mee's death was sudden and wholly unexpected and it cut short a life he had hoped would continue until he had seen the world he dreamt of materialise and until his imagination had run dry. He had once said to Hammerton, "Sandy, I must remember that I may live to be ninety."[76] Typically Mee had made sure that those left behind would be secure. He had invested his money well and insurance policies ensured financial support for his family.

His death was greeted with the kind of regret and sorrow reserved for iconic public figures. An obituary in *The Times* announced that he had held a "pre-eminent position" in the writing and editing of educational publications for children, through which he had "exerted great influence".[77] *The Daily Mirror* said, "There are few adults today who have not learned something from his works at some time in their lives, and he has left a contribution to education that will long survive him."[78] As with nearly everything in his life, Mee planned for the end, even down to his obituary. It had been written some years before by John Derry and was placed in the safe in Mee's office. It was published as Derry wrote it on the front page of *The Children's Newspaper* on 12 June 1943.[79] In it Derry claimed for him the status of "one of the most successful journalists in the world".[80]

Mee's death was reported across the world; typical was a letter of sympathy from an Australian schoolboy, like thousands that flooded into his London office:

> On behalf of children I write this letter expressing our sadness at the death of our friend Arthur Mee. He has given us many wonderful things to guide us on the road of life; books that we may become wise; knowledge that we may become learned; the arts that we may appreciate the beautiful; and advice that we may possess good characters. He loved everything that was good and beautiful, and he shared that love with us. Arthur Mee influenced the characters of thousands of children. Our friend has passed from this world, but he has left a heritage that will be dear to our hearts for ages to come.[81]

John Hammerton felt that Mee left a significant heritage of writing that would never be bettered; it was an output that had been of "incalculable good to many millions".[82] Officiating at Mee's memorial service in London, the Rev. A.J. Macdonald claimed that, apart from J.M. Barrie and Robert Baden-Powell, few of Mee's generation could match his work for children, concluding, "His name will stand for ever as the greatest writer for children of our day and generation."[83] Mee's friend the artist Frank Salisbury dedicated his autobiography to Mee, describing him as a "loveable genius" and a "hero to the youth of the world".[84] Other admirers, friends and colleagues wrote of his "goodness of heart" and "impulsive generosity", of his tolerance and loyalty to friends, and of his kindness, sensitivity and honesty.[85]

Two of Mee's articles appeared in *The Children's Newspaper* after his death. His final contribution was published on 19 June 1943 and urged Hitler to sue for peace to avoid the inevitable destruction of Germany. It is characteristically Mee in its buoyant view that the tide had turned and the defeat of the Nazis was imminent.[86] But it is "The Touchstone", which appeared on 5 June 1943, that has so much to say about Mee and his values. It was a call to arms in support of the re-generation of Christianity as a social doctrine, in which he wrote,

> It cannot be said too often that it is the only way. It is not the letter of Christianity that we fight for, not this creed or that, this church or that; it is not theology with all its mysteries and obscurities that will save us, but the spirit of Christianity that a child can understand. Forms and rituals are for those who need them; the spirit is for us all. There is not one of us who cannot subscribe to the Prophet Micah's kindly definition of our duty, To do justice, love mercy, and walk humbly with thy God; and it is enough. . . . Let us make the Golden Rule of Christianity our touchstone. We need not bow down to this creed or that. It is enough if we accept the Sermon on the Mount, and play the game.[87]

Amy Mee continued to live at Eynsford Hill and shared it with her sister Lena until she died on 14 August 1956. Amy Mee died on 9 November 1960 in King's College Hospital, Denmark Hill; she was eighty-two and following her death Eynsford Hill was sold. Marjorie Mee had lived with her parents until 1938 when her father had bought her the "Little House" next to their home; both houses are reached by the same drive from the main road. In a poem signed "Daddie", Mee welcomed his daughter to her new home:

> May nothing evil cross your door
> And may ill-fortune never pry,
> About your windows; may the roar
> and rains go by.
>
> Strengthened by faith your prayers will
> withstand the battering of the storm;
> Your hearth, though all the world grow chill
> Will keep you warm.

Peace shall walk softly through your rooms,
However blares the world's great din;
Your walls, up which the red rose blooms
Will keep hate out and keep love in.[88]

The unmarried Marjorie lived in the Little House for over forty years. She died on 22 November 1982, aged eighty-one, at which time she was living in South Darenth near Dartford, Kent. Today Eynsford Hill House is a Grade II listed building and, together with the Little House, remains a private home.

There is one recollection of Arthur Mee that reminds us of the core of the man. In *The British Weekly*, Robert Percy Hodder-Williams, Chairman of Mee's publisher Hodder & Stoughton, wrote,

> Arthur Mee was a little man in stature, with a good forehead and a quick look through his glasses. He always walked very busily like a boy looking for something. There was the eternal boy in his eagerness and in his sense of fun. Mee was a very modest man with no pretensions. He was often on the tip-toe of expectancy. He was always discovering new beauty and courage in men and books and things. But, he was a true Englishman, and there was nothing mystical about his dreams or his influence. When a challenge in some good cause was laid upon him, or he saw some iniquity on the prowl, he would be quick to take off his coat. He believed in the Empire; he was sure of its destiny and of its Shining future. There was one flag that stood above all other flags for freedom and liberty – the British flag; and he always flew it from his hill-top. He never doubted the outcome of this war. To him it was just a plain issue between good and evil. He was certain of the ultimate victory of right over wrong. His was always a soaring spirit.[89]

Had he read this, Mee would probably have blushingly dismissed it as being overly flamboyant, embarrassing and sentimental, but he would undoubtedly have allowed himself a quiet and satisfied smile.

Notes

Abbreviations

CN: *The Children's Newspaper*
CE: *The Children's Encyclopaedia*

Preface *(pp. xiii–xx)*

1. John Hammerton (1946), *Child of Wonder: An Intimate Biography of Arthur Mee*, London, Hodder & Stoughton, 13.
2. Maisie Robson (2002), *Arthur Mee's Dream of England*, Rotherham, The King's England Press.
3. Hammerton, *Child of Wonder*, 34.
4. Barbara Stoney (1974), *Enid Blyton: The Biography*, London, Hodder & Stoughton, 23.
5. Hammerton, *Child of Wonder*, 12-13.
6. Michel Foucault (1986), *The Uses of Pleasure: The History of Sexuality: Volume Two*, New York, Random House, 13.
7. David Cannadine (1995), "British History as a 'new subject': Politics, perspectives and prospects" in Alexander Grant & Keith Stringer (eds) (1995), *Uniting the Kingdom?: The Making of British History*, London, Routledge, 16.

1. Beginnings *(pp. 1-17)*

1. "The Census", *Derby Mercury*, 4 May 1881, 4.
2. Cornelius Brown (1891), *A History of Nottinghamshire*, London, Elliot Stock, 234.
3. David W. Bebbington (1984), "Nonconformity and electoral sociology, 1867-1918", *Historical Journal*, Vol. 27, 633-656.
4. David W. Bebbington (2007), *Victorian Nonconformity*, Milton Keynes, Paternoster.
5. David W. Bebbington (1982), *The Nonconformist Conscience: Chapel and Politics 1870-1914*, London, George Allen and Unwin.
6. Hammerton, *Child of Wonder*, 23.
7. "Stone-Laying Ceremony at Stapleford", *Nottingham Evening Post*, 4 December 1883, 4.

8. D.R. Pugh (1990), "English Nonconformity, education and passive resistance 1903-6", *History of Education,* Vol. 19, Issue 4, 355-373.

9. G.W. Byrt (1947), *John Clifford: A Fighting Free Churchman,* London, The Kingsgate Press, 18.

10. Charles T. Bateman (1904), *John Clifford: Free Church Leader and Preacher,* London, National Council of the Evangelical Free Churches.

11. John Clifford (1905), "Passive Resistance in England and Wales", The North *American Review,* March, 430-439, 438.

12. "More Nottm. Martyrs", *Nottingham Evening Post,* 15 June 1905, 4.

13. "Nottm Minister and Layman's Goods at Auction", *Nottingham Evening News,* 21 April 1910, 5; see also "Passive Obedience", *Nottingham Evening Post,* 11 March 1910, 6.

14. "Nottm Passive Resister's Protest", *Nottingham Evening Post,* 23 April 1923, 1.

15. *Nottinghamshire Guardian,* 27 August 1880, 2.

16. *Nottinghamshire Guardian,* 2 January 1885, 7.

17. "Stapleford School Board", *Nottinghamshire Guardian,* 10 March 1882, 5.

18. Hammerton, *Child of Wonder.*

19. Robson, *Arthur Mee's Dream of England,* 13.

20. Hammerton, *Child of Wonder,* 32.

21. "Editorial", *Nottinghamshire Guardian,* 22 June 1889, 4; "Nottingham Lace Trade", *Nottingham Evening Post,* 9 November 1889; "The Crisis in the Lace Trade", *Nottingham Evening Post,* 27 July 1889, 3.

22. "News Echoes", *Nottingham Evening Post,* 5 April, 1910, 4. Later in life Mee bought a Bible for use in services at the Woodborough Road Chapel which was used in a remembrance service for him in June 1943. See "Late Mr. Arthur Mee", *Nottingham Evening Post,* 21 June 1943, 4.

23. Hammerton, *Child of Wonder,* 44.

24. "Arthur Mee By His First Editor", *CN,* 12 June 1943.

25. Ibid.

26. "Former Bourne Headmaster", *Grantham Journal,* 27 February 1937, 2.

27. "Bourne", *Stamford Mercury,* 25 January 1889, 4.

28. "Bourn", *Grantham Journal,* 21 December 1878, 2.

29. "Quite a Striking portrait", *Grantham Journal,* 20 August 1898, 4.

30. "Bourne", *Grantham Journal,* 12 March 1887, 6; "Meeting of the Bourn Liberal Two Hundred", *Grantham Journal,* 4 June 1887, 6.

31. "Local Intelligence", *Sheffield Independent,* 1 July 1895, 6.

32. "Who's Who in Sheffield: Jottings about People", cuttings from the *Sheffield Independent,* 8-20 August 1902, 63.

33. John Hammerton (1944), *Books and Myself,* London, Macdonald, 9.

34. Ibid., 124.

35. Hammerton, *Child of Wonder,* 22.

36. Letter, Hancock to Mee, 27 July 1927.

37. Letter, Hancock to Derry, 30 March 1928.

38. Ernest A. Bryant (1908), *A New Self-Help,* London, Cassell.

39. Kate Jackson (1997), "The Tit-Bits Phenomenon: George Newnes, New Journalism and the Periodical Texts", *Victorian Periodicals Review,* Vol. 30, No. 3, 201-226.

40. Arthur Mee (1906), "The Freelance Journalist", *The Harmsworth Self-Educator*, 3934.

41. Ford Madox Hueffer (1905), *The Soul of London*, London, Alston Rivers, 111.

42. Charles Masterton (1909), *The Condition of England*, London, Methuen & Co., 77.

43. Mee, "The Freelance Journalist", 3934.

44. Herbert G. Wells (1934), *Experiment in Autobiography*, Volume I, London, Macmillan, 506.

45. *London Daily News*, 22 April 1898, 7.

46. Arthur Mee, "The Pleasure Telephone", *The Strand Magazine*, September, 1898, 339-345. It was *The Strand Magazine* that gave the world Sherlock Holmes.

47. Arthur Mee, "B. P. Hero of Mafeking", *Chums*, 23 May 1900, 631.

48. *Western Daily Press*, 29 April 1901, 3.

49. Arthur Mee, "The Making of Sherlock Holmes", *The Young Man*, 14, No. 10, October 1900, 335-337.

50. *Lloyd's Weekly Newspaper*, 10 September 1899; *Pall Mall Gazette*, 31 August 1899, 8.

51. Hammerton, *Books and Myself*, 163.

52. Arthur Mee (1900), *Joseph Chamberlain: A Romance of Modern Politics*, London, S.W. Partridge & Co.; *Lord Salisbury: The Record Premiership of Modern Times* (1901), London, Hood, Douglas & Howard; *King and Emperor: The Life-history of Edward VII* (1901), London, S.W. Partridge & Co.

53. *Spectator*, 3 October 1903, 13; Arthur Mee (1903), *England's Mission by English Statesmen*, London, Grant Richards.

2. Caught in the Harmsworth Web *(pp. 18-34)*

1. J. Lee Thompson (2000), *Northcliffe: Press Baron in Politics, 1865-1922*, London, John Murray.

2. Max Pemberton (1922), *Northcliffe: A Memoir*, London, Hodder & Stoughton, 29-30.

3. Reginald Pound and Geoffrey Harmsworth, *Northcliffe*, New York, Praeger, 65-90.

4. Thompson, *Northcliffe*, 12-14; H. Simonis (1917), *The Street of Ink: An Intimate History of Journalism*, London, Cassell & Company Ltd, 61.

5. John Springhall (1994), "Disseminating Impure Literature: The 'Penny Dreadful' Publishing Business since 1860", *Economic History Review*, Vol. 47 (3), 567-584.

6. William E. Carson (1918), *Northcliffe: Britain's Man of Power*, Toronto, G.J. McLeod, 111.

7. Ibid.

8. Peter Bailey (1999), "White Collars, Gray Lives? The Lower Middle Class Revisited", *Journal of British Studies*, Vol. 38, No. 3, 273-290.

9. Cited in Hugh Cudlipp (1980), *The Prerogative of the Harlot: Press Barons and Power*, London, Bodley Head, 290.

10. Pound and Harmsworth, *Northcliffe*, 200.

11. William Kennedy Jones (1920), *Fleet Street and Downing Street*, London, Hutchinson, 145.

12. "Amalgamated Press", *The Daily Mail*, 15 December 1905, 8.

13. Letter, Mee to Derry, 31 December 1908.

14. Letter, Harmsworth to Mee, 16 October 1907.

15. Hammerton, *Child of Wonder*, 92.

16. *The South Eastern Gazette*, 14 October 1902, 4.

17. When Jack died he received a glowing obituary in *The Children's Newspaper* written by Ernest Bryant. Jack was buried in the wood at Eynsford Hill. See "Good-bye Jack", *CN*, 25 October 1919, 6.

18. Harold Begbie (1921), *The Mirrors of Downing Street: Some Political Reflections by a Gentleman with a Duster*, London, G.P. Putnam & Sons, 50.

19. Hammerton *Books and Myself*, 175.

20. Ibid., 179.

21. John Hammerton (1932), *With Northcliffe in Fleet Street*, London, Hutchinson & Co., 124.

22. "Books and Bookmen", *The Manchester Guardian*, 25 March 1905, 7; "The Harmsworth Encyclopaedia", *Manchester Courier and Lancashire General Advertiser*, 20 March 1905, 8.

23. "The Harmsworth Encyclopaedia", *The Practical Teacher*, April 1905, 537.

24. For example, on the dangers of the young smoking, see J.R. Johnson, "Children who Smoke", *The Daily Mail*, 8 January 1903, 4; a satire on the fashion of make-up, "The Beauty Doctor", *The Daily Mail*, 4 February 1903, 4; walks through the English countryside, "A Whitsuntide Tramp", *The Daily Mail*, 1 June 1903, 4; an attack on game shooting and fox hunting, "The Modern Lust for Slaughter", *The Daily Mail*, 16 December 1903, 4; an article critical of income tax, "The Fleecing of the Middle Classes", *The Daily Mail*, 26 July 1904, 4; and articles by Harold Begbie such as "A Silent Game", *The Daily Mail*, 18 January 1905, 4.

25. John Maynard Keynes (1920), *The Economic Consequences of the Peace*, New York, Harcourt, Brace and Howe, 12.

26. George Orwell (1952), "Such, Such Were the Joys", *Partisan Review*, September-October.

27. Mee, *The Harmsworth Self-Educator*, 1.

28. Ibid.; "An Education for ½d. a Day", *The Daily Mail*, 17 March 1905, 3.

29. Mee, *The Harmsworth Self-Educator*, 1.

30. "Which is to Be your Room?", *The Daily Mirror*, 7 November 1905, 2.

31. "The Fountain of Brain Power", *The Daily Mail*, 23 October 1905, 2.

32. *Manchester Courier and Lancashire General Advertiser*, 7 November 1905, 8.

33. "Harmsworth Self-Educator", *The Daily Mail*, 7 November 1905, 1.

34. "The Public Tribute to the Harmsworth Self-Educator", *The Daily Mail*, 18 June 1906, 5.

35. Pound and Harmsworth, *Northcliffe*, 294; Hammerton, *Child of Wonder*, 99.

36. Letter, Mee to Northcliffe, 27 August 1908.

37. Letter, Harmsworth to Mee, 16 October 1907.

38. Hammerton, *Child of Wonder*, 111.

39. Letter, Mee to Derry, 9 December 1932.

40. Letter, Mee to Harmsworth, 13 May 1909; Letter, Mee to Harmsworth, 8 November 1910.

41. Letter, Harmsworth to Mee, 1 August 1908.

42. Hammerton, *Books and Myself*, 41.

43. Simon Gunn and Rachel Bell (2002), *Middle Classes: Their Rise and Sprawl*, London, Cassell, 54.

44. Olive Anderson (1987), *Suicide in Victorian and Edwardian England*, Oxford, Oxford University Press.

45. Herbert G. Wells (1897), *The War of the Worlds*, Rockville, Arc Manor, 138.

46. Letter, Mee to Northcliffe, 26 May 1908.

47. Ibid.

48. Letter, Mee to Derry, undated.

49. "The World's Great Books", *The Hull Daily Mail*, 5 October 1909, 4.

50. Letter, Mee to Harmsworth, 13 May 1909; *The Hull Daily Mail*, 5 October 1909, 4.

51. Hammerton, *Books and Myself*, 199.

52. Letter, Mee to Derry, 1 September 1909.

53. Letter, Mee to Derry, 8 November 1909.

54. Letter, Mee to Derry, 17 January 1930.

55. Letter, Mee to Harmsworth, 30 October 1910.

56. "News Echoes", *Nottingham Evening Post*, 29 July 1910, 4.

57. Letter, Northcliffe to Mee, 10 November 1910.

58. Letter, Mee to Harmsworth, 30 October 1910.

59. Letter, Mee to Harmsworth, 30 October 1910.

60. Letter Northcliffe to Mee, 1 November 1910; Pound and Harmsworth, *Northcliffe*, 398.

61. Sir Victor Horsley was a pioneer in neurological surgery and the treatment of cerebral tumours and aneurisms. Like Mee he was a temperance activist and co-authored a popular anti-alcohol textbook. Mee writes of Horsley as the greatest brain surgeon in the world. See Arthur Mee (1913), *Arthur Mee's Talks to Girls*, London, Hodder & Stoughton, 119. Horsley was also Alfred Harmsworth's doctor; see Pound and Harmsworth, *Northcliffe*, 298, 340.

62. Letter, Mee to Derry, 12 June 1910.

63. "Funeral of a Young Nottingham Journalist", *Nottingham Evening Post*, 14 July 1910, 2.

64. Arthur Mee (1923), *Arthur Mee's Wonderful Day*, London, Hodder & Stoughton, 226-227.

65. Letter, Northcliffe to Mee, 20 July 1910.

66. "Joan Comes Into Her Own", *CN*, 24 September 1921, 7.

67. For differing views on Harmsworth's state of mind towards the end of his life, see Pound and Harmsworth, *Northcliffe*, 859-887.

68. "Lord Northcliffe", *CN*, 26 August 1922, 6.

69. Hammerton, *Child of Wonder*.

70. Gilbert Keith Chesterton (1905), *Heretics*, London, John Lane, 44.

71. Hammerton, *Books and Myself*, 150.

72. Ibid., 193.

73. Ibid., 176.

74. Donovan Pedelty, "Mee and Him", *The Guardian*, 1 September 2007.

75. Letter, Mee to Derry, 19 January 1909; Letter, Mee to Derry, 25 June 1926; Letter, Hancock to Derry, 17 October 1930.

76. Letter, Mee to Derry, 27 September 1911.
77. "New Scottish Comedy", *The Daily Mail*, 19 July 1911, 3; "Why Men and Women like Bunty", *The Daily Mail*, 15 December 1911, 11.
78. Letter, Mee to Derry, 23 March 1923.
79. Quoted in *Hastings and St Leonard's Observer*, 20 June 1931, 13.
80. "Arthur Mee, the Christian Gentleman of Fleet Street", *This England*, Spring 1981, 22.
81. Letter, Mee to Derry, 2 April 1910; Letter, Stella Hancock to Derry, 27 May 1929.
82. Hammerton, *Child of Wonder*, 100-101.
83. Letter, Mee to Derry, 4 April 1910.
84. Letter, Mee to Derry, 7 April 1910.
85. Letter, Mee to Derry, 9 August 1911.
86. Letter, Mee to Derry, 16 January 1922.
87. Hammerton, *Child of Wonder*, 229.
88. Letter, Mee to Derry, 14 January 1935.
89. Letter, Mee to Derry, 9 August 1915.
90. Letter, Mee to Derry, 18 August 1913.
91. Letter, Mee to Derry, 18 August 1913.
92. Letter, Hancock to Derry, 30 April 1931.
93. Letter, Mee to Derry, undated, but the letter fits a chronology of Wednesday 6 May 1931.

3. Manufacturing A Brand *(pp. 35-57)*

1. Philipp Blom (2008), *The Vertigo Years: Change and Culture in the West, 1900-1914*, London, Weidenfeld & Nicolson, Introduction.
2. John A. Hobson (1909), *The Crisis of Liberalism*, London, King & Sons, 271.
3. Charles F.G. Masterman (1905), *In Peril of Change: Essays Written in Time of Tranquillity*, New York, B.W. Huebsch, xii.
4. Board of Education (1905), *Suggestions for the Consideration of Teachers, and Others concerned in the work of Elementary Schools*, London, HMSO, 68.
5. James Henry Yoxall and Ernest Grey (1905), *Companion to the NUT Code*, London, Educational Supply Association, 21, 25.
6. John Dewey (1902), *The Child and the Curriculum*, Chicago, Chicago University Press; Edwin A. Kirkpatrick (1903), *Fundamentals of Child Study: a discussion of instincts and other factors in human development with practical applications*, London, Macmillan; Margaret McMillan (1904), *Education Through the Imagination*, London, Swan Sonnenschein & Co. Ltd.
7. James Barrie (1860-1937) was a journalist on *The Nottingham Journal* for eighteen months in 1883 and 1884. The impressions Barrie gained from this period took tangible form in his novel of provincial life, *When A Man's Single*, which first appeared as a serial in *The British Weekly*.
8. James M. Barrie (1911), *Peter Pan*, London, Hodder & Stoughton, 19.
9. John Springhall (1994), "'Pernicious Reading'? 'The Penny Dreadful' as Scapegoat for Late-Victorian Juvenile Crime", *Victorian Periodicals Review*, Vol. 27, No. 4, 326-349.

10. *Sunday at Home: a family magazine for Sabbath reading*, Vol. 1, No. 1, 1854, 320, 16, 89.

11. "A Minister's Address to the Children of his Congregation on the New Year", *Child's Companion*, 1:1, January 1824, 5.

12. *Child's Companion and Juvenile Instructor*, No. 181, January 1860.

13. William Jones and George Baxter (1850), *The Jubilee Memorial of the Religious Tract Society: Containing a Record of Its Origin, Proceedings, and Results, A.D. 1799 to A.D. 1849*, 127; Dennis Butts and Pat Garrett (eds) (2006), *From the Dairyman's Daughter to Worrals of the WAAF: The Religious Tract Society, Lutterworth Press and Children's Literature*, Cambridge, Lutterworth Press.

14. John Springhall (1994), "Disseminating impure literature: the 'penny dreadful' publishing business since 1860", *Economic History Review*, XLVII, 567-684, 568.

15. Gilbert K. Chesterton (1901), "A Defence of Penny Dreadfuls", *The Defendant*, London, J.M. Dent & Sons Ltd, 8.

16. Edwin J. Brett (1866), *Boys of England*, I, 2.

17. Joseph Bristow (1991), *Empire Boys: Adventures in a Man's World*, London, HarperCollins Academic.

18. *RTS Record*, No. 11, June 1879, 37.

19. Marjory Lang (1980) "Childhood's Champions: Mid-Victorian Children's Periodicals and the Critics", *Victorian Periodicals Review* 13, 1/2, 17-31, 22.

20. Harriet Martineau (1865), "Life in the Criminal Classes", *Edinburgh Review*, 122, 347.

21. *Morning Post*, 18 April 1876, 4.

22. Quoted in Jack Cox (1982), *Take A Cold Tub Sir!: The History of the Boy's Own Paper*, Guildford, The Lutterworth Press, 18.

23. Patrick Dunae (1976), "Boy's Own Paper: Origins and Editorial Policies", *The Private Library*, IX, 120-158.

24. Edward Salmon, "What Girls Read", *Nineteenth Century*, XX, October 1886, 520.

25. "Pictured Annuals", *Pall Mall Gazette*, 21 November 1899, 9.

26. Cox, *Take A Cold Tub Sir!*, 12.

27. Robert H. MacDonald (1994), *The Language of Empire: Myths and Metaphors of Popular Imperialism, 1880-1918*, Manchester, Manchester University Press, 10.

28. Hammerton, *Books and Myself*, 20.

29. Interview with G.M. Fenn, *Chums*, 13 September 1893, 41.

30. Arthur Mee, "B.P. Hero of Mafeking", *Chums*, 23 May 1900, 631.

31. *Little Folks*, Vol. 2, 1871-72, v; Simon Nowell Smith (1959), *The House of Cassell, 1848-1958*, London, Cassell.

32. Pemberton, *Lord Northcliffe*, 29-30.

33. *The Boys' Realm*, 14 June, 1902, 4; see also *Halfpenny Marvel*, 24 September 1895, 5.

34. Diana Dixon (1986), "From Instruction to Amusement: Attitudes of Authority in Children's Periodicals before 1914", *Victorian Periodicals Review*, Vol. 19, No. 2, 63-67, 63; Kirsten Drotner (1988), *English Children and Their Magazines, 1751-1945*, New Haven and London, Yale University Press, 123.

35. Arthur Mee (ed.) (1908), *The Children's Encyclopaedia*, Volume 1, London, The Educational Book Company, 2.

36. Letter, Mee to Northcliffe, 6 April 1908.
37. Letter, Harmsworth to Mee, 23 March 1908.
38. Mee, *CE*, 2.
39. Ibid., 1.
40. Barbara Lamming, *The Trident*, December 1982. *The Trident* is the monthly magazine of the Anglican Churches of Eynsford, Farningham and Lullingstone. I am grateful to Dr Susan Pittman, Archivist at the Farningham & Eynsford Local History Society, for providing this information.
41. See Valerie Lawson (2010), *Mary Poppins, She Wrote: The true story of Australian writer P.L. Travers, creator of the quintessentially English nanny*, London, Simon & Schuster.
42. Maud Pember Reeves (1914), *Round About a Pound a Week*, London, G. Bell & Sons Ltd.
43. Letter, Mee to Harmsworth, 6 April 1908.
44. Mee, *CE*, 2.
45. "Children's Encyclopaedia", *The Daily Mail*, 13 March 1908, 3; see also Hammerton, *Child of Wonder*, 127-128.
46. "Reviews", *Bath Chronicle and Weekly Gazette*, 2 April 1908, 6.
47. "Notes", *Norfolk Chronicle*, 21 March 1908, 3.
48. "The Children's Encyclopaedia", *The Review of Reviews*, April 1908, 397.
49. "The Children's Encyclopaedia", *Illustrated London News*, 3 September 1910, 372.
50. Letter, Northcliffe to Mee, 23 March 1908.
51. Letter, Mee to Northcliffe, 6 April 1908.
52. Mee, *CE*, 2; Letter, Mee to Northcliffe, 6 April 1908.
53. Letter, Mee to Derry, 1 June 1911.
54. Letter, Mee to Derry, 9 December 1908.
55. Letter, Mee to Derry, 19 January 1909.
56. Letter, Mee to Derry, 31 December 1908.
57. Letter, Mee to Derry, 15 June 1910.
58. Letter, Mee to Derry, 31 December 1908.
59. Letter, Mee to Derry, 15 November 1910.
60. "Reviews", *Bath Chronicle and Weekly Gazette*, 22 October 1908, 6.
61. Hammerton, *Books and Myself*, 204.
62. Letter, Mee to Derry, 11 December 1929.
63. Letter, Mee to Derry, 31 December 1908.
64. Hammerton, *Child of Wonder*, 96.
65. See Arthur Mee, "Harold Begbie", *CN*, 26 October 1929, 4.
66. See David H. Lawrence (1910), "The Goose Fair", *The English Review*, No. 15, February, 399-409, 400.
67. James T. Boulton (ed.) (2002), *The Letters of D.H. Lawrence*, Cambridge, Cambridge University Press.
68. Letter, Mee to Derry, 12 October 1909.
69. Letter, Mee to Derry, 9 November 1911.
70. Letter, Mee to Northcliffe, 13 May 1909.
71. Letter, Mee to Northcliffe, 30 October 1910.
72. Letter, Mee to Northcliffe, 8 November 1910.
73. Letter, Northcliffe to Mee, 10 November 1910.

74. "New Children's Magazine", *The Daily Mail*, 14 February 1910, 5; "New Children's Encyclopaedia", *The Daily Mail*, 15 February 1910, 1; "Publishing Record", *The Daily Mail*, 16 February 1910, 1.
75. *The Daily Mirror*, 19 February 1910, 10.
76. "A Great Pleasure and a Great Disappointment", *The Daily Mirror*, 26 February 1910, 10; *The Daily Mirror*, 19 March 1910, 10.
77. "How A Million Children Are Being Educated", *The Daily Mirror*, 20 August 1910, 10.
78. Letter, Northcliffe to Mee, 15 December 1910.
79. Letter, Mee to Derry, 31 December 1914.
80. *The Daily Mirror*, 19 October 1915, 12.
81. Letter, Mee to Derry, 16 March 1933.
82. Letter, Mee to Derry, 20 March 1933.
83. "Visit of Mr Arthur Mee", *Derby Daily Telegraph*, 5 December 1912, 4.
84. "Hero worship", *The Sunday Times*, 6 November 1921, 9.
85. *Derby Daily Telegraph*, 5 December 1912, 4.
86. "Arthur Mee's Children's Hour", *The Bookman*, December 1928, 186.
87. Dixon, *From Instruction to Amusement*, 63-67.
88. "Your Editor's Advice", *Boy's Herald*, 1:1, August 1903.
89. *Every Boy's Monthly*, I, 1905.
90. Mee, *CE*, 3.
91. Letter, Mee to Derry, 8 December 1909.
92. Mee, *CE*, 2.
93. "The World From Which Peter Pan Came", *CN*, 16 February 1924, 2.
94. Adrienne E. Gavin & Andrew F. Humphries (2009), "Worlds Enough and Time: The Cult of Childhood in Edwardian Fiction" in Adrienne E. Gavin and Andrew F. Humphries (eds) (2009), *Childhood in Edwardian Fiction, Worlds Enough and Time*, London, Palgrave Macmillan, 2.
95. Hammerton, *Child of Wonder*, 35.
96. Quoted in Margaret Summerton, "He Taught Children the Magic of 'Why?'", *The Daily Mail*, 29 May 1943, 1.
97. Arthur Mee (1913), *Arthur Mee's Letters to Boys*, London, Hodder & Stoughton, 116.
98. Mee, *Arthur Mee's Wonderful Day*, 339.
99. Letter, Mee to Derry, 7 August 1925.
100. Letter, Mee to Derry, 21 November 1930.
101. Pound and Harmsworth, *Northcliffe*, 340.
102. Letter, Mee to Northcliffe, 13 May 1909.
103. Letter, Mee to Northcliffe, 13 May 1909.
104. Letter, Mee to Northcliffe, 30 October 1910.
105. Letter, Mee to Derry, 14 October 1910.
106. Letter, Mee to Derry, 12 October 1910.
107. Letter, Mee to Derry, 15 November 1910.
108. Letter, Mee to Derry, 14 October 1910.
109. Letter, Mee to Derry, 31 October 1910; Letter, Mee to Northcliffe, 30 October 1910.
110. Hammerton, *Child of Wonder*, 173.

111. Ibid., 174.
112. Thomas Herbert Darlow (1925), *William Robertson Nicoll: Life and Letters*, London, Hodder & Stoughton, 58-59.
113. Dixon Scott (1916), *Men of Letters*, London, Hodder & Stoughton, 205.
114. "Thank You, World", *CN*, 12 April 1919, 6.
115. See for example *CN*, 22 March 1919; *CN*, 29 March 1919; *CN*, 5 April 1919; and *CN*, 12 April 1919.
116. *The Times*, 11 August 1919, 15.
117. *The Times*, 26 March 1919, 14; 2 May 1919, 6.
118. "The Children's Newspaper", *Western Daily Press*, 22 March 1919, 4.
119. John Simpson (2005), *Days from a Different World*, London, Pan.
120. Harry Secombe, "To Be Honest", *Punch*, 18 October 1972, 533.
121. William Hardcastle, "Hardcastle", *Punch*, 4 October 1972, 458.
122. Roy Hattersley, "Tragi-Comic cuts", *Punch*, 28 March 1984, 24.
123. Hunter Davies, "Father's Day", *Punch*, 4 November 1981, 798.
124. Gillian Avery (2008), "Popular Education and Big Money: Mee, Hammerton and Northcliffe" in Julia Briggs, Dennis Butts, and Matthew Orville Grenby (eds), *Popular Children's Literature in Britain*, Aldershot, Ashgate Publishing Ltd, 229-247, 242.
125. Eric Hobsbawm (2003), *Interesting Times: A Twentieth-Century Life*, University of Virginia, Knopf Doubleday, 19.
126. Bob Bartholomew quoted in Steve Holland (2006), *Look and Learn: A History of the Classic Children's Magazine*, London, Look and Learn Magazine Ltd, 49.
127. Muriel M. Green (1948), "The Children's Magazine in Britain Today", *Library Review*, Vol. 11, 8, 464-467, 464.
128. "The Children's Treasure House", *The Daily Mail*, 27 August 1921, 6; "Lands & Peoples", *The Daily Mail*, 11 February 1926, 1; "Children's Pictorial", *The Daily Mail*, 5 November 5, 1924, 14.
129. Letter, Mee to Northcliffe, 8 May 1909.
130. Letter, Mee to Derry, 2nd January, 1924.
131. Letter, Mee to Derry, 2 November 1924.
132. Ibid.
133. Robert Bellah (1985), *Habits of the Heart: Individualism and Commitment in American Life*, Berkeley, University of California Press, 39.

4. God, Faith and Evolution *(pp. 58-73)*

1. William K. Lowther Clarke (ed.) (1911), *Facing the Facts*, London, James Nisbet.
2. George Haw (ed.) (1906), *Christianity and the Working Classes*, London, Macmillan.
3. Hugh McLeod (1999), "Dissent and the peculiarities of the English, c1870-1914" in Jane Shaw and Alan Kreider (eds), *Culture and the Nonconformist Tradition*, Cardiff, University of Wales Press.
4. James Anthony Froude (2011), *Thomas Carlyle: A History of the First Forty Years of His Life, 1795-1835*, Cambridge, Cambridge University Press, 2.
5. Mee, *Arthur Mee's Wonderful Day*, 88-89; Arthur Mee (1917), *Who Giveth Us the Victory*, Toronto, William Briggs, 58.

6. Mee, *Who Giveth Us the Victory*, 12.

7. Ibid., 313, 315.

8. Ibid., 77, 313.

9. "Arthur Mee's Ride Around England", *CN*, 7 September 1935, 4; see also Mee, *Arthur Mee's Letters to Boys*, 150-151.

10. Letter, Mee to Derry, 18 February 1924.

11. Letter, Mee to Derry, 19 February 1924.

12. Mee, *Arthur Mee's Letters to Boys*, 145; see also Arthur Mee, *Arthur Mee's Book of the Flag*, London, Hodder & Stoughton, 367.

13. Mee, *Arthur Mee's Book of the Flag*, 367.

14. Letter, Mee to Derry, 8 November 1909.

15. "Mr P.L. Parker", *The Times,* 4 April 1925, 17.

16. Letter, Mee to Derry, 2 April 1925.

17. Mee, *Arthur Mee's Wonderful Day*, 52.

18. Arthur Mee, *Arthur Mee's Book of Heroes*, London, Hodder & Stoughton, 239.

19. Mee, *Arthur Mee's Wonderful Day*, 83.

20. Ibid., 309.

21. William Paley (1802), *Natural Theology*, New York, American Tract Society, 15-16.

22. Mee, *Arthur Mee's Wonderful Day*, 310-311, 312.

23. Mee, *Who Giveth Us the Victory?*, 18.

24. Mee, *Arthur Mee's Wonderful Day*, 311.

25. Mee, *Who Giveth Us Victory?*, 33.

26. Mee, *Arthur Mee's Wonderful Day*, 309.

27. See 1883 letter to Charles A. Watts, editor of *The Agnostic Annual*, in *Life and Letters of Thomas Henry Huxley* (1913), 3 vols, London, Macmillan, 97.

28. B. Lightman, "Ideology, Evolution and Late-Victorian Agnostic Popularisers", in J. Moore (ed.) (1989), *History, Humanity and Evolution*, Cambridge, Cambridge University Press, 285-309.

29. Herbert Spencer (1904), *An Autobiography*, Volume 1, New York, D. Appleton & Co., 171.

30. Spencer, *An Autobiography*, 397.

31. Mee, *Arthur Mee's Wonderful Day*, 309.

32. See Ursula DeYoung (2011), *A Vision of Modern Science: John Tyndall and the Role of the Scientist in Victorian Culture*, New York, Palgrave Macmillan.

33. John Tyndall (1879), *Fragments of Science*, London, Longman, Green & Co.

34. Mee, *Who Giveth Us Victory?*, 33.

35. Mee, *Arthur Mee's Hero Book*, 316-317.

36. Mee, *Arthur Mee's Wonderful Day*, 333.

37. Ibid., 90.

38. Mee, *Arthur Mee's Hero Book*, 316-317.

39. "Brave, Beautiful, Wonderful World", *CN*, 20 October 1934, 9.

40. "The Power Forever Working in the World", *CN*, 3 November 1934, 9.

41. "God is Working Out his Purposes", *CN*, 17 January 1942, 1.

42. Frederick Burkhardt and Sydney Smith (1985, 1990 edn), *Correspondence of Charles Darwin*, 9 vols, Volume 5, Cambridge, Cambridge University Press, 32.

43. Mee, *Arthur Mee's Book of Heroes*, 83-84.

44. Mee, *Arthur Mee's Wonderful Day*, 341.

45. Mee, *Letters to Boys*, 86.
46. "Be of Good Courage", *CN*, 17 June 1922, 6.
47. "We Are Ten", *CN*, 23 March 1929, 6.
48. "Ten Ideas that must be beaten", *CN*, 10 December 1938, 9.
49. Mee, *Arthur Mee's Wonderful Day*, 329.
50. Mee, *Letters to Boys,* 10-11.
51. Mee, *Arthur Mee's Book of the Flag*, 360.
52. Mee, *Who Giveth Us the Victory?*, 61, 79.
53. Mee, *Who Giveth Us the Victory?*, 13.
54. Richard Soloway (1995), *Demography and Degeneration: Eugenics and the Declining Birthrate in Twentieth-Century Britain*, Chapel Hill, University of North Carolina, xvii-xviii.
55. *Report of the Inter-Departmental Committee on Physical Deterioration* (1904), London, HMSO.
56. Dan Stone (2002), *Breeding Superman: Nietzsche, Race and Eugenics in Edwardian and Interwar Britain*, Liverpool, Liverpool University Press, 115.
57. Geoffrey Searle (1990), *The Quest for National Efficiency: A Study in British Politics and Political Thought, 1899-1914*, London, Ashfield Press, 61.
58. Samuel Hynes (1968), *The Edwardian Turn of Mind: First World War and English Culture*, London, Pimlico, 45.
59. Dan Stone (2001), "Race in British Eugenics", *European History Quarterly*, Vol. 31, No. 3, 397-425.
60. Herbert Spencer (1891, 1967 edn), *The Study of Sociology*, New York, Appleton.
61. Spencer, *The Study of Sociology*, 314.
62. Francis Galton (1904), "Eugenics: Its Definitions, Scope and Aims", *The American Journal of Sociology*, Vol. 10, No. 1, 1-25, 1.
63. "Eugenics", *The Times*, 13 April 1910, 11.
64. "The Herbert Spencer Lecture", *The Times*, 8 June 1907, 7.
65. Greta Jones (1986), *Social Hygiene in Twentieth Century Britain*, New York, Croom Helm.
66. Sam Pryke (1998), "The Popularity of Nationalism in the Early British Boy Scout Movement", *Social History*, Vol. 23, No. 3, 309-324; Michael Rosenthal (1986), *The Character Factory, Baden-Powell and the Origins of the Boy Scout Movement*, New York, Pantheon Books.
67. It is as well to be careful not to confuse what Victorians and Edwardians meant by "race". The society within which Mee lived and worked was racist, but there is a need to differentiate between cultural racism and biological racism. Claims of racial supremacy were part of an established discourse of belonging to a culture within which race was intractably identified with the English nation. Consequently when some commentators wrote of "race" they were invariably defining what they considered to be the nation and its racial identity. This of course does not mean that biological racism was absent and there were a number of texts published, such as Arnold White's *Efficiency and Empire* (1901), Robert Reid Rentoul's *Race Culture or Race Suicide* (1906) and Charles Armstrong's *The Survival of the Unfittest* (1910). Among eugenics supporters the majority used the term "race" as an indicator of cultural identity, although for some, including at times H.G. Wells and Beatrice Webb, race was a biological category.

68. "The Science Of Race Building", *The Times*, 26 July 1912, 4.

69. Jones, *Social Hygiene in Twentieth Century Britain*, 18-21.

70. Thomas P. O'Connor, "The Busy Man's Reference Book", *The Daily Mail*, 18 November 1912, 6.

71. Gerald K. Chesterton (1922), *Eugenics and Other Evils*, London, Cassell & Co., 1.

72. Ibid., 180. In *What's Wrong with the World*, Chesterton writes, "Mr Saleeby would honestly like to have Eugenics; but I would rather have rheumatics."

73. Sidney Webb, "Regeneration or Race Suicide", *The Times*, 11 October 1906, 17; Sidney Webb & Beatrice Webb (1907), *The Decline of the Birth Rate*, London, Fabian Tract no. 131.

74. "Mr. Francis Galton On Eugenics", *The Times*, 17 May 1904, 14; see also Herbert G. Wells, "The Endowment of Motherhood", *The Daily Mail*, 22 June, 1910, 6; "Nonsense about Eugenic Babies", *The Daily Mail*, 18 October 1913, 4. In *The Time Machine* Wells presents a vision of evolutionary theory in its depiction of a future world in which humankind is divided between two degenerate races: the dissolute, apathetically and mentally corrupt Eloi, living on the surface, and the barbaric and savage subterranean Morlocks. Eugenics is also a feature of Wells' *The New Machiavelli* (1911).

75. Bernard Shaw's *Man and Superman* (1903) evokes fears of racial degeneration and explores Shaw's views on radical social and sexual reform through selective breeding and a biological approach to race improvement. It is important to be careful with Shaw's views on eugenics as he condemned negative eugenics and often satirised and undermined some of its claims.

76. Mee, *Who Giveth Us Victory?*, 77.

77. Letter, Mee to Northcliffe, 30 October 1910.

78. See Caleb Saleeby (1906), *Evolution, the Master-Key*, London, Harper.

79. Grant Rodwell (1997), "Dr Caleb Williams Saleeby: the Complete Eugenicist", *History of Education*, 26, 1, 23-40, 24.

80. "Kent County Temperance Federation", *Kent & Sussex Courier*, 19 April 1918, 5; "The Temperance Congress", *Kent & Sussex Courier*, 31 May 1918, 4; "Climbing Up to Higher Things", *CN*, 13 March 1920, 3; "Dr. Saleeby", *CN*, 23 December 1940, 2; "Child Welfare Conference", *Kent & Sussex Courier*, 24 November 1916, 5.

81. "Kent County Temperance Federation", *Kent Messenger*, 26 May 1917, 3.

82. Caleb Saleeby (1909), *Parenthood and Race Culture*, London, Cassell & Co.

83. Ronald Campbell Macfie (1912), *Heredity, Evolution, and Vitalism*, New York, William Wood & Co, 254-261; see also "Ronald Macfie", *Times Literary Supplement*, 1 December 1932, 914.

84. "Collected Poems of Dr Macfie", *CN*, 28 December 1929, 13. Macfie also wrote on health-related issues. See Ronald Campbell Macfie (1909), *Air and Health*, London, Methuen & Co.

85. "The Song of the Girl Guides", *CN*, 22 March 1930.

86. Letter, Mee to Derry, 11 June 1931; 16 July 1931; see Mee's *CN* obituary, "One More Old Friend of Ours", *CN*, 27 June 1931, 2.

87. "Life and the Lungs", *The Children's Encyclopaedia*, Vol. 2, 1320.

88. Ibid., 1323.

89. Arthur Mee and John Hammerton (eds) (1910), *The World's Greatest Books*, New York, McKinlay, Stone & Mackenzie, 111.
90. "Nation's Ladder", *CN*, 3 March 1920, 3.
91. "The Herbert Spencer Lecture", *The Times*, 8 June 1907, 7; Francis Galton (1909), "Eugenic qualities of primary importance", *Eugenic Review*, 1 (2), 74-76.
92. Rodwell, "Dr Caleb Williams Saleeby", 28-30.
93. Mee, *Arthur Mee's Book of the Flag*, 363.
94. Letter, Mee to Derry, 9 February 1926.
95. Nathan Roberts (2004), "Character in the mind: citizenship, education and psychology in Britain, 1880–1914", *History of Education*, Vol. 33, No. 2, 177-197, 177.
96. Board of Education (1904), *Codes of Regulations for Public Elementary Schools with Schedules*, London, HMSO, Introduction.
97. Florence H. Ellis (1907), *Character Forming in School*, London, Longmans, Green & Co., v.
98. Michael Sadler (ed.) (1908), *Moral Instruction and Training in Schools. Report of an International Inquiry: Volume One: The United Kingdom*, London, Longmans, Green & Co., xvii.
99. Mee, *Arthur Mee's Talks to Boys*, 115-127.
100. Ibid., 117-122.
101. Ibid., 20.
102. "Right and Left", *CN*, 29 July 1922, 6.
103. Mee, *Arthur Mee's Talks to Girls*, 111-112.
104. "Work and Play", *CN*, 24 March 1928, 6.
105. "Well Played", *CN*, 21 February 1925, 6.
106. "Drifting", *CN*, 17 December 1927, 6.
107. Geoffrey Searle (1976), *Eugenics and Politics in Britain, 1900-1914*, Leyden, Noordhoff.
108. "Alcohol, the enemy of life", *CE*, Volume 2, 2679.
109. Ibid., 2681.
110. Mee, *Arthur Mee's Talks to Boys*, 47.
111. Letter, Mee to Derry, 26 October 1914.
112. Hammerton, *Child of Wonder*, 161.
113. Letter, Mee to Sir William Robertson Nicoll, 3 August 1916, MS 3518/1/1/24, Special Collections, University of Aberdeen.
114. Darlow, *William Robertson Nicoll: Life and Letters*, London, Hodder & Stoughton, 243; see also W. Robertson Nicoll (1907), *The Lamp of Sacrifice: sermons preached on special occasions*, New York, A.C. Armstrong & Co.
115. Hammerton, *Books and Myself*, 163.
116. Arthur Mee and Stuart Holden (1917), *Defeat or Victory?: The Strength of Britain Book* with an introduction by C.W. Saleeby; *The Fiddlers: Drink in the Witness Box* (1917), London, Morgan and Scott; *The Parasite* (1917), London, Morgan and Scott.
117. Mee, *The Fiddlers*.
118. "Censorship", HC debate, 25 June 1917, Vol. 95, cc30-131.
119. Mee, *Defeat or Victory?*.

120. "Barred Book Seized in Canada", *The Christian Science Monitor*, 15 March 1918, 9; "Today in Parliament", *Derby Daily Telegraph*, 20 June 1917, 3; *Manchester Evening News*, 19 June 1917, 3.

121. Mee, *Who Giveth Us Victory?*, 147-148.

122. "The Case for Prohibition", *The Daily Mail*, 22 December 1916, 2; *Cheltenham Looker-On*, 9 March 1918, 14; "The Truth About Alcohol and the War", *Daily Express*, 14 December 1916, 1; *Daily Express*, 22 December 1916, 1.

123. "Publicans and Prohibition", *Nottingham Evening Post*, 3 May 1917, 2.

124. *The Daily Mail*, 31 May 1917, 1; *The Daily Mail*, 17 January 1917, 6; "Our Threatened Food", *The Daily Mail*, 5 February 1917, 2; *The Daily Mail*, 30 March 1917, 6; "Sugar Waste", *The Daily Mail*, 5 January 1918, 7; "Manifesto", *Church Times*, 8 June 1917, 500.

125. "The Nation Speaks at the Albert Hall", *The Daily Mail*, 24 May 1917, 1.

126. "Strength of Britain Movement", *The Daily Mail*, 3 August 1917, 5.

127. Quoted in "Beer and Food", *The Daily Mail*, 25 July 1917, 5.

128. "Strength of Britain", *The Daily Mail*, 19 August 1917, 4.

129. Arthur Mee, "The Strength of Britain Movement", *The Daily Mail*, 16 August 1917, 2.

130. Richard Henry Tawney (1931), *Equality*, London, Unwin Books.

5. A Matchless England *(pp. 74-85)*

1. Letter, Mee to Derry, 5 January 1931; Letter, Mee to Derry, 9 August 1915.

2. Arthur Mee (1936), *Enchanted Land*, London, Hodder & Stoughton, 4.

3. Letter, Mee to Derry, 28 July 1927.

4. Mee, *Arthur Mee's Book of the Flag*, 24.

5. Ibid., 19-20.

6. Ibid., 315.

7. Ibid., 357, 359; "What Are You-Doing in the World Arthur Mee?", *CN*, 21 May 1938, 10.

8. Arthur Mee (1941), *1940: Our Finest Hour*, London, Hodder & Stoughton, 113.

9. Mee, *Arthur Mee's Book of the Flag*, 366.

10. Ibid., 313.

11. "Where They Love Shakespeare", *CN*, 12 August 1922, 7.

12. "Shakespeare's Day", *CN*, 2 April 1923, 6.

13. Letter, Mee to Derry, 11 February 1926.

14. Letter, Mee to Derry, 2 February 1922.

15. John Derry made a significant contribution to this publication and chose many of the individuals to be included. See letter, Mee to Derry, 24 August 1933. Originally intended to consist of fifty parts, the magazine came to an end with part thirty-eight.

16. Mee, *1940: Our Finest Hour*, 37.

17. Mee, *Letters to Boys*, 5.

18. Mee, *Arthur Mee's Book of the Flag*, 366; Mee, *1940: Our Finest Hour*, 113.

19. "What Are You-Doing-in the World Arthur Mee?", *CN*, 21 May 1938, 11; Mee, *Arthur Mee's Book of the Flag*, 367. Mee's heroes included explorers, writers, social reformers, scientists and inventors. The list is long and includes Captain James

Cook, Grace Darling, Walter Raleigh, William Shakespeare, Elizabeth Fry, Florence Nightingale, Edith Cavell, Thomas Carlyle, Alfred Russel Wallace, Charles Darwin, Shakespearean characters like Henry V.

20. Mee, *Arthur Mee's Talks to Boys*, 102-103.

21. Mee, *Arthur Mee's Hero Book*, 47-48.

22. Ibid., 93.

23. Ibid., 177.

24. Ibid., 272

25. Ibid., 64. See *The Spectator*, 3 November 1917, for an account of Greenaway's exploits.

26. Mee occasionally turned over the editorial of *The Children's Newspaper* to Baden-Powell, on which occasions the Chief Scout wrote of improving the health, strength and character of the young and of shielding them from foreign films, "slackness", watching professional sport and "general unrest", an agenda with which Mee vigorously agreed. See "The Chief Scout Speaks", *CN*, 12 December 1936, 6.

27. Mee, *Arthur Mee's Hero Book*, 275.

28. Ibid., 233-234.

29. "What Are You-Doing in the World Arthur Mee?", *CN*, 21 May 1938, 10.

30. Martin J. Wiener (2004 edn), *English Culture and the Decline of the Industrial Spirit, 1850-1980*, Cambridge, Cambridge University Press.

31. Charles Masterman (1904), "The English City" in Lucian Oldershaw (ed.), *England: A Nation*, London, R. Brimley Johnson, 49.

32. Robert C.K. Ensor (1904), "The English Countryside" in Oldershaw, *England: A Nation*, 97.

33. Ernest C. Pulbrook (1915), *The English Countryside*, London, Batsford Ltd, 2.

34. Stanley Baldwin, "What England means to me", speech to the Royal Society of St George, Hotel Cecil, London, 6 May 1924; see also Stanley Baldwin (1937), *On England and Other Addresses*, London, Books for Libraries Press.

35. Henry V. Morton (1927), *In Search of England*, London, Methuen & Co., 14.

36. Vera Brittain (1940), *England's Hour*, London, Macmillan & Co. Ltd, 257-258.

37. Mee, *Enchanted Land*, Introduction; Mee, *Little Treasure Island: Her Story and Her Glory*, London, Hodder & Stoughton, Prelude. The book was published in 1920 but elements of it were written as far back as 1914.

38. Mee, *Arthur Mee's Book of the Flag*, 365.

39. Mee, *Enchanted Land*, 1936, 1.

40. "The Great House of a Great People", *CN*, April 26 1919, 6.

41. "The Glory of the Earth", *CN*, 8 May 1920, 6.

42. Editorial, "Are We Good Tenants", *CN*, 4 November 1939, 6.

43. Mee, *Enchanted Land*, 29.

44. Letter, Mee to Derry, 29 August 1928.

45. Mee, *Enchanted Land*, 156.

46. David Matless (1998), *Landscape and Englishness*, London, Reaktion Books; Roger Ebbatson (2005), *An Imaginary England: Nation, Landscape and Literature, 1840-1920*, Aldershot, Ashgate Publishing Ltd; Robert Burden and Stephan Kohl (eds) (2006), *Landscape and Englishness*, Amsterdam, Rodopi.

47. Fred Inglis (1981), *The Promise of Happiness*, Cambridge, Cambridge University Press.

48. Anne Helmreich (2002), *The English Garden and National Identity: The Competing Styles of Garden Design, 1870-1914*, Cambridge, Cambridge University Press, 3.

49. F.E. Green (1909), "The architect in the garden", *The World's Work*, Vol. 17, April, 508.

50. Mee, *Arthur Mee's Wonderful Day*, 38.

51. Mee, *Enchanted Land*, 284.

52. Hammerton, *Child of Wonder*, 165.

53. "Down in Somerset", *CN*, 3 September 1927, 6.

54. "Arthur Mee's Broadcast", *CN*, 1 December 1934, 9.

55. Mee, *Little Treasure Island*, 178.

56. Mee, *Enchanted Land*, 282.

57. Mee, *Little Treasure Island*, 108.

58. Arthur Mee, "A Garden-Owner's Privilege", *The Times*, 5 August 1930, 11; "Gardens Open to the Public", *The Times*, 1 August 1938, 15; "Kent Gardens on View", *Dover Express*, 29 July 1938, 14.

59. Arthur Mee, "A Country Garden", *The Times*, 22 April 1941, 5.

60. "To a Friend Far Away", *CN*, 30 September 1939, 1.

61. Susan Ang (2000), *The Widening World of Children's Literature*, London, Palgrave Macmillan; Peter Hunt (ed.) (1995), *Children's Literature: An Illustrated History*, Oxford, Oxford University Press.

62. Mee, *Little Treasure Island*, 202.

63. *The Daily Herald*, 31 July 1914, 1; "More Anti-War Protests", 6 August 1914, 5.

64. Herbert G. Wells, "Why Britain Went to War", *The War Illustrated*, 22 August 1914, 2.

65. Cited in Mary Kertesz (1992), "The Enemy: British images of the German people during the Second World War", unpublished PhD thesis, Sussex University, 33.

66. Mee, *Little Treasure Island*, 202.

67. Pound & Harmsworth, *Northcliffe*, 327; see also Sally J. Taylor (1996), *The Great Outsiders: Northcliffe, Rothermere and the Daily Mail*, London, Weidenfeld & Nicolson.

68. Letter, Northcliffe to Mee, 22 August 1908.

69. Letter, Mee to Northcliffe, 27 August 1908.

70. Letter, Northcliffe to Mee, 23 March 1908.

71. Arthur L. Frothingham (1919), *Handbook of War Facts and Peace Problems*, New York, Committee on Organised Education National Security League.

72. The Bryce Report (1915), *Report of the Committee on Alleged German Outrages*, London, HMSO. See John Horne and Alan Kramer (2001), *German Atrocities, 1914: A History of Denial*, Yale University Press, New Haven, CT.

73. Cited in Ian Cawood and David McKinnon-Bell (2010), *The First World War: Questions and Analysis in History*, London, Routledge, 29.

74. John Clifford (1917), *Our Fight for Belgium and What it Means*, London, Hodder & Stoughton, 7.

75. Mee, *Little Treasure Island*, 236.

76. Ibid., 203-214.

77. Letter, Mee to Derry, 12 October 1914.

78. Letter, Mee to Derry, 10 November 1914.

79. Mee, *Little Treasure Island*, 216-217.
80. Letter, Mee to Derry, 10 November 1914.
81. See Richard Van Emden and Steve Humphries (2004), *All Quiet on the Home Front: An Oral History of Life in Britain During the First World War*, London, Headline Books.
82. Letter, Mee to Derry, 10 November 1914.
83. Mee, *Little Treasure Island*, 232-249, 246.

6. An Accidental Empire *(pp. 86-101)*

1. Quoted in J.A. Spender (1923), *The Life of the Right Hon. Sir Henry Campbell Bannerman*, Volume 1, London, GCB, 257.
2. S.C. Smith (1998), *British Imperialism, 1750-1970*, Cambridge, Cambridge University Press, 34.
3. George Orwell, "The Lion and the Unicorn: Socialism and the English Genius" in Sonia Orwell and Ian Angus (eds) (1970), *The Collected Essays, Journalism and Letters of George Orwell*, Harmondsworth, Penguin Books, 80.
4. Bernard Porter (2005), *The Absent-Minded Imperialists: Empire, Society, and Culture in Britain*, Oxford, Oxford University Press, 307.
5. Catherine Hall and Sonya O. Rose (eds) (2006), *At Home With The Empire: Metropolitan Culture and the Imperial World*, Cambridge, Cambridge University Press.
6. Michael Billig (1995), *Banal Nationalism*, London, Falmer Press.
7. John M. MacKenzie (1984), *Propaganda and Empire: The Manipulation of British Public Opinion, 1880-1960*, Manchester, Manchester University Press; John M. MacKenzie (ed.) (1986), *Imperialism and Popular Culture*, Manchester, Manchester University Press.
8. Kathryn Castle (1996), *Britannia's Children*, Manchester, Manchester University Press, 7-8.
9. Lawrence James (1994), *The Rise and Fall of the British Empire*, Cheltenham, Pickaback Books, 207; see also George Orwell's essay on the impact of weekly magazines for boys written in 1939 in Orwell and Angus (eds), *Collected Essays, Journalism and Letters*, 566-567.
10. John A. Hobson (1902), *Imperialism: A Study*, London, J. Nisbet.
11. John George Godard (1905), *Racial Supremacy: Being Studies in Imperialism*, London, Simpkin, Marshall & Co. Ltd, 8, 31.
12. Frederick Harrison (1908), *National & Social Problems*, London, Macmillan.
13. Francis W. Hirst, Gilbert Murray & J.L. Hammond (1900), *Liberalism and the Empire*, London, Brimley Johnson, 4.
14. Quoted in Paul Kennedy (1980), *The Rise of Anglo-German Antagonism*, 1860-1914, London, George Allen & Unwin, 467.
15. See for example Francis W. Hirst, Gilbert Murray and J.L. Hammond (1900), *Liberalism and the Empire*, London, R. Brimley Johnson.
16. Mee, *Arthur Mee's Book of the Flag*.
17. Mee, *Little Treasure Island*, Preface.
18. Mee, *Arthur Mee's Book of the Flag*, 19.
19. "The Foundation Stones of Happiness", *CN*, 26 January 1935, 4.

20. "The Rise of Britain Overseas", *CE*, Volume 3, 1946, 2076.

21. Mee, *Arthur Mee's Book of the Flag*, 72; "The Amazing Empire", *CN*, 1 December 1923, 3; "A Splendid Heritage", *CN*, 23 May 1925, 7.

22. Arthur Mee (1939), *Why We Had to Go to War*, London, Hodder & Stoughton, 8.

23. "God's Witness", *CN*, 9 September 1939, 1-2.

24. Mee, *1940: Our Finest Hour*, 50.

25. Sir John Robert Seeley (1883), *The Expansion of England: Two Courses of Lectures*, Boston, Roberts Brothers, 8.

26. Arthur Mee, "Twenty Fourth of May", *CN*, 21 May 1943, 1.

27. Mee, *Arthur Mee's Book of the Flag*, 72.

28. "A Splendid Heritage", *CN*, 23 May 1925, 7.

29. Mee, *Arthur Mee's Book of the Flag*, 72.

30. "Our Valuable Empire", *CN*, 17 January 1935, 5.

31. Mee, *Arthur Mee's Book of the Flag*, 78.

32. Ibid., 86.

33. Ibid., 93; "Crime In India", *CN*, 22 November 1924, 4.

34. "Editorial, A Master Problem of Our Race", *CN*, 8 March 1924, 6.

35. Letter, Mee to Derry, 30 September 1921.

36. *The Times*, 25 May 1907, 8.

37. Arthur Mee, "Arthur Mee Twenty Fourth of May", *CN*, 21 May 1943, 1.

38. Ibid.

39. "A Splendid Heritage", *CN*, 23 May 1925, 7.

40. "The Island in the middle of the world and the Peoples of the Flag", *CN*, 22 May 1920, 5.

41. *The Manchester Guardian*, 24 May 1908.

42. F. Clement and C. Egerton (1914), *The Future of Education*, London, G. Bell and Sons Ltd, 49.

43. Jim English (2006), "Empire Day in Britain, 1904-1958", *The Historical Journal*, 49, 1, 247-276; Jonathan Rose (2001), *The Intellectual Life of the British Working Classes*, New Haven, Yale University Press.

44. Hall and Rose, *At Home With The Empire*, 22-23.

45. Niall Ferguson (2004), *Empire: How Britain Made the Modern World*, London, Penguin, originally published by Allen Lane.

46. Arnold White (1901), *Efficiency and Empire*, London, Methuen.

47. A Biologist, "A Biological View of English Foreign Policy", *Saturday Review*, February 1896.

48. *Western Mail*, 4 December 1893, 3.

49. *Sunderland Daily Echo and Shipping Gazette*, 28 May 1894, 2.

50. *Burnley Express*, 13 June 1894, 2.

51. "The Parts of the Brain", *CE*, Vol. 5, 3047.

52. "The Head and the Limbs", *CE*, Vol. 3, 1692.

53. Ibid.

54. "Possibilities of the Race that Once Owned Australia", *CN*, 14 May 1927, 8.

55. Ibid.

56. Ibid.

57. Mee, *Arthur Mee's Book of the Flag*, 191.

58. Ibid.
59. "Portrait of a Gentleman", *CN*, 27 July 1929, 4.
60. "Should Men be Made to Work?", *CN*, 7 August 1926, 8.
61. Mee, *Arthur Mee's Book of the Flag*, 219.
62. Ibid., 221; "Peter Pan is a Soldier", *CN*, 12 July 1941, 1.
63. Mee, *Arthur Mee's Book of the Flag*, 141.
64. Bernard Smith (1985), *European Vision and the South Pacific*, New Haven, Yale University Press, 167.
65. "A Beautiful Chair in an Ugly House", *CN*, 30 October 1926, 7.
66. "Topsy-Turvy Country", *CN*, 22 August 1942, 7.
67. "An Exile Thinks of Home", *CN*, 24 November 1928, 9.
68. "Western Australia is 100 Years Old", *CN*, 22 June 1929, 12.
69. "Beautiful Australia", *CN*, 8 October 1928, 9.
70. "The Mixing Up of Peoples", *CN*, 14 February 1925, 7.
71. Ibid.
72. "Sir Leonard Hill", *CN*, 26 September 1931, 5.
73. Mee to Derry, 27 September 1929.
74. Letter, Arthur Mee to John Derry, 17 February 1925.
75. "Boys for the Empire", *CN*, 25 March 1922, 9.
76. "A Boy's Hope", *CN*, 16 August 1924, 9.
77. "Big Brother's Waiting", *CN*, 21 November 1925, 9; "Little Brother's First Friend", *CN*, 8 October 1927; "Wonderful Spaces", *CN*, 16 July 1924, 9.
78. "Career of an East End Boy", *CN*, 20 October 1928, 2.
79. "To Be a Farmer's Boy", *CN*, 10 October 1935, 4.
80. "Big Brother's Waiting", *CN*, 21 November 1925, 9; "Little Brother's First Friend", *CN*, 8 October 1927, 3.
81. "Little Brother's First Friend", *CN*, 8 October 1927, 3.
82. Ibid.
83. "Kookaburras from Cockneys", *CN*, 11 July 1931, 8.
84. "A Place in the Sun For All", *CN*, 28 September 1935, 7.
85. "The Children's Farm", *CN*, 30 June 1934, 2.
86. "Kingsley Fairbridge's Farm Schools", *CN*, 16 July 1938, 2.
87. Roger Kershaw & Janet Sacks (2008), *New Lives for Old: The Story of Britain's Child Migrants*, London, The National Archives.
88. Legislative Assembly Former Child Migrants Statement by Minister for Family and Children's Services, Western Australia Parliament, 13 August 1998: http://www.parliament.wa.gov.au/hansard.
89. "Prime Minister's Statement: Child Migration", *Parliament UK*, 25 February 2010: http://www.parliament.uk/business/news/2010/02/prime-ministers-statement-child-migration.
90. Joseph Catanzaro, "Farmed out to fear", *The West Australian*, 26-27 May 2012, 63-65.
91. Mee, *Arthur Mee's Book of the Flag*, 161.
92. "In the Empty Heart of Australia", *CN*, 22 August 1925, 7.
93. Bob Reece (2007), *Daisy Bates: Grand Dame of the Desert*, Canberra, National Library of Australia.

94. Henry Reynolds (2005), *Nowhere People: How International Race Thinking Shaped Australia's Identity*, Melbourne, Penguin; Richard Hall (1998), *Black Armband Days: Truth from the Dark Side of Australia's Past*, Sydney, Vintage, 149.

95. Visits by royalty brought her celebrity and in 1934 she was awarded a CBE. See "Waiting for the King's Son", *CN*, 13 October 1934, 2; "King's Son Calls on Daisy Bates", *CN*, 24 November 1935, 1.

96. "Children in the Stone Age", *CN*, 5 May 1928, 8.

97. Mee, *Arthur Mee's Book of the Flag*, 163.

98. Letter, Hancock to John Derry, 8 September 1927.

99. "The Stone Age Man Coming On", *CN*, 24 December 1927, 3; "Men Appear Out of the Stone Age", *CN*, 3 March 1928, 7.

100. "The Stone Age Man Coming On", *CN*, 24 December 1927, 3.

101. "Children in the Stone Age", *CN*, 5 May 1928, 8.

102. Letter, Mee to Derry, 2 January 1929.

103. Letter, Mee to Derry, 7 July 1930.

104. Mee, *Arthur Mee's Book of the Flag*, 164.

105. "Kabbarli, the solitary spectator of a vanishing race", *CN*, 26 November 1938, 8.

106. Daisy Bates (1938), *The Passing of the Aborigines: A Lifetime Spent Among the Natives of Australia*, London, Murray.

107. Quoted in Bob Reece, *Daisy Bates: Grand Dame of the Desert*, 123.

108. "Our Cannibals", *The Sydney Morning Herald*, 30 January 1930, 6; "Our Cannibals", *The Sydney Morning Herald*, 27 January 1930, 2.

109. Bob Reece (2007), "'You Would Have Loved Her for Her Lore': The Letters of Daisy Bates", *Australian Aboriginal Studies*, No. 1, 51-70.

110. Hall, *Black Armband Days*, 169.

111. Ann Standish, "Devoted Service to a Dying Race?: Daisy Bates and the Passing of the Aborigines" in Joy Damousi and Katharine Ellinghaus (eds) (1999), *Citizenship, Women and Social Justice*, History Department, The University of Melbourne, 59.

112. Rowena Mohr (1999), "Neo-colonialist Hagiography and the Making of an Australian Legend: Daisy Bates", *Lateral*, Issue 2, 2.

7. Society, Humanity and Order *(pp. 102-123)*

1. "Work Hard and Play Hard", *CN*, 11 March 1922, 6.

2. Mee, *1940: Our Finest Hour*.

3. Hammerton, *Child of Wonder*, 102.

4. Ian Packer (2003), "Religion and the New Liberalism: The Rowntree Family, Quakerism and Social Reform", *Journal of British Studies*, Vol. 42, No. 2, 236-257, 240.

5. Letter, Mee to Derry, 1 June 1911.

6. Arthur Mee (1898), "The Transformation in Slumland: The Remarkable Story of a London Clergyman", *Temple Magazine*, 2, 181, 449-454, 451.

7. Mee, *Arthur Mee's Letters to Boys*, 150.

8. John Clifford (1898), *Socialism and the Teaching of Christ*, London, Fabian Tract No. 78, 5; John Clifford (1906), *The Ultimate Problems of Christianity*, London, James Clarke & Co., 291-292.

9. Quoted in Hammerton, *Child of Wonder*, 163.

10. "John Clifford the Factory Boy", *CN*, 8 December 1923, 6.

11. Mee, *Who Giveth Us the Victory?*, 125.

12. Ibid., 71.

13. Ibid., 139.

14. Ibid., 101.

15. Ibid., 146.

16. Ibid., 140-141.

17. Ibid., 152.

18. "Give Them Something To Do", *CN*, 2 February 1929, 6; "Work For Every Man", *CN*, 6 August 1932, 7.

19. Letter, Mee to Derry, 7 February 1929.

20. Letter, Mee to Derry, 19 March 1928.

21. "To the National Government", *CN*, 31 December 1932, 6; "The Million With Nothing to Do", *CN*, 22 September 1923, 8.

22. "Work Waiting for Idle Men", *CN*, 16 July 1932, 10.

23. "Two Million Men Doing Nothing", *CN*, 18 February 1939, 1.

24. Hammerton, *Books and Myself*, 176.

25. "More Troops and Tanks to End Liverpool Strikes", *The Daily Mirror*, 5 August 1919, 3.

26. "Government Strikes and the Public", *The Sunday Times*, 9 February 1919, 6.

27. "Bolshevist Gold Paid to Ferment Strikes Here", *The Daily Mirror*, 7 August 1919, 3.

28. Kingsley Martin (1966), *Father Figures*, London, Hutchinson, 88. See also *The Times*, 8 May 1919, 12, for a report of Bolshevik "terror" and "wholesale executions" in Petrograd.

29. Paul Ward (1998), *Red Flag and Union Jack: Englishness, Patriotism and the British Left, 1881-1924*, Woodbridge, Boydell & Brewer Ltd, 166.

30. Quoted in Paul B. Johnson (1968), *Land Fit for Heroes: The Planning of British Reconstruction, 1916-1919*, Chicago, Chicago University Press, 30.

31. Mee, *Arthur Mee's Talks to Girls*.

32. Ibid., 81

33. "The Ten Dark Days", *CN*, 18 October 1919, 1.

34. "Our Country Over All", *CN*, 18 October 1919, 6.

35. "The Rules of the Game", *CN*, 7 February 1920, 6.

36. "The Sanity of Labour", *CN*, 15 July 1922, 2.

37. "The Troubles of Old King Coal", *CN*, 11 September 1920, 7.

38. "Moscow Orders to our Reds", *The Daily Mail*, 25 October 1924, 9; Ibid., 8.

39. Letter, Mee to Derry, 2 November 1924. Ramsey MacDonald's election speech in Glasgow accused the Liberals and Conservatives of forcing an election. Part of the speech focussed upon explaining why the government had abandoned the prosecution of Mr J.R. Campbell, the editor of the communist *Workers Weekly* newspaper. Campbell was accused of sedition by enticing mutiny among soldiers and sailors. The charge was withdrawn after Labour members in Parliament threatened to abandon their support for MacDonald's government. It is entirely possible that Mee saw this as unacceptable partisan politics bordering on corruption and explains his comment that "They are ready to sacrifice the country for a party any day". See "Dirty Indeed", *The Daily Mail*, 15 October 1924, 8.

40. "The Dramatic Change in Parliament", *CN*, 15 November 1924.

41. Letter, Mee to Derry, 2 November 1924; Letter, Mee to Derry, 7 August 1925.

42. "British Ideas for Britain", *CN*, 17 October 1925, 6; "Impatience", *CN*, 8 September 1923, 6.

43. Letter, Mee to Derry, 12 August 1925.

44. "Our Duty", *The Times*, 6 May 1926, 3; "For King and Country", *The Daily Mail*, 3 May 1926, 8; "The Illegal Strike", *The Daily Mail*, 8 May 1926, 2.

45. "A Fight to a Finish", *Manchester Guardian*, 7 May 1926, 1.

46. *The Daily Express*, 4 May 1926, 1.

47. *The Daily Express*, 7 May 1926, 1.

48. Letter, Mee to Derry, 7 May 1926.

49. Ibid.

50. Ibid. In this passage Mee is referring to the fact that on 2-3 May typesetters in the print room of *The Daily Mail* refused to set the paper for publication unless passages of an anti-strike editorial were removed. This action was seen by some as the first act of the General Strike. See "No Fumbling", *The Daily Mail*, 4 May 1926, 4.

51. The 1910 Osborne Judgement held that the law did not allow trade unions to collect a levy for political purposes, specifically, to fund the Labour Party's organisational and electoral efforts. The judgement was reversed by the Trade Union Act 1913. This restored the legitimacy of union political funding but required unions to ballot all their members and to allow individual members to opt out of contributing to the levy.

52. Letter, Mee to Derry, 7 May 1926.

53. Ibid.

54. Ibid.

55. Ibid.

56. Ibid.

57. Roy Hattersley (2007), *Borrowed Time: The Story of Britain Between the Wars*, London, Abacus Books, 128.

58. Tony Cliff and Donny Gluckstein (1986), *Marxism and Trade Union Struggle: The General Strike of 1926*, London, Bookmarks; Chanie Rosenberg (1919), *Britain on the Brink of Revolution*, London, Bookmarks; "Soviet Money for General Strike", *The Times*, 11 June 1926, 9; "British Note To Moscow", *The Times*, 12 June 1926, 14; "The General Strike", *The Times*, 5 May 1926, 1; "Mr. Macdonald on The General Strike", *The Times*, 28 May 1926, 12.

59. "The Nation's Victory", *The Financial Times*, 13 May 1926, 2.

60. "Volunteers Keep the Country Going: Scenes of the Great Strike", *Illustrated London News*, 14 May 1926, 867.

61. "For King and Country!", *The Daily Mail*, 13 May 1926, 2.

62. "The County's Nine Day Wonder", *CN*, 22 May 1926, 1.

63. Ibid.

64. "The Great Crisis", *CN*, 22 May 1926, 2.

65. "Editorial", *CN*, 22 May 1926, 2.

66. Julia Bush (2002), "British Women's Anti-Suffragism and the Forward Policy, 1908-14", *Women's History Review*, Vol. 11, 3, 431-454.

67. Violet Markham (1912), *Miss Violet Markham's Great Speech at the Albert Hall*, London, National League for Opposing Woman Suffrage.

68. Julia Bush (2007), *Women Against the Vote: Female Anti-Suffragism in Britain*, Oxford, Oxford University Press.
69. Letter, Mee to Derry, 22 December 1909.
70. Mee, *Arthur Mee's Letters to Girls*, 75.
71. Ibid., 77.
72. Ibid., 78.
73. Ibid., 30-32.
74. Ibid., 128.
75. Ibid., 110.
76. Mee, *Arthur Mee's Letters to Girls*, 25, 45.
77. Caleb Saleeby (1911), *Women and Womanhood: A Search for Principles*, New York, M. Kennerley, 7, 260.
78. Caleb Saleeby (1909), "Psychology of parenthood", *Eugenics Review*, April, 1(1), 37-46, 44.
79. Mee, *Letters to Girls*, 27, 31-33.
80. Arthur Mee (1924), *Talks to Girls*, 113. *Talks to Girls* was a revised edition of Mee's 1913 *Arthur Mee's Letters to Girls*, but the content is almost identical.
81. Mee, *Letters to Girls*, 142.
82. Mee, *Talks to Girls*, 97.
83. Ibid., 102-103; see also Arthur Mee, "The Girl Who Wants Her Chance", *CN*, 15 May 1920, 9.
84. Mee, *Talks to Girls*, 93.
85. Letter, Hancock to Derry, 22 May 1922.
86. "Girls Doing Great Things", *CN*, 10 June 1922, 7.
87. Letter, Hancock to Derry, 12 September 1932.
88. Lucy Delap (2005), "Feminist and Anti-Feminist Encounters in Edwardian Britain", *Historical Research* 78, 201, 377-399, 381; Bush, *Women Against the Vote*, 23-139.
89. "In Memoriam", *The Times*, 20 July 1946, 1; *The Times*, 21 July 1950; "In Memoriam", *The Times*, 24 December 1957, 1.
90. Letter, Mee to Derry, 18 August 1913.
91. Letter, Mee to Derry, 22 December 1909.
92. *Western Gazette*, 11 February 1927, 8; *Yorkshire Post and Leeds Intelligencer*, 29 June 1933, 2.
93. Letter, Mee to Derry, 11 December 1921.
94. "Big and Little Eggs", *CN*, 13 May 1922, 8; *CN*, 3 June 1922, 5.
95. Barbara Lamming, *The Trident*, December 1982.
96. Letter, Mee to Derry, 11 April 1929.
97. Hammerton, *Books and Myself*, 171.
98. Letter, Mee to Derry, 29 May 1911; Letter, Mee to Derry, 1 June 1911.
99. Letter, Mee to Derry, 26 November 1913; Letter, Mee to Derry, 7 August 1925.
100. Letter, Mee to Derry, 31 July 1930.
101. Letter, Mee to Derry, 7 May 1926.
102. Letter, Hancock to Derry, 13 November 1930; see also "Deaths", *Nottingham Evening Post*, 13 November 1930, 8.
103. Letter, Mee to Derry, 2 December 1930.

8. The Challenge of the Modern *(pp. 124-141)*

1. Samuel Hynes (1990), *A War Imagined: The First World War and English Culture*, London, Bodley Head, ix.
2. "Arthur Mee's Jubilee", *CN*, 11 October 1941, 5.
3. "The Miracle That is Being Born", *CN*, 17 July 1937, 1.
4. Susan Pedersen and Peter Mandler (eds) (1994), *After the Victorians: Private Conscience and Public Duty in Modern Britain: Essays in Memory of John Clive*, London, Psychology Press, 10.
5. "Impatience", *CN*, 8 September 1923, 6.
6. "Young England and Old England", *CN*, 3 November 1923, 6.
7. "From the Editor's Desk", *CN*, 2 September 1939, 6.
8. D.H. Lawrence (2003), *Studies in Classic American Literature*, Volume 2, Cambridge, Cambridge University Press, 30.
9. Brendon O'Connor (2004), "A Brief History of Anti-Americanism: from cultural criticism to terrorism", *Australasian Journal of American Studies*, Vol. 23, No. 1, 77-92.
10. National Council of Public Morals (1917), *The Cinema: Its Present Position and Future Possibilities*, London, Williams & Norgate, xxi.
11. "The Cinematograph in Education", *The Times*, 27 October 1913, 11; "Films and the Child", *The Times*, 29 May 1914, 15.
12. Dean Rapp (2002), "Sex in the Cinema: War, Moral Panic, and the British Film Industry, 1906-1918", *Albion: A Quarterly Journal Concerned with British Studies*, Vol. 34, No. 3, 422-451.
13. Mark Glancy (2006), "Temporary American citizens? British audiences, Hollywood films and the threat of Americanization in the 1920s", *Historical Journal of Film, Radio and Television*, Vol. 26, Issue 4, 461-484.
14. "At the Cinema: A World of Inanity", *The Times*, 25 February 1916, 11.
15. Ella Hepworth Dixon, "Foolish Films", *The Daily Mail*, 21 February 1916, 4.
16. "Kinema Trash", *The Manchester Guardian*, 9 December 1926, 20.
17. "Sex Films Plague", *The Daily Express*, 7 May 1932, 3.
18. Mee, *Talk to Girls*, 57; "Film-Poison", *CN*, 6 February 1926, 6.
19. "Cruelty to Make A Film", *CN*, 5 June 1926, 4; "Truth and Fiction on the Film", *CN*, 28 February 1931, 6.
20. "Can the Kinema Be Saved?", *CN*, 23 October 1926, 2.
21. Letter, Mee to Derry, 31 December 1925.
22. "The Great Kinema Danger", *CN*, 6 September 1930, 6; "The Kinema is Becoming a Danger", *CN*, 17 March 1934, 7.
23. *The Daily Mirror*, 13 June 1932, 16.
24. "The Mangling Business", *CN*, 6 August 1932, 6.
25. *The Daily Mirror*, 27 December 1933, 22.
26. "Our Films", *CN*, 20 January 1934, 10.
27. *Punch*, 7 October 1931, 392.
28. "The Amazing Kinema", *CN*, 17 May 1919, 3; "Kinema on a Savage Island", *CN*, 12 May 1919, 3.
29. "Films to teach around the Earth", *CN*, 6 September 1919, 2.
30. "Children and the Cinema", *The Times*, 20 December 1922, 10.

31. "The Films Again", *CN*, 3 February 1923, 6.

32. R.G. Burnett and E.D. Martell (1932), *The Devil's Camera: Menace of a Film-ridden World*, London, Epworth Press, 15.

33. "The Films Fit For No Day", *CN*, 30 April 1932, 6.

34. "Peace Jazzing", *The Daily Mirror*, 27 March 1919, 5.

35. Joseph B. Priestley (1962), *Margin Released: A Writer's Reminiscences and Reflections*, London, Harper & Row, 66-67.

36. Julian Hare, "Jazz to Cure that Tired Feeling", *The Daily Mirror*, 25 March 1919, 7.

37. Jack Hylton, letter, *Liverpool Echo*, 17 February 1926, 11.

38. Constant Lambert (1934), *Music Ho: A Study of Music in Decline*, New York, Charles Scribner's & Sons; Catherine Parsonage (2005), *The Evolution of Jazz in Britain, 1880-1935*, Aldershot, Ashgate.

39. "Savoy Bands' Concert", *The Guardian*, 10 December 1925, 6.

40. "Week-Day Concerts in Churches", *The Guardian*, 1 September 1926, 11.

41. Jason Toynbee (2013), "Race, History, and Black British Jazz", *Black Music Research Journal* 33, 1, 1-25.

42. "Jazz not fit for white races, Sir Henry Cowards' Criticism", *The Guardian*, 20 September 1927, 3; see also "Further Anti-Jazz Cowardisms", *The Guardian*, 31 January 1929, 22; "Sir H. Coward On B.B.C. Music That Debases", *The Daily Mail*, 3 September 1936, 9.

43. "The Savagery of Jazz", *The Guardian*, 20 April 1927, 4.

44. "Nigger Music Comes From the Devil", *The Guardian*, 6 August 1927, 14.

45. "Why I Would Broadcast (or Ban) Jazz!", *The Guardian*, 30 December 1929, 8.

46. "Radio Listeners Preferences", *The Guardian*, 1 January 1930, 10.

47. "The Noise of the B.B.C.", *CN*, 4 December 1937, 6.

48. "B.B.C. and Jazz Stuff", *CN*, 29 November 1930, 2.

49. "Singing in the Train", *CN*, 21 January 1933, 4.

50. "The Gospel of Jazz", *CN*, 29 April 1939, 6.

51. "Bored to Death?", *CN*, 31 August 1935, 1.

52. "Good News From the B.B.C.", *CN*, 20 March 1937, 10.

53. Ibid.

54. "We Agree With Hitler", *CN*, 14 May 1938, 6.

55. "Civilization is Passing By", *CN*, 28 June 1941, 1.

56. Letter, Mee to Derry, 12 September 1935.

57. Letter, Mee to Derry, 18 July 1930.

58. Ibid.

59. "A Thing That Beats the Novelists", *CN*, 14 January 1928, 6.

60. Mee, *Talks to Boys*, 131.

61. Ibid., 132.

62. Letter, Mee to Derry, 12 September 1935.

63. "The Mental Slum", *CN*, 25 February 1928, 6.

64. Mee, *Talks to Boys*, 131.

65. "The Mental Slum", *CN*, 25 February 1928, 6.

66. "Our Beautiful Language", *CN*, 17 November 1928, 6.

67. "State Control of Broadcasting", *The Times*, 29 July 1930, 12.

68. John Reith (1924), *Broadcast over Britain*, London, Hodder & Stoughton, 34.

69. "Broadcasting", *CN*, 2 May 1925, 8.
70. "The Most Powerful Man in the World", *CN*, 15 February 1930, 6.
71. "Just An Idea", *CN*, 6 February 1937, 6.
72. Mee is referring to the novelist Gertrude Stein (1874-1946) and the poet Edith Sitwell (1887-1964). See "The Most Powerful Man in the World", *CN*, 15 February 1930, 6.
73. Jennifer Ruth Doctor (1999), *The BBC and Ultra-Modern Music, 1922-1936: Shaping a Nation's Tastes*, Cambridge, Cambridge University Press, 40.
74. "Broadcasting", *The Times*, 26 January 1924, 8; "Broadcasting", *The Times*, 12 October 1926, 7; "Programmes", *The Times*, 15 August 1930, 10; "Programmes", *The Times*, 13 September 1932, 10.
75. "One Word More to the B.B.C", *CN*, 29 October 1927, 6.
76. "Clean Speaking", *CN*, 5 November 1921, 4.
77. "Slang", *CN*, 22 January 1921, 6.
78. "Protection Wanted, Why Not Banish Vulgar English?", *CN*, 31 October 1931, 2.
79. "The Great Kinema Danger", *CN*, 6 September 1930, 6.
80. "The Word Killers", *CN*, 3 May 1937, 6.
81. "O.K. With Mee!", *Punch*, 27 May 1931, 584. Mrs Partington, an elderly lady from Sidmouth in Devon, is said during a severe storm in 1824 to have attempted, Canute-like, to turn back the ocean tide with her mop to prevent flooding. Her actions came to form an anecdotal description of a person involved in futile resistance.
82. Letter, Mee to Derry, 25 March 1930.
83. "John Galsworthy", *CN*, 5 January 1929, 4.
84. "Straws in the Wind", *CN*, 10 January 1931, 9.
85. "The Abuse of the Library Rate", *CN*, 1 February 1930, 2.
86. Clare Ravenwood & John Feather (2011), "Censorship and Book Selection in British Public Librarianship 1919-1939: Professional Perspectives", *Library and Information History*, Vol. 26, Issue 4, 258-271, 265.
87. "The Wrong Use of a Library", *CN*, 9 May 1931, 6.
88. "Not Quite Nice", *The Daily Mirror*, 17 August 1928, 9.
89. Letter, Mee to Derry, 25 March 1930.
90. Letter, Mee to Derry, 31 March 1930.
91. "Evil on the Rates", *CN*, 10 May 1930, 7.
92. Ibid.
93. "The Abuse of the Library Rate", *CN*, 1 February 1920, 2.
94. "Kansas Burns the C.E.", *CN*, 11 July 1925, 2; "What Tennessee Does Not Like", *CN*, 11 July 1925, 4; "Dayton Against the World", 15 January 1927, 6.
95. Peter Mandler (1999), *Fall and Rise of the Stately Home*, London, Yale University Press, 226-227.
96. Trevor Rowley (2006), *The English Landscape in the Twentieth Century*, London, Continuum; Alan Jackson (1986), *London's Metropolitan Railway*, London, David & Charles; Oliver Green (ed.) (2004), *Metro-Land*, British Empire Exhibition, 1924, reprinted edn, Southbank Publishing; Tom Sharpe (1936), *English Panorama*, London, J. Dent and Co.
97. David H. Lawrence, "Nottingham and the Mining Countryside 1929" in James T. Boulton (ed.) (2004), *D.H. Lawrence Late Essays and Articles, Volume 2*, Cambridge, Cambridge University Press, 291.

98. Edmund Blunden (1929), *Nature in English Literature*, London, Hogarth Press, 10.

99. Joseph B. Priestley (1934), *English Journey*, London, Penguin, 375.

100. Frank Trentmann (1994), "Civilization and Its Discontents: English Neo Romanticism and the Transformation of Anti-Modernism in Twentieth-Century Western Culture", *Journal of Contemporary History*, Vol. 29, No. 4, 583-625, 608.

101. Mee, *Enchanted Land*, 284-285.

102. Letter, Mee to Derry, 30 March 1930.

103. Mee, *Enchanted Land*, 4.

104. "The Beast in the Beautiful Countryside", *CN*, 22 October 1927, 6.

105. "Turning Us into a Circus", *CN*, 19 May 1928, 6; "Aunt Sally From America", *CN*, 20 April 1929, 2; "Aunt Sally", *CN*, 1 June 1929, 2.

106. "How to Vote", *CN*, 25 May 1929, 6.

107. David Matless (2001), *Landscape and Englishness*, London, Reaktion Books, 47.

108. "The C.N. Bill for the Countryside", *CN*, 5 March 1932, 6.

109. "The Proper Way With Litter Louts", *CN*, 23 July 1932, 6; "How are the Litter Louts Getting On?", *CN*, 24 August 1935, 8; "Broken Glass, the Worst Kind of Litter Lout", *CN*, 16 August 1930, 5; "On the Spot Fines the Only Way With the Litter-Lout", *CN*, 2 September 1939, 6; "The Litter Lout", *CN*, 25 June 1927, 8.

110. "How to Vote", *CN*, 25 May 1929, 6.

111. "Where Shall We Find Rest?", *CN*, 26 November 1929, 6.

112. Letter, Mee to Derry, 16 June 1930.

113. See *Kent Today*, c. 1936/7, the Committee for the Preservation of Rural Kent of the Kent Council of Social Service, 34-36.

114. Letter, Mee to Derry, 15 April 1935.

115. Letter, Mee to Derry, 4 May 1930.

9. "A Heartbreaking World" *(pp. 142-156)*

1. "A Hard Blow for the Pessimist", *CN*, 17 May 17 1919, 6.

2. "The One Hope for the World", *CN*, 22 March 1919, 5; "The Rich Man in His Castle, The Poor Man at His Gate", *CN*, 7 August 1926, 6; "The Turning of the Tide", *CN*, 25 October 1924, 6; "The New Birthday of the World", *CN*, 31 January 1920, 6.

3. "Like Gentlemen", *CN*, 31 December 1927, 6.

4. Letter, Mee to Derry, 13 January 1922.

5. "A Round Table for the World", *CN*, 2 January 1932, 1.

6. "Wanted, 400 Million Good Europeans", *CN*, 28 July 1928, 6.

7. Letter, Mee to Derry, 31 December 1925.

8. Ibid. See letter, Mee to Derry, 25 December 1925.

9. Letter, Mee to Derry, 11 January 1926.

10. "Letters to the Editor, League of Nations Union", *The Times*, 17 December 1929, 10.

11. "An Army of Revenge: Munich 'Fascist' Threats", *The Times*, 15 January 1923, 10; see also *The Times*, 2 November 1923; 5 and 12 November 1923, 14.

12. Ian Kershaw (2002), *Hitler 1889-1936: Hubris*, London, Penguin.
13. "The Jews in Germany, Persecution at a New Pitch", *The Times*, 8 November 1935, 15.
14. *The Guardian*, 10 March 1933; *The Guardian*, 16 March 1933; *The Guardian*, 29 March 1933.
15. *The Guardian*, 26 July 1933; *The Guardian*, 13 November 1933; *The Guardian*, 1 January 1934; *The Guardian*, 11 November 1938.
16. "Fight Against Fascism", *The Daily Worker*, 22 June 1933, 1.
17. "Germany's Election Surprise", *CN*, 4 October 1930, 4; "A Wild Man and His Words", *CN*, 11 October 1930, 2.
18. "Dramatic Change in Europe", *CN*, 1 April 1933, 7; "The Meanest of all Revolutions", *CN*, 15 April 1933, 2; "The New Tyranny Over Germany", *CN*, 6 May 1933, 7; "Plain Tale From a Nazi Camp", *CN*, 7 October 1933, 8; "Shall a Tyrant Rule the Earth?", *CN*, 9 September 1939, 1.
19. "Germany", *CN*, 22 April 1933, 2.
20. "The Jew in the Grip of Terror", *CN*, 17 December 1938, 2.
21. Mee, *1940: Our Finest Hour*, 49.
22. Ibid., 72.
23. Letter, Mee to Derry, 16 March 1933.
24. Letter, Mee to Derry, 17 January 1936.
25. Ibid.
26. Ibid.
27. "Shall a Tyrant Rule the Earth?", *CN*, 9 September 1939, 2.
28. Letter, Mee to Derry, 6 December 1925.
29. Letter, Mee to Derry, 27 September 1929.
30. Letter, Mee to Derry, 5 January 1931. The idea was not original and during the time Mee was working on what was to become *The King's England*, Shell Oil Company had employed John Betjeman to be the general editor of a series of guidebooks to be known as *Shell County Guides*. The first of that series on Cornwall, quite different in style and length from Mee's books, was published in June 1934, two years before Mee's first volume, *Enchanted Land*, was ready.
31. Peter Lowe (2012), *English Journeys: National and Cultural Identity in 1930s and 1940s England*, Amherst, NY, Cambria Press.
32. Letter, Mee to Derry, 2 September 1930.
33. Letter, Mee to Derry, 25 February 1931.
34. Letter, Mee to Derry, 27 January 1931.
35. Letter, Mee to Derry, 17 March 1931.
36. Letter, Mee to Derry, 31 December 1931.
37. Letter, Mee to Derry, 3 February, 1932.
38. Letter, Mee to Derry, 2 December 1930.
39. Letter, Mee to Derry, 27 April 1933; 3 November 1933; 16 November 1933.
40. Letter, Mee to Derry, 15 January 1933.
41. Ibid.
42. *CN*, 21 October 1933, 2; "Arthur Mee's 1000 Heroes", *The Daily Mail*, 20 October 1933, 20.
43. Letter, Mee to Derry, 20 January 1933; Letter, Mee to Derry, 15 January 1933.
44. Letter, Mee to Derry, 22 January 1933.

45. Letter, Mee to Derry, 6 February 1933.

46. Letter, Mee to Derry, 18 April 1934.

47. Eva Derry outlived her husband by over sixty years, dying in Bournemouth in 1991 aged 101.

48. *Hull Daily Mail*, 4 January 1939, 8. Gee called his home in Bridlington, Yorkshire, "Eynsford".

49. John Cuming Walters (1863-1933), a journalist and author, edited *Manchester City News* and *The Manchester Evening Chronicle*. Walters wrote and edited works on Charles Dickens, Alfred Tennyson and Marie Corelli and was a central figure in the Lancashire Shakespeare community.

50. Tyerman claimed that he visited 150 villages and wrote 30,000 words. Letter, Tyerman to Derry, 29 July 1931.

51. Letter, Mee to Derry, 21 April 1932.

52. "Cain Against the World", *CN*, 16 September 1939, 2; "To a Friend Far Away", *CN*, 30 September 1939, 1; "O Little Island With a Mighty Heart", *CN*, 6 July 1940, 2.

53. Mee, *1940: Our Finest Hour*, 69.

54. "Arthur Mee's Jubilee", *CN*, 11 October 1941, 5.

55. Ibid.

56. Angus Calder (1992), *The People's War: Britain 1939-1945*, London, Pimlico.

57. Mee, *1940: Our Finest Hour*, 33, 66, 159.

58. Ibid., 153.

59. Ibid., 158.

60. "The history of Eynsford Baptist Church, 1938-1940", *Eynsford Christian Fellowship*: www.webpages.free online.co.uk/ebc/hist4.htm.

61. Mee, *1940: Our Finest Hour*, 153-154; "The Voice Eternal in the Heavens", *CN*, 31 August 1940, 1.

62. Mee, *1940: Our Finest Hour*.

63. Ibid., 153.

64. "John Talks It Over with Daddie", *CN*, 29 December 1934, 13; "The Story of Twelve Young Men", *CN*, 6 June 1942, 4; "A Man of Good Conscience", *CN*, 18 September 1943, 4.

65. Mee, *1940: Our Finest Hour*, 80.

66. Ibid., 102.

67. Ibid., 103, 90.

68. Barbara Lamming, *The Trident*, December 1982.

69. This was first published in *The Children's Newspaper* in 1941. See "Civilization's Second Chance", *CN*, 13 December 1941, 1-2.

70. These attacks upon aspects of modernity first appeared in *The Children's Newspaper* in August 1943. See "Nobleness Walks in Our Ways Again", *CN*, 8 August, 1942, 1.

71. This was first published in *The Children's Newspaper* under the title "Never did So Much Depend Upon So Many" (*CN*, 15 March 1941, 1).

72. Robson, *Arthur Mee's Dream of England*, 7

73. Ibid., 8.

74. "Mr Arthur Mee", *The Times*, 29 May 1943, 6.

75. "Arthur Mee's Will", *Brisbane Sunday Mail*, 8 August 1943, 2.

76. Hammerton, *Child of Wonder*, 244.
77. "Mr Arthur Mee", *The Times*, 29 May 1943, 6.
78. *The Daily Mirror*, 29 May 1943, 5.
79. "Arthur Mee, By His First Editor", *CN*, 12 June 1943, 1.
80. "Hail and Farewell", *CN*, 12 June 1943, 4.
81. "Boy Thanks Author", *The Brisbane Courier Mail*, 31 May 1943, 2.
82. *CN*, 12 June 1943, 4.
83. *Nottingham Evening Post*, 4 June 1943, 4.
84. Frank O. Salisbury (1944), *Portrait and Pageant Kings, Presidents, and People*, London, John Murray. Salisbury, a devout Methodist, was a highly regarded artist who specialised in portrait painting. Among the international figures he painted were Benito Mussolini, Franklin D. Roosevelt, Winston Churchill and Queen Elizabeth II. Salisbury and Mee were close friends and he painted the portrait of Mee that appears on the cover of this book, as well as that of John Hammerton's 1946 biography. Mee gifted the original oil on canvas portrait to Nottinghamshire County Library Service to commemorate his fifty years in journalism. On Mee's death he left Salisbury an original statuette of a Tang Dynasty priest.
85. Quoted in "Arthur Mee", *CN*, 19 June 1943, 2.
86. "Why Not Peace Tomorrow, Corporal Hitler?", *CN*, 19 June 1943, 1.
87. "The Touchstone", *CN*, 5 June 1943, 1.
88. Letter, Mee to Marjorie Mee, dated Christmas 1938.
89. Quoted in "Arthur Mee", *CN*, 19 June 1943, 2.

Bibliography

Anderson, Olive (1987), *Suicide in Victorian and Edwardian England*, Oxford, Oxford University Press

Ang, Susan (2000), *The Widening World of Children's Literature*, London, Palgrave Macmillan

Avery, Gillian (2008), "Popular Education and Big Money: Mee, Hammerton and Northcliffe" in Briggs, Julia, Butts, Dennis & Grenby, Matthew Orville (eds), *Popular Children's Literature in Britain*, Aldershot, Ashgate Publishing Ltd

Bailey, Peter (1999), "White Collars, Gray Lives?: The Lower Middle Class Revisited", *Journal of British Studies*, Vol. 38, No. 3, 273-290

Baldwin, Stanley (1937), *On England and Other Addresses*, London, Books for Libraries Press

Barrie, James M. (1911), *Peter Pan*, London, Hodder & Stoughton

Bateman, Charles T. (1904), *John Clifford: Free Church Leader and Preacher*, London, National Council of the Evangelical Free Churches

Bates, Daisy (1938), *The Passing of the Aborigines: A Lifetime Spent among the Natives of Australia*, London, Murray

Bebbington, David W. (1982), *The Nonconformist Conscience: Chapel and Politics 1870-1914*, London, George Allen & Unwin

—— (1984), "Nonconformity and electoral sociology, 1867-1918", *Historical Journal*, Vol. 27, 633-656

—— (2007), *Victorian Nonconformity*, Milton Keynes, Paternoster

Begbie, Harold (1921), *The Mirrors of Downing Street: Some Political Reflections by a Gentleman with a Duster*, London, G.P. Putnam & Sons

Bellah, Robert (1985), *Habits of the Heart: Individualism and Commitment in American Life*, Berkeley, University of California Press

Billig, Michael (1995), *Banal Nationalism*, London, Falmer Press

Blom, Philipp (2008), *The Vertigo Years: Change and Culture in the West, 1900-1914*, London, Weidenfeld & Nicolson

Blunden, Edmund (1929), *Nature in English Literature*, London, Hogarth Press

Board of Education (1904), *Codes of Regulations for Public Elementary Schools with Schedules*, London, HMSO

—— (1905), *Suggestions for the Consideration of Teachers, and Others concerned in the work of Elementary Schools*, London, HMSO

Boulton, James T. (ed.) (2002), *The Letters of D.H. Lawrence*, Cambridge, Cambridge University Press

Bristow, Joseph (1991), *Empire Boys: Adventures in a Man's World*, London, HarperCollins Academic

Brittain, Vera (1940), *England's Hour*, London, Macmillan & Co. Ltd

Brown, Cornelius (1891), *A History of Nottinghamshire*, London, Elliot Stock

Bryant, Ernest A. (1908), *A New Self-Help*, London, Cassell

The Bryce Report (1915), *Report of the Committee on Alleged German Outrages*, London, HMSO

Burden R. & Kohl, S. (eds) (2006), *Landscape and Englishness*, Rodopi, Amsterdam

Burkhardt F. & Smith S. (1985, 1990 edn), *Correspondence of Charles Darwin*, 9 vols, Cambridge, Cambridge University Press

Bush, Julia (2002), "British Women's Anti-Suffragism and the Forward Policy, 1908-14", *Women's History Review*, Vol. 11, 3, 431-454

—— (2007), *Women Against the Vote: Female Anti-Suffragism in Britain*, Oxford, Oxford University Press

Butts, D. & Garrett, P. (eds) (2006), *From the Dairyman's Daughter to Worrals of the WAAF: The RTS, Lutterworth Press and Children's Literature*, Cambridge, Lutterworth Press

Byrt, G.W. (1947), *John Clifford: A Fighting Free Churchman*, London, The Kingsgate Press

Campbell Macfie, Ronald (1912), *Heredity, Evolution, and Vitalism*, New York, William Wood & Co.

Cannadine, David (1995), "British History as a 'new subject': Politics, perspectives and prospects" in Grant, A. & Stringer, K. (eds) (1995), *Uniting the Kingdom?: The Making of British History*, London, Routledge

Carson, William E. (1918), *Northcliffe: Britain's Man of Power*, Toronto, G.J. McLeod

Castle, Kathryn (1996), *Britannia's Children*, Manchester, Manchester University Press

Cawood, Ian & McKinnon-Bell, David (2010), *The First World War: Questions and Analysis in History*, London, Routledge

Chesterton, Gilbert K. (1901), "A Defence of Penny Dreadfuls", *The Defendant*, London, J.M. Dent & Sons Ltd

—— (1905), *Heretics*, London, John Lane

—— (1922), *Eugenics and Other Evils*, London, Cassell & Co.

Clement, F. & Egerton, C. (1914), *The Future of Education*, London, G. Bell and Sons, Ltd

Cliff, T. & Gluckstein, D. (1986), *Marxism and Trade Union Struggle: The General Strike of 1926*, London, Bookmarks

Clifford, John (1905), "Passive Resistance in England and Wales", *The North American Review*, March, 430-439

—— (1917), *Our Fight for Belgium and What it Means*, London, Hodder & Stoughton

Cox, Jack (1982), *Take A Cold Tub Sir!: The History of the Boy's Own Paper*, Guildford, Lutterworth Press

Cudlipp, Hugh (1980), *The Prerogative of the Harlot: Press Barons and Power*, London, Bodley Head

Darlow, Thomas H. (1925), *William Robertson Nicoll: Life and Letters*, Hodder & Stoughton, London

Delap, Lucy (2005), "Feminist and anti-Feminist Encounters in Edwardian Britain", *Historical Research* 78, 201, 377-399

Dewey, John (1902), *The Child and the Curriculum*, Chicago, Chicago University Press

DeYoung, Ursula (2011), *A Vision of Modern Science: John Tyndall and the Role of the Scientist in Victorian Culture*, New York, Palgrave

Dixon, Diana (1986), "From Instruction to Amusement: Attitudes of Authority in Children's Periodicals before 1914", *Victorian Periodicals Review*, Vol. 19, No. 2, 63-67

Doctor, Jennifer (1999), *The BBC and Ultra-Modern Music, 1922-1936: Shaping a Nation's Tastes*, Cambridge, Cambridge University Press

Drotner, Kristen (1988), *English Children and Their Magazines, 1751-1945*, New Haven and London, Yale University Press

Dunae, Patrick (1976), "Boy's Own Paper: Origins and Editorial Policies", *The Private Library*, IX, 120-158

Ebbatson, Roger (2005), *An Imaginary England: Nation, Landscape and Literature, 1840-1920*, Aldershot, Ashgate Publishing Ltd

Ellis, Florence H. (1907), *Character Forming in School*, London, Longmans Green

English, Jim (2006), "Empire Day in Britain, 1904-1958", *The Historical Journal*, 49, 1, 247-276

Ensor, Robert (1904), "The English Countryside" in Oldershaw, Lucien, *England, a Nation: Being the Papers of the Patriots' Club*, London, R.B. Johnson

Ferguson, Niall (2004), *Empire: How Britain Made the Modern World*, London, Penguin

Foucault, Michel (1986), *The Uses of Pleasure: The History of Sexuality: Volume Two*, New York, Random House

Frothingham, Arthur L. (1919), *Handbook of War Facts and Peace Problems*, New York, Committee on Organised Education National Security League

Froude, James A. (2011), *Thomas Carlyle: A History of the First Forty Years of His Life, 1795-1835*, Cambridge, Cambridge University Press

Galton Francis (1904), "Eugenics: Its Definitions, Scope and Aims", *The American Journal of Sociology*, Vol. 10, No. 1, 1-25

Gavin, A.E. & Humphries, A.F. (2009), *Childhood in Edwardian Fiction: Worlds Enough and Time*, London, Palgrave

Glancy, Mark (2006), "Temporary American citizens?: British audiences, Hollywood films and the threat of Americanization in the 1920s", *Historical Journal of Film, Radio and Television*, Vol. 26, Issue 4, 461-484

Godard, John G. (1905), *Racial Supremacy, being studies in imperialism*, London, Simpkin, Marshall & Co. Ltd

Green, Oliver (ed.) (2004), *Metro-Land: British Empire Exhibition 1924*, London, Southbank Publishing

Green, M. Muriel (1948), "The Children's Magazine in Britain Today", *Library Review*, Vol. 11, 8, 464-467

Gunn, S. & Bell, R. (2002), *Middle Classes: Their Rise and Sprawl*, London, Cassell

Hall, Catherine & Rose, Sonya O. (eds) (2006), *At Home With The Empire: Metropolitan Culture and the Imperial World*, Cambridge, Cambridge University Press

Hall, Richard (1998), *Black Armband Days: Truth from the Dark Side of Australia's Past*, Sydney, Vintage

Hammerton, John (1932), *With Northcliffe in Fleet Street*, London, Hutchinson & Co.

—— (1944), *Books and Myself*, London, Macdonald

—— (1946), *Child of Wonder: An Intimate Biography of Arthur Mee*, London, Hodder & Stoughton

Harrison, Frederic (1908), *National & Social Problems*, London, Macmillan

Hattersley, Roy (2007), *Borrowed Time: The Story of Britain Between the Wars*, London, Abacus Books

Haw, George (ed.) (1906), *Christianity and the Working Classes*, London, Macmillan

Helmreich, Anne (2002), *The English Garden and National Identity: The Competing Styles of Garden Design, 1870-1914*, Cambridge, Cambridge University Press

Hirst, F.W., Murray, G. & Hammond, J.L. (1900), *Liberalism and the Empire*, London, R. Brimley Johnson

Hobsbawm, Eric (2003), *Interesting Times: A Twentieth-Century Life*, University of Virginia, Knopf Doubleday

Hobson, John A. (1902), *Imperialism: A Study*, London, J. Nisbet

—— (1909), *The Crisis of Liberalism*, London, King & Sons

Holland, Steve (2006), *Look and Learn: A History of the Classic Children's Magazine*, London, Look and Learn Magazine Ltd

Holmes, Robert (1996), *Footsteps: Adventures of a Romantic Biographer*, London, Vintage

Horne, J. & A. (2001), *German Atrocities, 1914: A History of Denial*, New Haven, CT, Yale University Press

Hueffer, Ford Madox (1905), *The Soul of London*, London, Alston Rivers

Hunt, Peter (ed.) (1995), *Children's Literature: An Illustrated History*, Oxford, Oxford University Press

Hynes, Samuel (1968), *The Edwardian Turn of Mind: First World War and English Culture*, London, Pimlico

—— (1990), *A War Imagined: The First World War and English Culture*, London, Bodley Head

Inglis, F. (1981), *The Promise of Happiness*, Cambridge, Cambridge University Press

Jackson, Alan (1986), *London's Metropolitan Railway*, London, David & Charles

Jackson, Kate (1997), "The Tit-Bits Phenomenon: George Newnes, New Journalism and the Periodical Texts", *Victorian Periodicals Review*, Vol. 30, No. 3, 201-226

James, Lawrence (1994), *The Rise and Fall of the British Empire*, Cheltenham, Pickaback Books

Johnson, Paul B. (1968), *Land Fit for Heroes: The Planning of British Reconstruction, 1916-1919*, Chicago, Chicago University Press

Jones, Greta (1986), *Social Hygiene in Twentieth Century Britain*, New York, Croom Helm

Jones, W. & Baxter, G. (1850), *The Jubilee Memorial of the Religious Tract Society: Containing a Record of its Origin, Proceedings, and Results, A.D. 1799 to A.D. 1849*, London, Religious Tract Society

Kennedy, Paul (1980), *The Rise of Anglo-German Antagonism, 1860-1914*, London, George Allen & Unwin

Kennedy Hones, William (1920), *Fleet Street and Downing Street*, London, Hutchinson

Kershaw, R. & Sacks, J. (2008), *New Lives for Old: The Story of Britain's Child Migrants*, London, The National Archives

Kertesz, Mary (1992), "The Enemy: British Images of the German People During the Second World War", unpublished PhD thesis, Sussex University

Kirkpatrick, Edwin A. (1903), *Fundamentals of Child Study: a discussion of instincts and other factors in human development with practical applications*, London, Macmillan

Lambert, Constant (1934), *Music Ho: A Study of Music in Decline*, New York, Charles Scribner's & Sons

Lang, Marjory (1980), "Childhood's Champions: Mid-Victorian Children's Periodicals and the Critics", *Victorian Periodicals Review* 13, 1/2, 17-31

Lawrence, D.H. (2003), *Studies in Classic American Literature*, Volume 2, Cambridge, Cambridge University Press

—— "Nottingham and the Mining Countryside 1929" in Boulton, James T. (ed.) (2004), *D.H. Lawrence: Late Essays and Articles, Volume 2*, Cambridge, Cambridge University Press

—— (1910), "The Goose Fair", *The English Review*, No. 15, February, 399-409

Lawson, Valerie (2010), *Mary Poppins She Wrote: The true story of Australian writer P.L. Travers, creator of the quintessentially English nanny*, London, Simon & Schuster

Lightman, B. (1989), "Ideology, Evolution and Late-Victorian Agnostic Popularisers" in Moore, J. (ed.), *History, Humanity and Evolution*, Cambridge, Cambridge University Press, 285-309

Lowther Clarke, William K. (ed.) (1911), *Facing the Facts*, London, James Nisbet

MacDonald, Robert H. (1994), *The Language of Empire: Myths and Metaphors of Popular Imperialism, 1880-1918*, Manchester, Manchester University Press

MacKenzie, John M. (1984), *Propaganda and Empire: The Manipulation of British Public Opinion, 1880-1960*, Manchester, Manchester University Press

—— (ed.) (1986), *Imperialism and Popular Culture*, Manchester, Manchester University Press

Mandler, Peter (1999), *Fall and Rise of the Stately Home*, London, Yale University Press

Markham, Violet (1912), *Miss Violet Markham's Great Speech at the Albert Hall*, London, National League for Opposing Woman Suffrage

Martin, Kingsley (1966), *Father Figures*, London, Hutchinson

Martineau, Harriet (1865), "Life in the Criminal Classes", *Edinburgh Review*, 122

Masterman, Charles (1904), "The English City", in Oldershaw, Lucien, *England, a Nation: Being the Papers of the Patriots' Club*, London, R.B. Johnson

—— (1905), *In Peril of Change: Essays Written in Time of Tranquillity*, New York, B.W. Huebsch

Masterton, Charles (1909), *The Condition of England*, London, Methuen & Co.

Matless, David (1998), *Landscape and Englishness*, London, Reaktion Books

Maynard Keynes, John (1920), *The Economic Consequences of the Peace*, New York, Harcourt, Brace and Howe

McLeod, Hugh (1999), "Dissent and the peculiarities of the English, c1870-1914" in Shaw, J. & Kreider, A. (eds), *Culture and the Nonconformist Tradition*, Cardiff, University of Wales Press

McMillan, Margaret (1904), *Education through the Imagination*, London, Swan Sonnenschein & Co. Ltd

Mee, Arthur, "The Pleasure Telephone", *The Strand Magazine*, September 1898, 339-345

—— "B. P. Hero of Mafeking", *Chums*, 23 May 1900, 631

—— (1900), *Joseph Chamberlain: A Romance of Modern Politics*, London, S.W. Partridge

—— (1900), "The Making of Sherlock Holmes", *The Young Man*, 14, No. 10, October, 335-337

—— (1901), *King and Emperor: The Life-History of Edward VII*, London, S.W. Partridge

—— (1901), *Lord Salisbury*, London, Hood, Douglas & Howard

—— (1903), *England's Mission by English Statesmen*, London, Grant Richards

—— (ed.) (1908), *The Children's Encyclopaedia*, London, The Educational Book Company

—— (1913), *Arthur Mee's Letters to Boys*, London, Hodder & Stoughton

—— & Holden, Stuart (1917), *Defeat or Victory: The Strength of Britain Book*, London, Morgan & Scott Ltd

—— (1917), *The Fiddlers: Drink in the Witness Box*, London, Morgan & Scott Ltd

—— (1917), *The Parasite*, London, Morgan & Scott Ltd

—— (1936), *Enchanted Land*, London, Hodder & Stoughton

—— (1941), *1940: Our Finest Hour*, London, Hodder & Stoughton

Mohr, Rowena (1999), "Neo-colonialist Hagiography and the Making of an Australian Legend: Daisy Bates", *Lateral*, Issue 2, 2

Morton, Henry V. (1927), *In Search of England*, London, Methuen & Co.

National Council of Public Morals, *The Cinema: Its Present Position and Future Possibilities*, London, Williams & Norgate

Nicoll, W. Robertson (1907), *The Lamp of Sacrifice: Sermons Preached on Special Occasions*, New York, A.C. Armstrong & Co.

O'Connor, Brendon (2004), "A Brief History of Anti-Americanism: from cultural criticism to terrorism", *Australasian Journal of American Studies*, Vol. 23, No. 1, 77-92

Orwell, George, "Such, Such Were the Joys", *Partisan Review*, September-October 1952

—— (1970), "The Lion and the Unicorn: Socialism and the English Genius" in Orwell, S. & Angus, I. (eds), *The Collected Essays, Journalism and Letters of George Orwell*, Harmondsworth, Penguin Books

Packer, Ian (2003), "Religion and the New Liberalism: The Rowntree Family, Quakerism and Social Reform", *Journal of British Studies*, Vol. 42, No. 2, 236-257

Paley, William (1802), *Natural Theology*, New York, American Tract Society

Parsonage, Catherine (2005), *The Evolution of Jazz in Britain, 1880-1935*, Aldershot, Ashgate

Pedersen, S. & Mandler, P. (eds) (1994), *After the Victorians: Private Conscience and Public Duty in Modern Britain: Essays in Memory of John Clive*, London, Psychology Press

Pember Reeves, Maud (1914), *Round About a Pound a Week*, London, G. Bell &
    Sons Ltd
Pemberton, Max (1922), *Northcliffe: A Memoir*, London, Hodder & Stoughton
Porter, Bernard (2005), *The Absent-Minded Imperialists: Empire, Society, and
    Culture in Britain*, Oxford, Oxford University Press
Pound, Reginald & Harmsworth, Geoffrey (1959), *Northcliffe*, New York, Praeger
Priestley, Joseph B. (1934), *English Journey*, London, Penguin
—— (1962), *Margin Released: A Writer's Reminiscences and Reflections*, London,
    Harper & Row
Pryke, Sam (1998), "The Popularity of Nationalism in the Early British Boy Scout
    Movement", *Social History*, Vol. 23, No. 3, 309-324
Pugh, D.R. (1990), "English Nonconformity, education and passive resistance
    1903-6", *History of Education*, Vol. 19, Issue 4, 355-373
Pulbrook, Ernest C. (1915), *The English Countryside*, London, Batsford Ltd
Rapp, Dean (2002), "Sex in the Cinema: War, Moral Panic, and the British Film
    Industry, 1906-1918", *Albion: A Quarterly Journal Concerned with British
    Studies*, Vol. 34, No. 3, 422-451
Ravenwood, C. & Feather, J. (2011), "Censorship and Book Selection in British
    Public Librarianship 1919-1939: Professional Perspectives", *Library and
    Information History*, Vol. 26, Issue 4, 258-271
Reece, Bob (2007), *Daisy Bates: Grand Dame of the Desert*, Canberra, National
    Library of Australia
—— (2007), "'You Would Have Loved Her for Her Lore': The Letters of Daisy
    Bates", *Australian Aboriginal Studies*, No. 1, 51-70
Report of the Inter-Departmental Committee on Physical Deterioration (1904),
    London, HMSO
Reynolds, Henry (2005), *Nowhere People: How International Race Thinking Shaped
    Australia's Identity*, Melbourne, Penguin
Roberts, Nathan (2004), "Character in the mind: citizenship, education and
    psychology in Britain, 1880-1914", *History of Education*, Vol. 33, No. 2, 177-
    197
Robson, Maisie (2003), *Arthur Mee's Dream of England*, Rotherham, King's
    England Press
Rodwell, Grant (1997), "Dr Caleb Williams Saleeby: the Complete Eugenicist",
    History of Education, 26, 1, 23-40
Rose, Jonathan (2001), *The Intellectual Life of the British Working Classes*, New
    Haven, Yale University Press
Rosenberg, Chanie (1919), *Britain on the Brink of Revolution*, London, Bookmarks
Rosenthal, Michael (1986), *The Character Factory: Baden-Powell and the Origins of
    the Boy Scout Movement*, New York, Pantheon Books
Rowley, Trevor (2006), *The English Landscape in the Twentieth Century*, London,
    Continuum
Sadler, Michael (1908 edn), *Moral Instruction and Training in Schools: Report of an
    International Inquiry: Volume One: The United Kingdom*, London, Longmans,
    Green
Saleeby, Caleb (1906), *Evolution, the Master-Key*, London, Harper
—— (1909), *Parenthood and Race Culture*, London, Cassell and Co.

—— (1909), "Psychology of parenthood", *Eugenics Review*, 1(1), April, 37-46

—— (1911), *Women and Womanhood: A Search for Principles*, New York

Salisbury, Frank (1944), *Portrait and Pageant Kings, Presidents, and People*, London, John Murray

Salmon, Edward, "What Girls Read", *Nineteenth Century*, XX, October 1886

Scott, Dixon (1916), *Men of Letters*, London, Hodder & Stoughton

Searle, Geoffrey (1976), *Eugenics and Politics in Britain, 1900-1914*, Leyden, Noordhoff

—— (1990), *The Quest for National Efficiency: A Study in British Politics and Political Thought, 1899-1914*, London, Ashfield Press

Seeley, John R. (1883), *The Expansion of England: Two Courses of Lectures*, Boston, Roberts Brothers

Sharpe, Tom (1936), *English Panorama*, London, J. Dent and Co.

Simonis, H. (1917), *The Street of Ink: An Intimate History of Journalism*, London, Cassell and Company Ltd

Simpson, John (2005), *Days from a Different World*, London, Pan

Smith, Bernard (1985), *European Vision and the South Pacific*, New Haven, Yale University Press

Smith S.C. (1998), *British Imperialism, 1750-1970*, Cambridge, Cambridge University Press

Soloway, Richard (1995), *Demography and Degeneration: Eugenics and the Declining Birthrate in Twentieth-Century Britain*, Chapel Hill, University of North Carolina

Spencer, Herbert (1891, 1967 edn), *The Study of Sociology*, New York, Appleton

—— (1904), *An Autobiography*, Volume 1, New York, D. Appleton & Co.

Spender, J.A. (1923), *The Life of the Right Hon. Sir Henry Campbell Bannerman*, London, GCB

Springhall, John (1994a), "Disseminating impure literature: the 'penny dreadful' publishing business since 1860", *Economic History Review*, Vol. 47, No. 3, 567-684

—— (1994b), "'Pernicious Reading'? 'The Penny Dreadful' as Scapegoat for Late-Victorian Juvenile Crime", *Victorian Periodicals Review*, Vol. 27, No. 4, 326-349

Standish, Ann (1999), "'Devoted Service to a Dying Race'?: Daisy Bates and The Passing of the Aborigines" in Damousi, J. & Ellinghaus, K. (eds) (1999), *Citizenship, Women and Social Justice*, History Department, The University of Melbourne

Stone, Dan (2001), "Race in British Eugenics", *European History Quarterly*, Vol. 31, No. 3, 397-425

—— (2002), *Breeding Superman: Nietzsche, Race and Eugenics in Edwardian and Interwar Britain*, Liverpool, Liverpool University Press

Stoney, Barbara (1974), *Enid Blyton: The Biography*, London, Hodder

Tawney, R.H. (1931), *Equality*, London, Unwin Books

Thompson, J. Lee (2000), *Northcliffe: Press Baron in Politics, 1865-1922*, London, John Murray

Toynbee, Jason (2013), "Race, History, and Black British Jazz", *Black Music Research Journal* 33, 1, 1-25

Trentmann, Frank (1994), "Civilization and Its Discontents: English Neo Romanticism and the Transformation of Anti-Modernism in Twentieth-Century Western Culture", *Journal of Contemporary History*, Vol. 29, No. 4, 583-625

Tyndall, John (1879), *Fragments of Science*, London, Longman, Green & Co.

Van Emden, Richard & Humphries, Steve (2004), *All Quiet on the Home Front: An Oral History of Life in Britain During the First World War*, London, Headline Books

Ward, Paul (1998), *Red Flag and Union Jack: Englishness, Patriotism and the British Left, 1881-1924*, Woodbridge, Boydell & Brewer Ltd

Wells, Herbert G. (1897), *The War of the Worlds*, Rockville, Arc Manor

—— (1934), *Experiment in Autobiography*, London, Macmillan

White, Arnold (1901), *Efficiency and Empire*, London, Methuen

Wiener, Martin J. (2004 edn), *English Culture and the Decline of the Industrial Spirit, 1850-1980*, Cambridge, Cambridge University Press

Yoxall, J.H. & Grey, E. (1905), *Companion to the NUT Code*, London, Educational Supply Association

Index

You may also be interested in

Voice of Nonconformity

*William Robertson Nicoll
and The British Weekly*

Keith A. Ives

Print ISBN: 978 0 7188 9222 7
PDF ISBN: 978 0 7188 4519 3
ePub ISBN: 978 0 7188 4520 9
Kindle ISBN: 978 0 7188 4521 6

Sir William Robertson Nicoll (1851–1923) was a journalist, writer and minister of the Scottish Free Church, who founded the highly influential nonconformist newspaper *The British Weekly*. An important figure in English nonconformity, Robertson Nicoll was a complex individual whose life and interests are difficult to sum up completely. While some commentators, even his authorised biographer T.H. Darlow, thought they captured much, others who also knew the subject felt that many important aspects of his life had been left out.

This new biography opens up significant areas of Robertson Nicoll's life that have been neglected by other studies, and sheds particular light on his influence on 'believing criticism' in Scotland during the late 19th and early 20th centuries. This book will appeal to anyone interested in the life and times of William Robertson Nicoll, as well as acting as a valuable resource for scholars of Christianity and nonconformity of this period.

Available now with more excellent titles in Paperback, Hardback, PDF and Epub formats from The Lutterworth Press

www.lutterworth.com

You may also be interested in

From the Dairyman's Daughter to Worrals of the WAAF
The RTS, Lutterworth Press and Children's Literature

Dennis Butts & Pat Garrett (eds)

ISBN: 978 0 7188 3055 7

A collection of essays based on the Children's Books History Society study conference marking the bicentenary of the Religious Tract Society and the Lutterworth Press. The book analyses the children's literature it produced, charting the development of the genre from the evangelical tract through to the popular school story, spanning the period from the late eighteenth to the mid-twentieth centuries. It shows how publishing worked within the context of a missionary society with a global reach.

The book details the nature and development of the tract genre both in Britain and America, before looking at the range of RTS and Lutterworth output of children's titles, including its movement into magazine publishing. The work studies the two great magazines for which the RTS and Lutterworth were known to generations of children, the *Boy's Own Paper* and the *Girl's Own Paper*, as well as other magazines and tracts.

Available now with more excellent titles in Paperback, Hardback, PDF and Epub formats from The Lutterworth Press

www.lutterworth.com

You may also be interested in

Living with Eagles
Marcus Morris, Priest and Publisher
Sally Morris & Jan Hallwood

ISBN: 978 0 7188 2982 7

Eagles seemed to dominate Marcus Morris's life. As a clergyman's son, he grew up with the eagle of the church lectern; as a priest himself he had his own lecterns. A brass inkwell topped by a flying eagle became the symbol of the most famous eagle of all – the children's magazine that influenced a generation.

Eagle and its sister papers *Girl*, *Swift* and *Robin* were read by millions throughout the 1950s and '60s. The religious and moral framework was strong, though not overstated, with Bible stories and lives of missionaries and saints featured regularly, and young readers were encouraged to become good citizens.

Each issue of *Eagle* had an Editor's Letter, signed by Marcus Morris, a name as widely known to his young readers as any modern pop idol. Morris was a radical priest, continually at odds with the Church establishment. He was a man of contrasts and his clerical status did not prevent him, or his actress wife, from indulging in extramarital affairs. After arguments with new masters in Fleet Street he left the company and spent the rest of his working life with the fourth eagle in his life, the symbol of the National Magazine Company which he made one of the most successful publishers in Britain. The fascinating story of this extraordinary man is told here for the first time.

Available now with more excellent titles in Paperback, Hardback, PDF and Epub formats from The Lutterworth Press

www.lutterworth.com

You may also be interested in

Charlotte Mason
Hidden Heritage and Educational Influence
Margaret A. Coombs

Print ISBN: 978 0 7188 9402 3
PDF ISBN: 978 0 7188 4407 3
ePub ISBN: 978 0 7188 4406 6
Kindle ISBN: 978 0 7188 4408 0

In her new and definitive biography, Margaret Coombs draws on years of research to reveal for the first time the hidden backdrop to Charlotte Mason's life, tracing the lives of her previously undiscovered Quaker ancestors to offer a better understanding of the roots of her personality and ideas. Coombs charts her rise from humble beginnings as an orphaned pupil-teacher to great heights as a lady of culture venerated within prestigious PNEU circles, illustrating how with determination she surmounted the Victorian age's rigid class divisions to achieve her educational vision.

A thorough analysis of Charlotte Mason's educational influences and key friendships challenges longstanding notions about the roots of her philosophy, offering a more realistic picture of her life and work than ever accomplished before.

Available now with more excellent titles in Paperback, Hardback, PDF and Epub formats from The Lutterworth Press

www.lutterworth.com

.